QUEST FOR SPEED

THE EPIC SAGA OF RECORD-BREAKING ON LAND

Published in September 2020

ISBN 978-1-910505-59-5

Published by Evro Publishing, Westrow House, Holwell, Sherborne, Dorset DT9 5LF, UK

Printed and bound in Slovenia by GPS

Illustrated, written and designed by Barry John

www.evropublishing.com

The author

Like every boy in the 1950s, Barry John knew the names of Cobb and Campbell and possessed battered Dinky toys of their cars. When he was 15, he discovered *Hot Rod* magazine and, instantly mesmerised, bought it when pocket money stretched that far. In the pages of *Hot Rod* he discovered the exploits of Breedlove and Arfons — and has been fascinated ever since. After studying at Harrow School of Art, he pursued a career as a graphic designer. Now retired, he has applied his professional skills to his passion and produced this book. He lives in Kent.

QUEST FOR SPEED
THE EPIC SAGA OF RECORD-BREAKING ON LAND

BARRY JOHN

Foreword by
DAVID TREMAYNE

EVRO
PUBLISHING

CONTENTS

FOREWORD • DAVID TREMAYNE

Anyone who knows me well, or cares about what I do, will be aware of my interest in — okay, obsession with — the Land Speed Record.

It began when I was a kid, when I stood on my tiptoes and peered over the gold flanks of a great big car at an exhibition in London, and took in the sleek, endless bonnet and what looked like a gun in front of the windscreen. It was Henry Segrave's *Golden Arrow*, and I wasn't yet four years old. Honestly, that's the first thing in my life that I remember.

That was all a subconscious thing back then, of course. What made it all blossom was watching Donald Campbell and *Bluebird* in their death throes on Coniston Water in January 1967, and being fired by something I still try and process sometimes. He wasn't just my first hero or a spiritual mentor and guide, but perhaps it's best that we leave it at that for now.

In my teens I used to draw land speed cars and dream of breaking the big record.

Of course, I never did. But I was blessed to be part of the team through which Richard Noble did with *Thrust 2*, at Black Rock Desert on 4 October 1983. And again when Andy Green took Richard's *Thrust SSC* through the sound barrier on 15 October 1997.

To be there when Andy drove *JCB Dieselmax* to its 350mph diesel record. To count these guys as friends. To do likewise with Craig Breedlove and Rocky Robinson. To have met the Art Arfons and Gary Gabelichs and Al Teagues of the world.

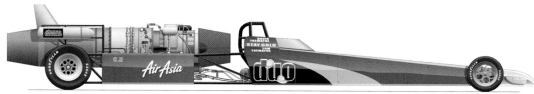

David Tremayne's STAY GOLD record car

To have crashed my own jetcar, *STAY GOLD*, at 260mph after peaking at 296.6mph during testing for an attack on the British Land Speed Record, to have walked away with just a scratched knuckle

on a steady hand, and to have found out who I really am.

So, yeah, speed on land (and water) goes deep with me. But so does the scribbling side of things, though that ride with *STAY GOLD* means more to me than everything put together that I've done in my journalistic career.

When Barry John first contacted me and I saw what sort of work he could do, I felt like I do when I hear Springsteen really on it; that sort of envious respect you have for somebody who can do something

so much better than you can yourself.

Then, not so long ago, he sent me the finished contents of this book. Holy moly! Of course I loved all the outright Land Speed Record holder renditions,

and their stories. It's great to keep such things in the public psyche, to inspire the next generation of daredevils. But I also loved the fact that old Al Teague (who still doesn't realise that he is right up there with his idols George Eyston and John Cobb) and Danny Thompson (a real hero whose familial story of loyalty and grit makes me want to cry, whom I am privileged to call a mate, and who is known in the Tremayne household as 'The Really Fast DT') were in there too. And they aren't the only ones, because Barry is a hot rodder at heart.

This is a wonderful book that celebrates passion. The passion of men and women (such as the much-missed Kitty O'Neil and Jessi Combs) to pursue their valorous dreams. And of a man creating such beautiful visual and mental images by deploying his own awesome skills to honour their memories.

The Land Speed Record, Barry John and Evro Publishing. Could it ever get better than this?

QUEST FOR SPEED

Until the advent of the industrial revolution the fastest that man could travel was on the back of a galloping horse. The invention of the steam engine, gas engine and electric motor would change that forever. By the late eighteenth century bystanders were treated to the amazing spectacle of vehicles travelling down the road without the aid of horses in front of them. These horseless carriages, or automobiles as they were known in France, caught the attention of the public with varying degrees of approval. Those with a positive view became captivated with the new technology and thus began a fascination with the motor car.

On 18 December 1898 this enthusiasm resulted in the French magazine *La France Automobile* organising a competition in which Count Gaston de Chasseloup-Laubat, driving a Jeantaud automobile, recorded the highest speed. Over a flying kilometre he was recorded with an average speed of 39.23mph. In most accepted histories of land speed record holders he appears as the first on the list. In fact the Count was a long way from being the fastest man on earth. He was not even as fast as a galloping horse but it was the first automobile record. An idea had been put into motion that would eventually result in the breaking of the sound barrier, a phrase that had not been coined at that time. To achieve success in this particular activity — some records lasted for decades, some just hours — the participants would need to put the following series of factors together in the best feasible combination.

MOTIVATION

From 1898 to the present day there have been many contenders for the land speed record, which is not a race as such and has no prize, not even an inscribed cup. So what is the motive? Early automobile manufacturers were well aware of the publicity that such activity could generate and how it could help to promote their products together with their chosen means of power. As speeds increased beyond the capability of modified road-going cars, vehicles specially built for the purpose contested the records, which created competition of a different kind. For some it was a source of national pride, for others it became a personal contest with their closest rivals, even members of their own family. Some simply aspired to the title of the 'fastest man on the planet' and then went on to break their own records. For many it would become an obsession or an addiction or simply the reason for living.

TECHNOLOGY

The technology of the day was not preordained but followed the conceptual thought of creative individuals whose ideas were brought to reality by shaping inanimate chunks of metal into complex machines. Born of the industrial revolution, it involved every aspect of maths, physics and chemistry.

It would seem obvious that increases in power go hand-in-hand with higher speeds but that is to over-simplify things. Once the piston engine became dominant in the challenge it also brought with it the problem of developing efficient clutches, transmissions and tyres to make the increased power effective. More power also meant ever larger engines with an ever greater weight penalty, which resulted in unwieldy monsters that could only be controlled with difficulty. As speeds approached 200mph more thought was given to the idea of streamlining, a subject of which most participants had but a sketchy understanding. Without the advantage of a wind tunnel, designs were based on what looked right or just common sense. The absolute land speed record is now the domain of rocket and jet technology and the cars contesting the piston-engine records use smaller, more efficient engines, proving that it is the best combination of all factors that will succeed rather than brute force.

FINANCE

The early enthusiasm of the French was

soon emulated by German, Italian, British and American automobile manufacturers who willingly underwrote the cost of challenging for the record. The publicity was deemed a valuable asset in selling their products. Racing on open roads had started soon after the automobile's appearance and developed into Grand Prix racing in the early 1900s. The manufacturers involved could use one of their racing cars, perhaps change the gearing, make slight engine modifications and exercise a little weight reduction to make a reasonable attempt at the record. This resulted in the record changing hands several times a year until the search for more power sidelined automotive engines in favour of aircraft engines. This became a British affair, with one notable exception, and was funded by private means and help from interested parties like component, tyre and ignition manufacturers. In the post-war years sponsorship by companies not related to motor vehicles gradually became more prominent. The cost of any attempt

at the absolute record is now so high that it is usual to see any challenger liberally decorated with logos of sponsors from all areas of the business world.

COURAGE

The drivers in this story faced mechanical setbacks, engine fires and the constant threat of disastrous tyre failure. As speeds increased the cars were notoriously difficult to control. They were faced with going into a world of speed where no one knew the limits of the machines. To climb into any of these cars required raw courage that took different forms ranging from calculated risk to recklessness. Some of the participants overcame disabilities that would demotivate the average person before they even sat behind the wheel.

Many suffered accidents only to recover and climb back in the car. Some lost their lives in the endeavour or met their end in some other speed-related event. Others faced the demon of speed just once and simply walked away.

REGULATING ORGANISATIONS

To claim a record it was necessary to be timed by a credible organisation. On 12 November 1895 the Automobile Club de France (ACF) was formed to set the regulations for motor racing. In the beginning there were no rules for speed records as such apart from a weight limitation and the means of timing was hand-held stopwatches with the results taken in good faith.

As motor racing became more wide-spread the new Association Internationale des Automobile Clubs Reconnus (AIACR) was established in 1904. This was an amalgam of European automobile clubs, including those of Britain and Germany, but the ACF persisted in trying to dictate the rules until 1922. The regulations had evolved to require contestants to make two runs (or passes) over a measured mile or kilometre in opposite directions with an interval of no more than an hour, to be timed with electronic equipment accurate

to a hundredth of a second, and to exceed the existing record by one per cent. After the Second World War the AIACR then became known as the Fédération Internationale de l'Automobile (FIA) and effectively regulated international land speed records.

The Fédération Internationale des Clubs Motocyclistes (FICM) was founded in 1904 to sanction motorcycle racing. This evolved into the Fédération Internationale de Motocyclisme (FIM), which seemingly would not have much to do with absolute records once cars became dominant. But that proved to be not quite the case.

On the other side of the Atlantic the American Automobile Association (AAA) was founded on 4 March 1902 to organise and oversee timing at speed events. Then in 1937 the Southern California Timing Association (SCTA) came into being to sanction land lpeed racing events held at El Mirage Dry Lake, California and at the Bonneville Salt Flats, Utah.

The early dominance of French vehicles

caused the ACF to cling to the idea that the land speed record was French property and they continued to call the shots from within the AIACR. This led to scepticism of results across the Atlantic. Americans did not see it that way. All that mattered was a credible speed. This led to many anomalies in the list of achievements and confused the issue as far as who the fastest man on earth might be at any particular point in time.

VENUES
In order to set a record any vehicle must have a suitable stretch of track to drive on. Straight sections of public highways sufficed to begin with but were superseded by longer stretches of flat beach. The beach straights were then found wanting in traction as speeds increased. They did not allow enough room to accelerate, enter the measured kilometre or mile and still leave room to slow down safely. The advent of the aero-engine cars through to rockets and jets required vast amounts of

open flat space that could be found only at the Bonneville Salt Flats in Utah, Lake Eyre in South Australia and the Black Rock Desert in Nevada. Strange as it seems, it is difficult to find 20-mile-long, perfectly flat stretches of the earth's surface that are relatively free of debris. There may well come a time when potential speeds will exceed the capacity for any location to accommodate them.

WEATHER CONDITIONS
After years spent raising the funds, building the car and travelling long distances, many contenders have been confounded by the elements. At Bonneville the annual Speed Week was cancelled in both 2014 and 2015 due to bad weather and deterioration of the salt surface. The condition of the salt would appear to spell the end of any absolute record attempts at this legendary venue. At Lake Eyre in Australia Donald Campbell's multi-million-pound attempt in 1963 was seriously affected by the weather as the track was covered in three inches of

water. Lake Eyre had not experienced any rainfall in the previous nine years.

FACTS AND FIGURES
Vehicle specifications were often in a state of flux. Some were as quoted by the manufacturer, some were not. Many went through a process of constant modification. Dimensions and weight in many cases are lost to time but in this book have been estimated wherever possible.

As far as horsepower is concerned it is impossible to verify figures as the way this was calculated in earlier days had more to do with taxation than actual output. The advent of aero engines gave rise to more confident figures as in many cases the manufacturers had to meet government specifications. It is also necessary to state the obvious fact that contenders in this activity would always look for ways to increase output and did not always share their secrets with competitors.

This plus the fact that many cars no longer exist and cannot be scrutinised

naturally leads to grey areas. We can, however, rely on simple science and graphs to make reasonable deductions about the specifications of the cars.

What remains is the speeds claimed if they are taken in good faith.

THE QUEST FOR SPEED
All the participants in this story had the determination, courage and perseverance to wrestle with the above factors in their search for speed. Luck was important and the goddess Fortuna smiled on some and not others. Many succeeded but were not officially recognised. This is the story not just of official record holders but also of extraordinary human endeavour in pushing the frontiers of the unknown, including some who failed yet made leaps in conceptual thought that also became woven into the fabric of the quest for speed. These designers and drivers constantly proved, often in the face of adversity, that there was more than one right way to do something.

JEANTAUD DUC • COUNT GASTON DE CHASSELOUP-LAUBAT

On 18 December 1898 an event at Achères in northern France initiated an activity that would grip the imagination of the industrial world. As part of a competition organised by *La France Automobile*, Count Gaston de Chasseloup-Laubat was timed on a 2km stretch in his electric Jeantaud car at 39.24mph. Camille Jenatzy, a Belgian, challenged this record and one month later he exceeded it with 41.42mph and sparked the idea that individuals would thus compete to set the highest speed.

SPECIFICATIONS

Vehicle	Jeantaud Duc
Origin	France
Weight	3,100lb (1,400kg)
Length	–
Width	–
Height	–
Transmission	Chain drive
Powerplant	Gramme electric motor
Horsepower	36hp
Power/weight ratio	1/86
Venue	Achères, France
Speeds	39.24mph & 43.69mph

Although both of these colourful characters appear on any list of land speed record holders, neither could truly claim to be the fastest man on earth. Thoroughbred racehorses were capable of speeds in excess of 40mph and American quarter horses could gallop at more than 50mph over short distances. On the mechanical side the development of the steam locomotive at the turn of the century resulted in speeds of 80mph and even more extravagant claims. In reality the early road vehicles were simply the fastest automobiles on earth but this did not seem to matter as public attention was captivated by the motor car.

Charles Jeantaud built his first electric carriage in 1881 and began manufacturing vehicles in Paris from 1883. His motive power was a direct-current electric motor designed by Belgian Zénobe Gramme, who had built a dynamo and found that it was reversible and would spin if connected to a DC supply. This motor was connected to the rear wheels via chain drive. The electricity was provided by lead-acid batteries that had first been invented in 1859 by Gaston Planté. His battery design was greatly improved by Camille Alphonse Faure in 1881. Faure used a

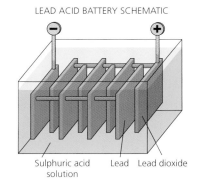

LEAD ACID BATTERY SCHEMATIC

Sulphuric acid solution   Lead   Lead dioxide

system of coated lead plates in a solution of sulphuric acid and water. The battery was rechargeable and this led to large-scale production by French manufacturer Fulmen. It is this basic design that can be found in every car in the modern world.

Jeantaud's automobile was also among the first to feature a steering wheel in place of a tiller.

However, it was a development of the combination of motor and batteries used by de Chasseloup-Laubat in the competition on a cold, wet day at Achères that was key to the Jeantaud Duc setting the first automobile record.

A French aristocrat, de Chasseloup-Laubat had a penchant for automobile races. He had won with a steam car in the 1897 Marseille-La Turbie long-distance race, the only major city-to-city event in which steam propulsion triumphed. The fact that he owned an automobile is

Steam locomotive 80mph

Horse 40mph+

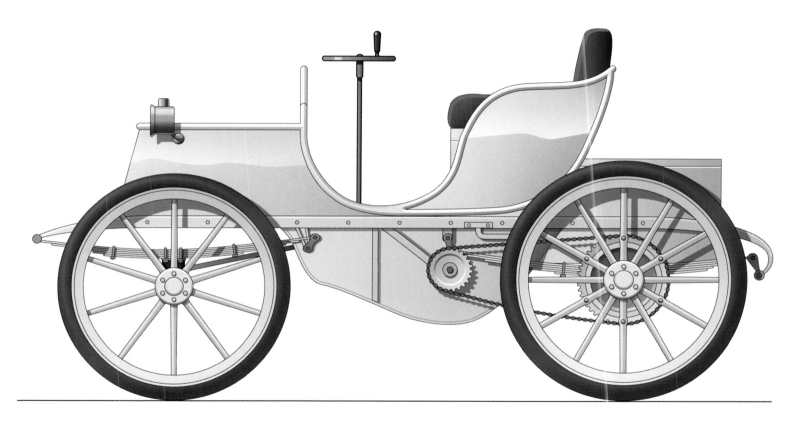

a reflection of a time when only the wealthy could afford one. This situation did not change much until the arrival in 1908 of Ford's Model T, which brought the motor car within the financial reach of ordinary people. And it did so with such unprecedented success that more than 16 million variants were produced.

The Count's record did not last long as Jenatzy, enthralled by the Achères event even though he had not been present, challenged the Count to a duel to be held on 17 January 1899.

Exactly how these speed trials were monitored has not been documented but the means to do it was available. In 1816 Louis Moinet created a mechanical timepiece, known as a chronograph, with the ability to time events to an accuracy of 1/60th of a second. This expensive masterpiece was a century ahead of its time but by the nineteenth century practicable, affordable stopwatches were in common use at sporting events and race tracks.

Motivation and means led to a never-ending quest for speed that was fraught with danger. Contenders from many different backgrounds were inspired to face this human and technical challenge for little reward, just a piece of paper with a few numbers on it — and immortality in automotive history.

JENATZY DOG CART • CAMILLE JENATZY

Camille Jenatzy was the son of the Hungarian Constant Jenatzy, who settled in Belgium and established Jenatzy Pneumatic, the first rubber factory in that country. The young Jenatzy studied as an engineer and was interested in the electric traction machines of the late nineteenth century. He was so interested, in fact, that he set up his own factory to produce such vehicles and went into competition with Jeantaud's electric automobiles.

Jenatzy was known for his sense of

SPECIFICATIONS

Vehicle	Dog cart
Origin	France
Weight	3,500lb (1,600kg)
Length	–
Width	–
Height	–
Transmission	Chain drive
Powerplant	Electric motor
Horsepower	36hp approx
Power/weight ratio	1/86
Venue	Achères, France
Speeds	41.42mph & 49.93mph

humour but was also a risk taker and was active in the popular sport of motor racing. He entered the Chanteloup hill climb near Nice in one of his electric cars and set the fastest time of the day, averaging 17mph over the 1.8km course. This may not sound that impressive but tarmac roads were things of the future and the course was simply mud and gravel, which was more suitable for a slow-moving horse than motorised wheels.

At this stage of the motor car's development, electric and steam cars were the main contenders with many more on the road than petrol-engine cars. Both were relatively quiet and reliable without such complications as clutch operation and gear changing. Although the range of electric vehicles was restricted by the limited duration of the batteries, they were popular for city driving where journeys were shorter and surfaces were smoother than the rugged routes in the countryside.

The internal combustion engine was a noisy, unreliable, oily machine that had

to be crank-started and as yet was not producing much useable power. This was soon to change once electric and steam power reached their practical limits and

Locations in France and Belgium where record attempts were made

the piston engine began its long era of dominance. But not quite yet.

On hearing of de Chasseloup-Laubat's accomplishment with the Jeantaud, Jenatzy immediately challenged his rival to a duel that took place on 17 January 1899, again at Achères, not far from Paris.

Jenatzy produced what were called dog carts. This was an apt description of his vehicle, which was a clumsy-looking, motorised cart but with plenty of room for batteries. It used the same type of carriage wheels with solid rubber tyres as the comparatively elegant Jeantaud but showed no visible concession to speed.

On the day of the duel at Achères, Jenatzy made the first run with a record speed of 41.42mph. But his success was short-lived. Within the hour de Chasseloup-Laubat had raised the record to 43.69mph but damaged his electric motor in the process. As the batteries of both cars were exhausted, Jenatzy proposed a rematch ten days later.

This time Jenatzy, equipped with an 80-cell Fulmen lead-acid battery, exceeded the record with a speed of 49.93mph while the Count experienced another burned-out motor and could not complete his run. Jenatzy now held pole position and intended to keep it that way. There was a shift in perception. This was no longer just

a case of which was the better vehicle: it had become a personal contest between the two men in a quest for speed. Their rivalry had captured the public's attention. From now on the bar would be continually raised and gradually involve more and more technical innovation.

Both Count Gaston de Chasseloup-Laubat and Camille Jenatzy had pushed their standard factory road machines to the limit but neither was willing to concede in this personal duel without further effort. Competition naturally breeds innovation and the question now was how to go faster.

The obvious solution was to reduce weight, which was relatively easy to do, and to increase power. This meant more voltage, a bigger motor, or even more motors. There were also some notions of how to slice through the air in a more efficient way. Making the vehicles less bulky was not a

great leap in technical thought. These basic ideas became the foundation of all that followed. Although the machinery looks very different, the fundamentals remain the same. The Count and Jenatzy had started something that man has continued to strive for — simply to go faster than anyone else.

JEANTAUD PROFILÉ • COUNT GASTON DE CHASSELOUP-LAUBAT

Count Gaston de Chasseloup-Laubat was now confronted with the problem of surpassing Jenatzy's speed of 49.93mph. His Jeantaud had suffered burned-out motors on previous attempts, which

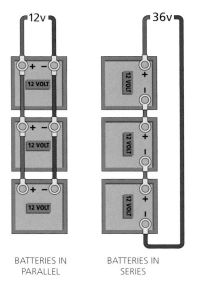

BATTERIES IN PARALLEL

BATTERIES IN SERIES

suggests that he had increased the voltage to this component beyond its capacity. Batteries connected in parallel maintained the voltage and increased duration.

Batteries connected in series increased the voltage at the same duration. Since he was to continue with the same vehicle he was forced to make modifications.

The limitations of the electric motor had been reached so instead of trying to increase power some advantage had to be gained elsewhere: the Count applied the science of common sense.

Little detail has survived but the few images of the machine that do exist suggest that an effort was made to reduce its weight and make its shape more functional. All unnecessary components, such as headlamps and bodywork, were removed. A framework, probably made of wood, was constructed and covered with a canvas material. This weight saving would have a beneficial effect on the power-to-weight ratio and put less stress on the motor. Then as now a vehicle has to actually complete the measured course to qualify for a recorded time.

Notably the Count gave some thought to the shape of the vehicle, resulting in a

chiselled nose with a rear end that could be described as an early fastback design. The rest of the main bodywork was devoid of any unnecessary protrusions. These features are a sign of an early consciousness of what today we would call aerodynamics or streamlining. At the

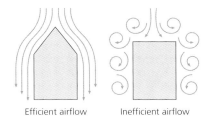

AIRFLOW SCHEMATIC

Efficient airflow   Inefficient airflow

time it probably would not have been a priority as the resistance of air was considered negligible if not non-existent at lower speeds. However, these changes to the bodywork did make the shape more efficient at passing through the air even if the gains were modest.

For decades to come the idea of streamlining cars was based on trial and

error or what looked right. Until designers had access to wind tunnels most of them applied the hit-and-miss science of 'eyeball aero' and experience through results.

The high ground clearance and exposed driver position of the Jeantaud remained in the overall specification. These flaws seem inconsistent with the new bodywork but from a practical point of view the high position of the driver was necessary for a good view when travelling at speed on a public road where surface irregularities or

SPECIFICATIONS

Vehicle	Jeantaud Profilé
Origin	France
Weight	2,500lb (1,150kg)
Length	–
Width	–
Height	–
Transmission	Chain drive
Powerplant	Gramme electric motor
Horsepower	36hp
Power/weight ratio	1/86
Venue	Achères, France
Speed	57.60mph

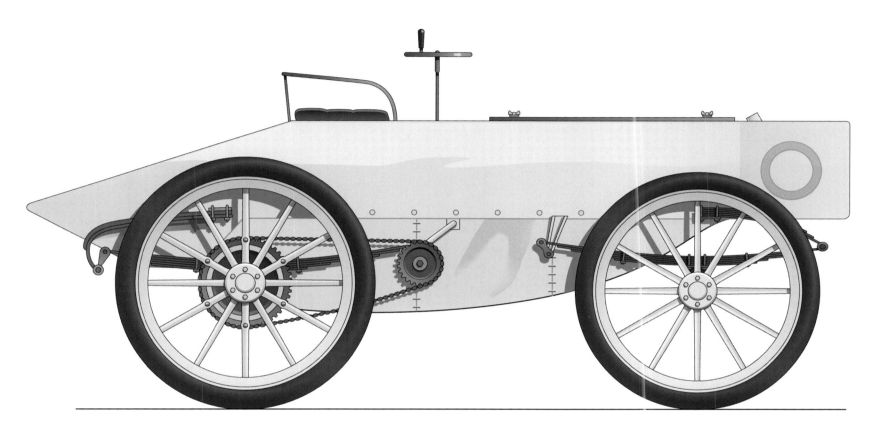

the sudden appearance of a pedestrian or animal were a constant hazard.

The problem of turbulent airflow beneath the body was not consciously considered at the time and drivers could always crouch forward, which they often did instinctively, if only to urge their machine on. The ground clearance was governed by the large-diameter wheels that were designed for a different purpose with the chassis set above the axles. In later cars the under-slung chassis was adopted. The large carriage wheels, originally created for horse-drawn vehicles, were better able to traverse bumps and ruts on unmade roads at lower speeds and, together with their narrow, solid rubber tyres, reduced rolling resistance.

On 4 March 1899, equipped with this new line of attack, Count Gaston de Chasseloup-Laubat regained the lead and stopped the clocks at 57.60mph.

In the background, having pushed his dog cart as far as it could go, Camille Jenatzy was working on something quite different. He had decided to build an automobile specifically for the purpose and completed it in two months.

LA JAMAIS CONTENTE • CAMILLE JENATZY

Within just three months the motives for the pursuit of speed underwent a perceptible change. The emphasis had moved from the vehicle itself to the person driving it. De Chasseloup-Laubat had modified his Jeantaud beyond recognition to reclaim the title. Jenatzy, meanwhile, had decided on another way of doing things and had designed a new car called *La Jamais Contente* with only one purpose in mind — simply to go fast with no other consideration. The publicity this

SPECIFICATIONS

Vehicle	La Jamais Contente
Origin	France
Weight	3,200lb (1,450kg)
Length	149.6in (3.80m)
Width	61.4in (1.56m)
Height	55.1in (1.40m)
Transmission	Chain drive
Powerplant	Postel-Vinay motors
Horsepower	68hp
Power/weight ratio	1/47
Venue	Achères, France
Speed	65.79mph

activity aroused was still very useful to manufacturers but neither car was ever to be offered for public consumption.

At this time the Automobile Club de France announced that it would regulate this interesting new activity and appoint

FIRST GENERATION AUTOMOBILE TYRE

Inflatable inner tube

Outer vulcanised rubber tyre

Tyre bolted to wheel rim

Wheel rim

official timekeepers to make the results more credible.

Due to his exploits and the colour of his hair, Jenatzy had earned the nickname *Le Diable Rouge* — The Red Devil — and he reappeared on the scene with a vehicle that

was a radical departure from his previous dog cart. Gone were the large, narrow carriage wheels, to be replaced with sturdy, small-diameter wooden wheels equipped with pneumatic tyres (from Édouard and André Michelin), which gave more traction. Michelin were the first to adapt pneumatic tyres for automobiles. These tyres consisted of a primitive outer rubber covering with an inflatable inner tube. The tyres of the period were often bolted to the wooden wheel rims and were prone to punctures or shredding.

The chassis was suspended on elliptical leaf springs and mounted with a light alloy bodywork called partinium, made of aluminium, tungsten and magnesium. Two Postel-Vinay motors, individually connected to the rear wheels, supplied the motive power. With enough batteries to provide 200 volts and 124 amps, the motors developed 68hp and propelled the purpose-built machine to a new record of 65.79mph on 29 April 1899. In metric France this speed exceeded the magic

figure of 100kph, causing a sensation. The Red Devil probably thought he had settled the matter once and for all.

La Jamais Contente is often described as having a torpedo shape, which was ground breaking visually but probably was not the prime factor in its success. The lightweight alloy body construction simply allowed for more heavy batteries that together with the two motors significantly improved the power-to-weight ratio in comparison with the Jeantaud. The shape

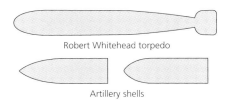

Robert Whitehead torpedo

Artillery shells

was certainly more functional than the dog cart and showed some similarity to Robert Whitehead's invention of the self-propelled torpedo, various artillery shells and bullets of the period.

Jenatzy also left us with some brief

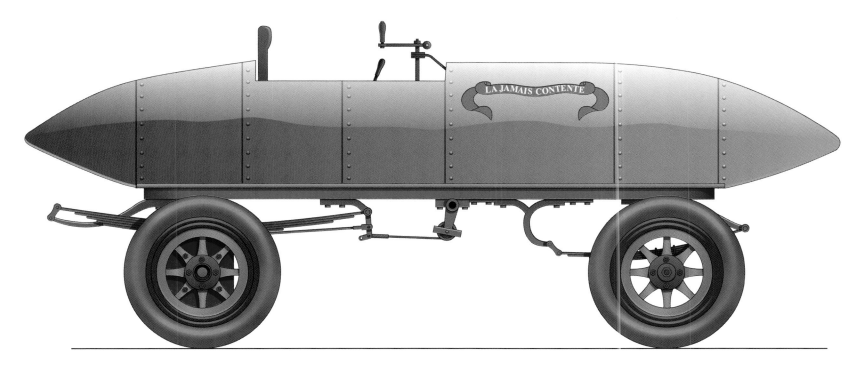

descriptions of what it was like to drive at the limit. He said that the car seemed to leave the ground and hurl itself forward like a projectile ricocheting along the ground while his gaze was steadfastly fixed about 200 metres ahead, his senses on the alert. The name *La Jamais Contente* — The Never Satisfied — became prophetic in

the quest for speed as it sums up the inherent reason for the activity to exist at all. Some future contestants were not satisfied with breaking the record and, in the absence of competition, continued to try to exceed their own endeavours.

The original car survives and now resides proudly in the Musée National de

la Voiture in Compiègne, north of Paris.

The Red Devil continued to participate in road-racing competitions, including the Gordon Bennett Cup, an annual event established by the American newspaper millionaire James Gordon Bennett Jr. In 1903, driving his favourite marque, a Mercedes, Jenatzy won the Cup

when it was staged at Athy in Ireland.

His sense of humour and risk taking finally became his undoing. When hosting a shooting party Jenatzy hid behind a bush, imitated a wild boar to frighten the guests and was promptly shot by one of them. He died on the way to hospital in a Mercedes ambulance. He was 45.

EASTER EGG • LÉON SERPOLLET

In the years following Camille Jenatzy's triumphant 65.79mph run, Léon and Henri Serpollet were busy perfecting the invention of the flash-tube boiler that was crucial to their efficient steam engine. Earlier in 1898 the brothers had gone into business with wealthy American Frank Gardner to form the Gardner-Serpollet Company and produce steam-powered automobiles. By 1902 they were ready to contest the record set by electric vehicles with Léon at the wheel of a steam-powered

SPECIFICATIONS

Vehicle	Easter Egg
Origin	France
Weight	1,650lb (750kg)
Length	136in (3.45m)
Width	–
Height	64.in (1.63m)
Powerplant	Steam engine
Transmission	Direct drive
Horsepower	30hp
Power/weight ratio	1/55
Venue	Nice, France
Speed	75.06mph

machine called *Oeuf de Pâques*, translated as *Easter Egg*.

The boiler used paraffin, fed by a pump, that was vaporised by pre-heating for combustion. This heated innovative flash tubes to produce instant steam that was fed to an equally efficient horizontally opposed

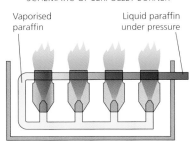

SCHEMATIC OF SERPOLLET BURNER

Vaporised paraffin
Liquid paraffin under pressure

four-cylinder engine. The appearance of the *Easter Egg*, described by one critic as looking like an upturned boat, was dictated by Léon Serpollet's view that at high speed it was more essential to diminish air resistance than to increase the power output. Although this was not entirely true, it was a perceptive observation on

a subject that was to take many years to be fully embraced. The pendulum would swing back and forth on the relationship between power, shape and weight in the decades to come.

It is interesting that although this was novel thinking as far as the automobile was concerned, it was in fact a science that many a great mind had wrestled with for centuries. Ship builders had studied the effect of positive and negative wind pressure on sails and agonised over the most efficient shape for ships' hulls for entire lifetimes. Eventually these same principles would be applied to land speed cars. As speeds rose in the second half of the century the movement of an object through the air was likened to passing through treacle and a great deal of thought was necessary with wind-tunnel testing becoming almost essential.

In 1902, after the initial dominance of the electric vehicles, Léon Serpollet was about to demonstrate that there was more than one right way to do something.

Having decided that the public road previously used at Achères was too rough and too short for his attempt, Léon Serpollet ran his *Easter Egg* on the Promenade des Anglais in Nice on 13 April 1902. Over the flying kilometre he recorded a new speed of 75.06mph, nearly 10mph faster than the three-year-old

CROSS SECTION OF BOILER PIPES

Conventional boiler pipes with thin walls and large water passages

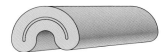

Flash boiler pipes have thick walls to retain heat and instantaneously create steam in the small water passages

record set by *La Jamais Contente*.

The Serpollet solution of small wheels with pneumatic tyres, efficient steam power and contoured bodywork that swept the air over a slightly lower driver position

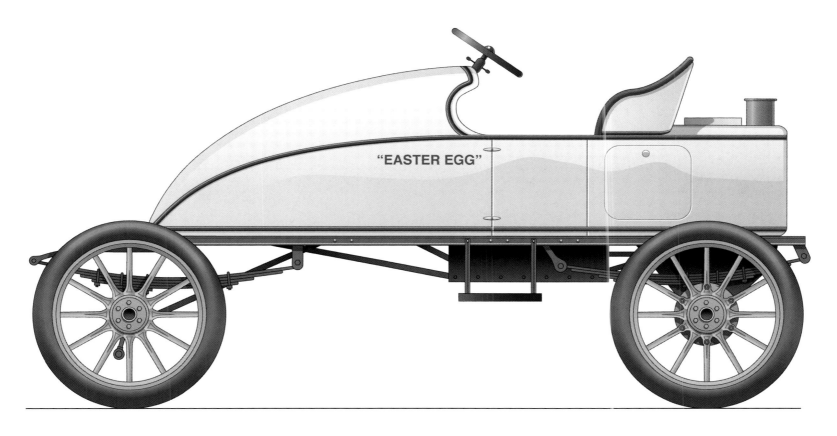

"EASTER EGG"

proved to be the best combination at that time, especially on a better surface. This put an end to the electric pioneers' early dominance in the quest for speed.

The key to this achievement and to the practicality of steam cars in general was Serpollet's own design of the flash tubes. These had much thicker walls than usual to retain more heat and the very narrow water channels helped convert water into steam more rapidly. This reduced the time it took to build up steam. As a result steam cars went on to capture a significant share of the automobile market in the first few decades of the twentieth century, especially in America, until finally overwhelmed by the rapidly developing internal combustion engine.

Intending to keep steam-powered cars in the public eye, Léon Serpollet entered cars in many of the early events until he retired from racing to concentrate his efforts on the production of steam trams. He suffered an early and untimely death aged 48 due to unknown illness.

The legendary *Easter Egg* now exists only in various replica forms. Although steam had taken the record, the rise of the internal combustion engine ensured that this supremacy was to be short-lived except for one last spectacular hurrah on the other side of the Atlantic.

ELECTRIC TORPEDO • WALTER C. BAKER

American Walter C. Baker, a 34-year-old engineering graduate of the Case School of Applied Science in Cleveland, made a fortune producing ball bearings for an ever-expanding industrial market before turning his attention to electric vehicles. Thomas Edison bought his first car from the Baker Electric Vehicle Company and began work on the nickel-iron batteries that Baker was to favour.

In 1902 the Automobile Club of America organised speed trials on the public roads of Staten Island. Like its French counterpart, the Automobile Club de France, the ACA required a one-way run only. At this event Baker unveiled a sinister machine the like of which had never been seen before, looking as if it had emerged from the pages of a Jules Verne science-fiction novel.

The 2,755lb *Electric Torpedo* fully enclosed the driver and brakeman, sitting in tandem, in a low-slung body made of pine covered with oil cloth and painted black. Its narrow spoked wheels were covered to reduce drag and it was motivated by a 14hp Elwell-Parker electric motor that was powered by Edison's new nickel-iron batteries. Other features included steering via cable, an early appearance of seat belts and a small cork-lined turret that gave the driver a restricted view of the road ahead through a tiny window. The whole machine was only 48in tall — low by any standard.

On 31 May 1902 Baker and his chief mechanic and brakeman, E. E. Denzer, climbed into this projectile and set off down the course. The events that followed are difficult to verify but as far as is known Baker built up speed in excess of 70mph, with some claims of over 100mph. He was still accelerating when he lost control while crossing some earth-covered trolley tracks. The Torpedo veered off the road, killing two spectators and injuring another. The car was a write-off but Baker and Denzer walked away unscathed.

Although it is generally accepted that Baker was officially timed at more than 70mph over the kilometre, he never entered the record books because the car failed to finish the course. He had been involved in racing accidents before and with new electric cars named *Torpedo Kids*, which also claimed unofficial records, he would experience more disaster and earn the sobriquet 'Bad Luck' Baker. He finally hung up the tinted goggles for which he was noted and thereafter concentrated on business. Speed events on public streets in America were deemed too dangerous and were banned.

Ascertaining accurate details of events

SPECIFICATIONS

Vehicle	Electric Torpedo
Origin	USA
Weight	2,755lb (1,250kg)
Length	224in (5.69m)
Width	–
Height	48in (1.22m)
Transmission	Chain drive
Powerplant	Electric motor
Horsepower	14hp
Power/weight ratio	1/196
Venue	Staten Island, USA
Speed	70mph

BAKER TORPEDO SCHEMATIC

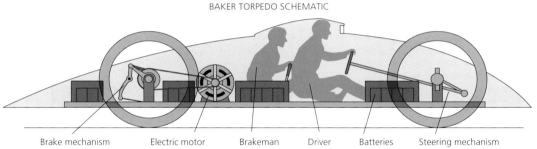

Brake mechanism   Electric motor   Brakeman   Driver   Batteries   Steering mechanism

held more than 100 years ago is difficult. It is possible only to make deductions from the few facts still available. For example, if *Electric Torpedo*'s weight of 2,755lb and the 14hp output of the motor are taken in good faith, the power-to-weight ratio is one horsepower to every 196lb. This is considerably inferior to the 1/47 ratio of *La Jamais Contente*. Therefore the performance of *Electric Torpedo* must have

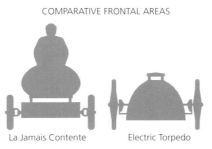

COMPARATIVE FRONTAL AREAS

La Jamais Contente   Electric Torpedo

been greatly enhanced by its aerodynamic shape (see diagram) plus the possibility

that it had a greater distance to build up speed in favourable conditions. Certainly streamlining and particularly reduced frontal area became critical areas of design in the latter part of the twentieth century.

Baker is not remembered as a record holder but rather as the man who made a quantum leap in vehicle design. Ironically his innovations were put to one side at the time, possibly because his extraordinary

designs were officially unsuccessful and associated with unmitigated disaster. Motive power was soon to become available in much larger quantities with the development of the internal combustion engine. For many years the ever-increasing horsepower that became available put other considerations into second place. 'Bad Luck' Baker and his futuristic *Electric Torpedo* designs were all but forgotten.

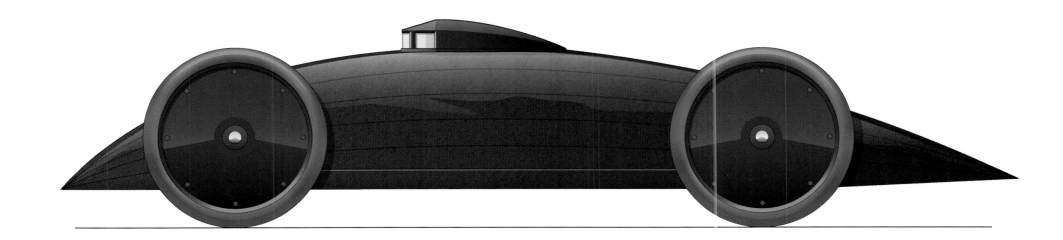

MORS TYPE Z • WILLIAM K. VANDERBILT II

William Kissam Vanderbilt II, known to his friends as Willie K, was a man of private wealth that allowed him to indulge in his enthusiasm for fast racing cars. In 1902 he set his sights on the automobile speed record held by Léon Serpollet in *Easter Egg*. Vanderbilt's chosen vehicle was the French-built Mors Paris-Vienna Type Z 9.2-litre petrol-engine car.

The early dominance of electric vehicles

SPECIFICATIONS

Vehicle	Mors Type Z
Origin	France
Weight	2,204lb (1,000kg)
Length	134in (3.40m)
Height	54in (1.37m)
Transmission	Clutch/gearbox
Powerplant	Four cylinders in-line
Engine capacity	9,232cc
Horsepower	60hp
BHP per litre	6.5/1
Power/weight ratio	1/34
Venue	Ablis, France
Speeds	76.08mph, 76.60mph & 77.13mph

had become limited by the weight of their batteries, which represented a large proportion of a car's overall weight. To increase the output of an electric motor also meant increasing the weight of batteries, which negated the desired effect. Steam-engine technology was also reaching a limit at that time, having undergone constant development for nearly 100 years.

Now it was the turn of the noisy internal combustion engine, which was in its infancy. The origins of the automobile can be traced back to the Patent Motorwagen designed by Carl Benz. Having already made stationary engines, Benz formed

1885 BENZ PATENT MOTORWAGEN

a company with Max Rose and Friedrich Wilhelm Eßlinge, who owned a bicycle repair shop. There, in 1885, he created his first purpose-built powered vehicle. This fragile-looking tricycle was constructed of a tube frame and spindly wheels that clearly showed its bicycle heritage. This was the first automobile to become commercially available.

As with many inventions, others were working on the same idea and within seven years automobiles had evolved into the image that we now know as the motor car. Hand-crafted cars such as the Mors appeared and by 1908 Ford's reliable Model T began its 19-year production run.

Road racing became very popular, running on public roads from city to city including the 900km race from Paris to Vienna that gave Vanderbilt's car its name. The Automobile Club de France regulated these events and many speed trials, enforcing the road-racing rule of a

maximum weight limit of 1,000kg. This gave the Mors, rated at 60hp, a power-to-weight ratio of 1/34, which was superior to all before it.

Dispensing with a little unwanted weight, Willie K became the first American to make a successful attempt on the record when he drove his Mors to 76.08mph at Ablis, about 65km south-west of Paris, on 5 August 1902, beating Léon Serpollet's speed of 75.06mph. This heralded the arrival of the piston engine as a serious contender and Vanderbilt's

SCHEMATIC OF CLUTCH OPERATION

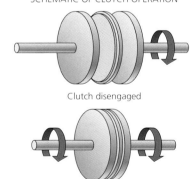

Clutch disengaged

Clutch engaged

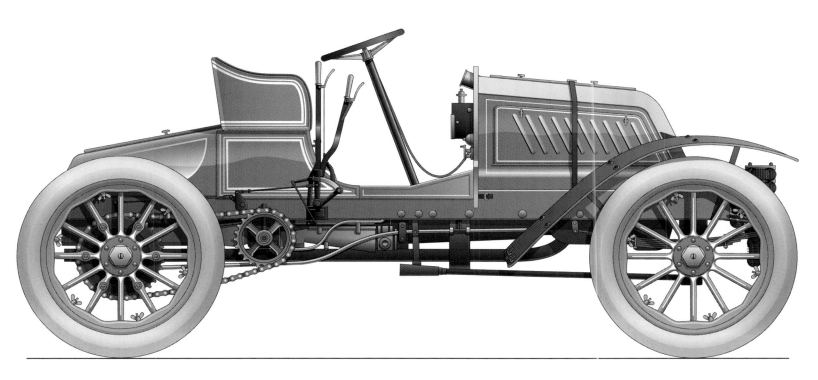

record did not last long. Others realised that the Mors Type Z was ready-made for more attempts. So it was that the laurels passed first to Henri Fournier with 76.60mph and then to Maurice Augières with 77.13mph in November, on the 5th and 17th respectively. Both drove a Mors Type Z at the French town of Dourdan.

The Mors Type Z engine was of a side-valve design with a bore of 140mm and stroke of 150mm, giving it a long-stroke designation. This meant that the distance the piston moved up and down was more than the diameter of the bore. This engine produced its thumping 60hp at 1,400rpm, a little over the tickover speed of a modern engine.

In the earlier vehicles the electric motor was controlled by a rheostat to monitor voltage and the steam engine by a regulating valve. But as the internal combustion engine is always turning over it brought with it such complications as gearboxes and differentials and the need to connect or disconnect the drive by means of a clutch. In its basic form the clutch consists of two discs that are pushed together to connect the engine to the wheels, usually with a friction plate between to make the transition relatively more gradual. The friction plate was coated with a composite such as asbestos to survive the intense heat that was generated by the slipping plates.

Overcoming these problems released the greater power potential of the piston engine. The power-to-weight ratio was so improved that streamlining was relegated to a secondary consideration for a further two decades. Finding more power became the overriding factor.

GOBRON-BRILLIÉ • ARTHUR DURAY

The Mors, in the now familiar form of a motor car with the engine in front and driver behind, had captured the record for piston engines. The publicity this generated attracted other manufacturers to enter the fray with their existing road-racing models. Next in line was the product of the now forgotten Société des Moteurs Gobron-Brillié, founded by Eugène Brillié and Gustave Gobron. Engineer Brillié decided that there was an alternative to the Mors four-cylinder in-line engine and created an unusual design featuring two opposed

SCHEMATIC OF CONE CLUTCH OPERATION

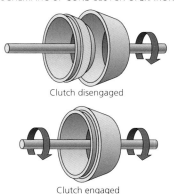

Clutch disengaged

Clutch engaged

pistons within each cylinder, known as the Système Gobron. Combustion took place when the pistons compressed the fuel mixture at the halfway mark in the cylinder. The cylinders were cast in pairs and two such units were mated together.

The Système Gobron engine was noted for its smooth running, a relative term in 1903, and it could also burn other fuels like benzine or alcohol besides petroleum spirit.

Engine evolution had come a long way in the nine years since Carl Benz had introduced his 2hp single-cylinder unit, with many different types appearing on the market.

Brillié also designed a variant on the clutch configuration that utilised cones instead of flat discs to ease the load on the transmission. The power then passed via a four-speed gearbox and chain drive to the rear wheels. As with the Mors, the earlier carriage wheels were discarded in favour

of stronger wooden artillery-type wheels fitted with pneumatic tyres.

This relatively advanced combination of motive power was in contrast to the

THE SYSTÈME GOBRON ENGINE

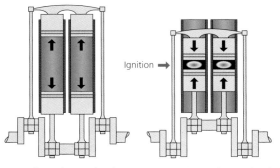

Intake stroke completed   Compression stroke completed

ramshackle appearance of the car as a whole. However, the weight regulations and the 100hp output gave the car a 1/22 power-to-weight ratio as compared to the Mors's 1/34. This was enough of an advantage for cosmetic appearance to need little attention.

A 22-year-old named Arthur Duray, a Belgian who later became a French citizen,

was making a name for himself as a racing driver. On 17 July 1904, he took the wheel of the Gobron-Brillié and drove it to a record of 83.46mph at Ostend in Belgium. Later that same year, on 5 November, he clocked a speed of 84.73mph at Dourdan, not far from Ablis. Other manufacturers took note of all the attention this created and felt inclined to get in on the action. After all it was simple: just build a bigger

SPECIFICATIONS

Vehicle	Gobron-Brillié
Origin	France
Weight	2,200lb (998kg)
Length	164in (4.17m)
Width	–
Height	60in (1.52m)
Transmission	Clutch and gearbox
Powerplant	Four-cyl opposed piston
Engine capacity	13.5 litres
Horsepower	100hp
BHP per litre	7.5/1
Power/weight ratio	1/22
Venues	Ostend & Dourdan
Speeds	83.46mph & 84.73mph

engine and remove all unnecessary weight to compensate.

Electric cars were now at a disadvantage. The problem was the battery banks. These could weigh up to 900lb and had very limited duration whereas petrol, containing more latent energy, weighs only 7lb per gallon, which allowed for a heavier power plant. The principal of the power-to-weight ratio was a simple one but at that time it was not fully understood that the power required was to prove exponential.

In other words, to gain an extra ten per cent in speed required considerably more than a ten per cent increase in power, eventually rising in the latter half of the twentieth century to astronomical proportions.

In the meantime the speed of 100mph, unthinkable for an automobile just a few years previously, was getting tantalisingly close. The audience and press were expectant, the automobile builders were willing and the pressure was on to conquer the magic ton.

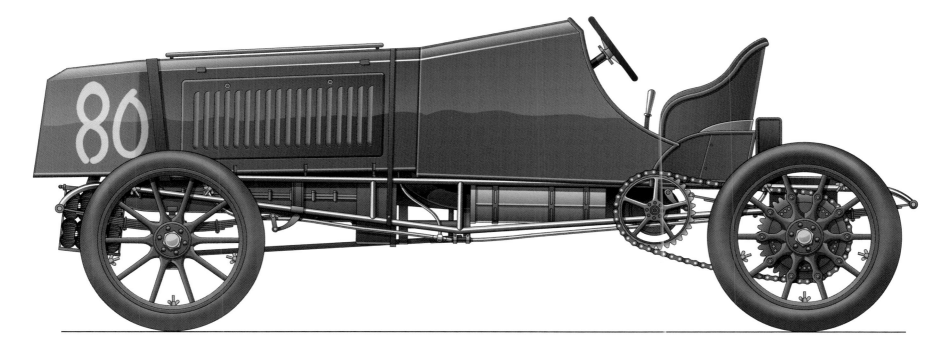

PIRATE • RANSOM E. OLDS

The seashore stretching from Ormond Beach south to Daytona Beach is 23 miles long and 500ft wide at low tide. The hard-packed sand is bordered on one side by sea and on the other by sand dunes, which provide a good view for spectators. The condition of the sand can vary according to the last tide and wind conditions but on a good day it provides a relatively smooth, straight, flat surface, a big improvement on the rough roads of the time. This remained the place to set records for more than 30 years, until speeds approached 300mph. After that the salt flats at Bonneville proved to be more practical.

When tycoon Henry Flagler bought the Ormond Hotel he thought racing on the beach would help to promote business. A contest was duly organised that became known as Speedweek. Alexander Winton agreed to bring one of his race cars and Ransom E. Olds promised a challenger.

Olds was mass-producing the Curved Dash Runabout but the 20mph car was not viable as a speed machine. So using the basic mechanicals, Olds built something more suitable and named it *Pirate*. Stripped down to the bare essentials and with an extended wheelbase, the car somewhat pre-dated slingshot dragsters with the driver hung out past the rear axle.

Winton and Olds driver H.T. Thomas

OLDSMOBILE CURVED DASH RUNABOUT

met on the sands in 1903 and both recorded a speed of 57mph, a tie that was amicably agreed upon in the days before competition took on an elemental, deadly seriousness.

SPECIFICATIONS

Vehicle	Pirate
Origin	America
Weight	850lb (386kg)
Length	138in (3.51m)
Width	–
Height	51in (1.29m)
Transmission	Chain drive
Powerplant	1,560cc single cylinder
Horsepower	7hp
BHP per litre	4.6/1
Power/weight ratio	1/120
Venue	Daytona
Speed	57mph

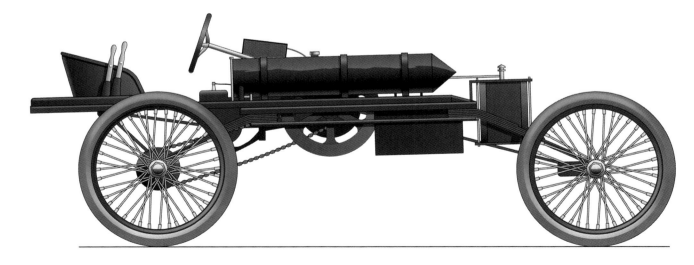

BULLET • ALEXANDER WINTON

Scottish immigrant Alexander Winton is the forgotten father of the American automobile. Like many contemporaries, he started with bicycle manufacture and progressed to self-propelled vehicles, becoming the first to sell an automobile, the Winton Six, in his adopted country. This was the first car to cross the continent from coast to coast. Winton was enthusiastic about racing for its publicity value and won often enough to be acclaimed as America's national track champion. He was also the first American to race an American car in Europe when he competed in the 1903 Gordon Bennett race.

For the inaugural contest at Ormond Beach he elected to drive himself and brought the four-cylinder 40hp *Bullet*. He continued building race cars with *Bullet* No. 2, which featured one of the first straight-eight engines, and recorded unofficial speeds of over 70mph. *Bullet* No. 3 followed with Barney Oldfield racing it across America.

As an inventor Winton held over 100 patents related to the car industry and on setting up the Winton Engine Corporation he produced the first American diesel engine with both locomotive and marine applications. He continued to manufacture quality cars until 1924, by which time he was no longer able to compete with the cheaper models mass-produced by Ford. In 1930 he sold the diesel company to General Motors and the Winton brand disappeared. The name Alexander Winton is largely unknown today but he rightly takes his place in the quest for speed.

Ormond Beach had now earned its title as the 'Birthplace of Speed' but in 1905 the American Automobile Association built a clubhouse on Daytona Beach just over the finish line and the events were thereafter said to be held at Daytona.

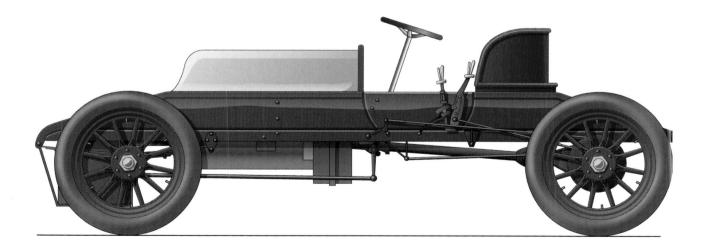

SPECIFICATIONS

Vehicle	Bullet
Origin	America
Weight	2,000lb (900kg) approx
Length	136in (3.45m)
Width	66in (1.68m)
Height	48in (1.22m)
Transmission	Two-speed gearbox
Powerplant	8-litre four-cylinder
Horsepower	40hp approx
BHP per litre	5/1
Power/weight ratio	1/50 approx
Venue	Daytona
Speed	57mph

FORD 999 • HENRY FORD

The intriguing story of the *999* began when motor racing enthusiast Henry Ford collaborated with the famous bicycle racer Tom Cooper, who provided the funds to build two race cars. They each consisted of a bare chassis carrying a huge 18.9-litre four-cylinder engine with a heavy flywheel and a clutch. There was no gearbox and the chain drive to the rear was replaced by a solid shaft drive to an exposed ring-

SPECIFICATIONS

Vehicle	Ford
Origin	America
Weight	2,730lb (1,238kg)
Length	146in (3.71m)
Width	56in (1.42m)
Height	50in (1.27m)
Transmission	Direct drive
Powerplant	Four-cylinder in-line
Engine capacity	18.9 litres
Horsepower	80–100hp
BHP per litre	5.3/1
Power/weight ratio	1/27
Venue	Lake St Clair, Michigan
Speed	91.37mph

and-pinion gear. Lighter wire spoke wheels replaced the wooden artillery wheels of the period and these were fitted with Firestone tyres. There was no rear suspension and the only concession to braking was a simple device acting on the rear axle. The concept was clear: maximum horsepower and minimum weight. One was the yellow-painted *Arrow* and the other, coloured red,

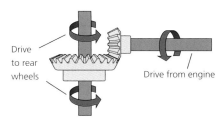

Drive to rear wheels

Drive from engine

SCHEMATIC OF RING AND PINION GEAR

was named *999* after the famed Empire State Express No. 999 steam locomotive that had claimed a speed in excess of 100mph. A car achieving the magic ton was no longer a chimera.

The claimed output of cars from this period is open to speculation. Horsepower, as defined by James Watt, is calculated by

multiplying the engine torque — twisting power — by the engine speed and dividing the result by 5,252. How these factors were arrived at is open to debate. Manufacturers often made optimistic claims to aid sales. However, it is reasonable to deduce that *999* had a better power-to-weight ratio than the previous record holder.

When the two cars were completed neither Ford nor Cooper felt inclined to take the controls so daredevil bicycle racer Barney Oldfield was hired. Having never driven an automobile before, Oldfield's only qualification was a total lack of fear. Curiously it was at this point that the cars proved to be temperamental and Ford sold his stake in the project before they actually raced, leaving Cooper and Oldfield as sole owners. The cigar-chomping Oldfield promptly proved his own and *999*'s worth by winning a race against Alexander Winton, recognised as America's top race driver. The indomitable

EARLY SPARK PLUG

Oldfield continued winning races to earn a national reputation.

In September 1903 *Arrow* was taking part in a race when it crashed, killing driver Frank Day. Henry Ford now bought back the damaged *Arrow* with the intention of breaking the speed record. It was repaired, painted red, renamed *999* and made ready for the attempt on the frozen lake of St Clair in Michigan. A four-mile section of the ice was cleared of snow to leave a bumpy track on the ice. On 12 January 1904 Ford, with his mechanic Ed 'Spider' Huff, who was instrumental in creating spark plugs for the *999* using dental porcelain, set a record speed of 91.37mph after claiming 100mph on an earlier test run.

The fact that the timing was done by the American Automobile Association and the Automobile Club de France refused to ratify it was of no concern to Ford as his interest was only in the market on his side of

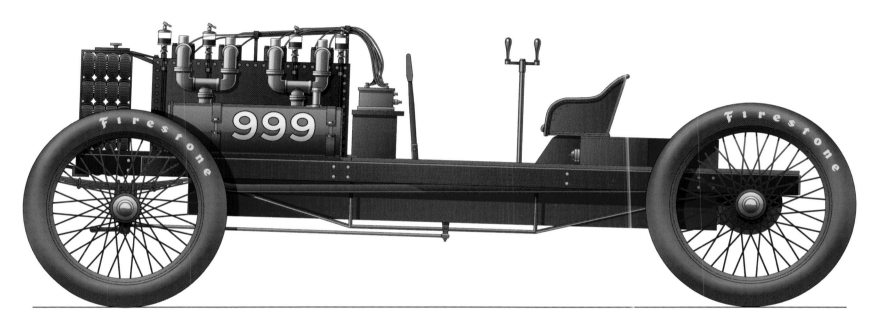

the Atlantic. The priceless publicity Ford gained from this feat helped to establish the Ford Motor Company, eventually leading to the sale of 16.5 million more modest Model Ts. Many decades later these workhorse vehicles, which boasted 20hp and a top speed of 45mph, were resurrected from scrapyards by hot rodders to have second lives screaming along the dry lakes and drag strips of America at speeds that would have astonished Henry Ford.

When reminiscing about *999* in his latter

HENRY FORD'S MODEL T

years, Henry's recollection of this fearsome machine of his own creation was that the roar of the cylinders was enough to half kill a man. Also, the car leaped into the air when it was not skidding on the ice and sprayed him with hot oil. Legend has it that mechanic 'Spider' Huff was clinging to the side of the engine operating the throttle to Ford's shouted instructions during the run despite every effort by the car to dislodge him from his perch. The poor traction between rubber and ice may well have deprived Ford of the magic ton but it seems that once was enough. The drive of his and Huff's life had scared him so badly that he never again wanted to climb into a racing car.

The illustration depicts the car as it looks today in the Henry Ford Museum in Dearborn, Michigan.

MERCEDES 90hp • WILLIAM K. VANDERBILT & PIERRE DE CATERS

Henry Ford's record-breaking run in Michigan did not stay intact for long. William K. Vanderbilt II was a wealthy man due to his father's success in the railroad business. This allowed him to indulge in his enthusiasm for speed with few financial restrictions. He had already become the first American to break the record with the French-made 60hp Mors at Dourdan and now took delivery of a 90hp Mercedes,

SPECIFICATIONS

Vehicle	Mercedes
Origin	Germany
Weight	2,204lb (1,000kg)
Length	144in (3.66m)
Width	56in (1.42m)
Height	50in (1.27m)
Transmission	Clutch and gearbox
Powerplant	Four-cylinder in-line
Engine capacity	12.7 litres
Horsepower	90hp
BHP per litre	7.09/1
Power/weight ratio	1/24
Venue	Daytona & Ostend
Speeds	92.3mph & 97.25mph

one of the most powerful automobiles available, the must-have car for those that could afford it. Ormond/Daytona Beach in Florida was chosen for the attempt with its 23 miles of firm sand. On 27 January 1904, just two weeks after the Ford *999* thundered to the record, Willie K raced the Mercedes over the measured mile and eight stopwatches clicked to record a time of 39 seconds. This was calculated to be 92.3mph, just a fraction faster than Ford's 91.37mph.

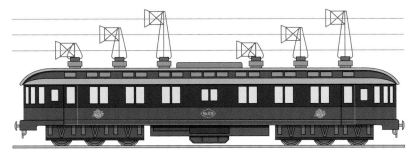

AEG RAILCAR - THE FASTEST WHEELED VEHICLE IN THE WORLD IN 1903

The reaction to this feat in France was lukewarm and a few months later the newly established, self-elected arbiters of

motoring events, the Automobile Club de France, chose not to recognise it as none of their timekeepers was present. Ignoring American claims became the norm in the ensuing years, adding to the debate as to who was the fastest at any given time.

Certainly neither Henry Ford nor Willie K was the fastest man in the world. Three months earlier, on 28 October 1903 in Marienfelde, Germany, an AEG electric railcar had been timed at an impressive 130.7mph under test conditions, and this was just as the piston-engine cars were making great strides.

Nonetheless the big Mercedes was

indisputably the fastest automobile in the world. Yet there was an anomaly. The Mercedes was undoubtedly heavier than the minimally basic Ford *999* and produced less horsepower, giving it an inferior power-

SCHEMATIC OF SHORT & LONG STROKE DESIGN

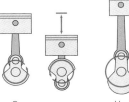

Over-square: large piston and short stroke   Under-square: small piston and long stroke

to-weight ratio. So how did it succeed? The explanation could be that it was running on a longer, more tractable surface. Ford could hardly have chosen a worse surface for the *999*, a combination of rubber on ice. The four-speed gearbox of the Mercedes also would have helped it to reach an optimum speed, wind conditions might have been more advantageous and, judging by Ford's comments, the experience was less dangerous. This is conjecture and cannot

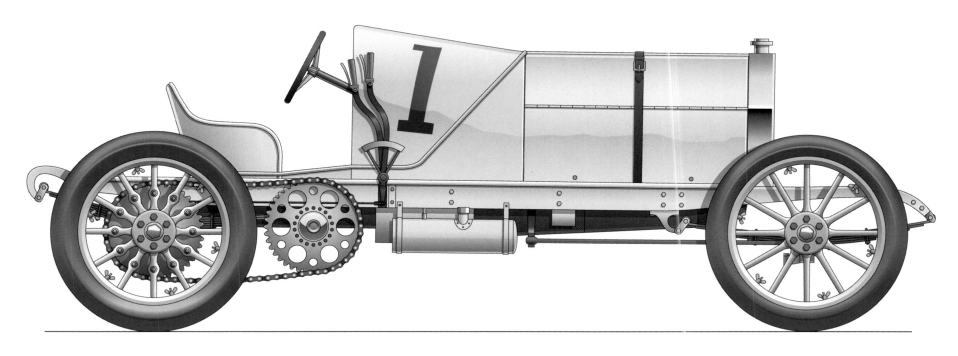

be verified but the record remains.

The big engine had been unusually modified to reduce its cylinder bore from 170mm to 165mm, decreasing the cubic capacity. However, the reduced piston weight enabled it to increase engine revolutions from 950 to 1,150rpm. As horsepower, simply put, is torque multiplied by engine revolutions (rpm), this increased the output. Like *999*, the stroke was less than the bore, giving the engine what is known as an over-square (short-stroke) configuration unlike most contemporary long-stroke designs.

Competition was strong in 1904, with Frenchman Louis Rigolly capturing the title in Nice just two months later, on 31 March, at 94.78mph. Then on 25 June Baron Pierre de Caters, driving a similar car to Vanderbilt, laid down the gauntlet with 97.25mph on a stretch of beach at Ostend in Belgium. With the record now officially back in Europe, Rigolly wasted no time in taking up the challenge to be the first to top the ton, 100mph, a speed that had been a fantasy figure for automobiles just a few years earlier.

After the adventurous Baron de Caters's brief foray on four wheels, he turned to aviation. Becoming Belgium's first pilot, he took part in many European air races until his inheritance ran out.

GOBRON-BRILLIÉ • LOUIS RIGOLLY

Louis Rigolly first beat Vanderbilt's record with his run of 94.78mph at Nice on 31 March 1904. His car was similar to the Gobron-Brillié driven by Arthur Duray the year before. The same Système Gobron engine was used but the bodywork had undergone drastic change. Gone was the scruffy appearance, to be replaced by a sleek form that featured a tapering chiselled prow. When Baron Pierre de Caters took the lead in June with a speed of 97.25mph at Ostend, Rigolly decided to respond.

Rigolly had enjoyed some success with his Gobron-Brillié in road racing but now had it specially prepared for the record attempt. Legend has it that the engine's capacity was increased to 15 litres and it was set up to run on alcohol, resulting in a claimed power output of 110hp, giving the car a favourable power-to-weight ratio of 1/20. These specifications cannot be verified but what happened next is on the record.

At Ostend on 21 July 1904 Rigolly

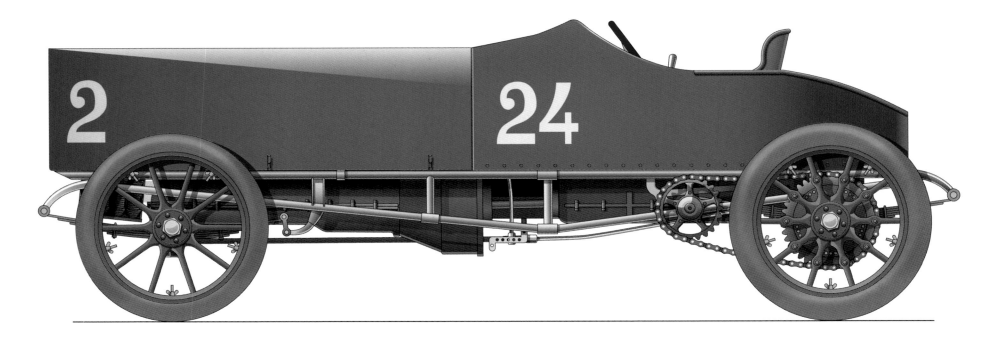

powered this combination through the measured kilometre in 21.6 seconds and became the first man to break the 100mph barrier with a speed of 103.55mph. Just a few years earlier this speed would have been beyond the comprehension of the average person. Amazingly, though, the record would not see the year out.

The reasons for the use of alcohol (CH_3OH) are not immediately apparent

SPECIFICATIONS

Vehicle	Gobron-Brillié
Origin	France
Weight	2,204lb (1,000kg)
Length	164in (4.17m)
Width	–
Height	60in (1.52m)
Transmission	Clutch & gearbox
Powerplant	Four-cyl. opposed piston
Engine capacity	13.5 litres
Horsepower	110hp
BHP per litre	8/1
Power/weight ratio	1/20
Venue	Nice & Ostend
Speed	94.78mph & 103.55mph

when compared with petrol (C_nH_{2n+2}). The piston engine acts as a pump sucking in fuel and air on the intake stroke. It then compresses this mixture on the compression stroke, causing it to ignite. The expanding hot gases push the piston downwards to create the power stroke. Petrol is able to release 18,400 British Thermal Units (BTUs) per pound when efficiently burned with 12.5lb of air. Alcohol on the other hand produces only 9,500 BTUs per pound of fuel but, as its chemical formula shows, alcohol contains oxygen and only needs about 4–5lb of air for complete combustion. Therefore an engine can burn up to three times more alcohol than petrol, resulting in a proportional power increase. Later in the twentieth century, nitromethane with an even lower heat value of 5,000 BTUs enabled even more dramatic power increases as it is composed of 50 per cent oxygen and needs only 1.7lb of air, or

even less, for complete combustion, giving power increases roughly in proportion to the percentage used. Dragsters eventually produced astronomical amounts of power and burned gallons of nitro faster than it can be poured from a bucket.

Although the opposed-piston layout

SCHEMATIC OF ATMOSPHERIC INTAKE VALVE

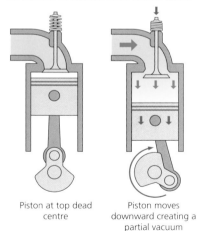

Piston at top dead centre

Piston moves downward creating a partial vacuum pulling in mixture

of the Gobron-Brillié was unusual, the engine employed devices common to large powerplants of the period. One such device was the atmospheric inlet valve, which was simply operated when the piston created a partial vacuum on its downward stroke, allowing atmospheric pressure to overcome the light spring that kept it in place. This valve never opened to any great extent and restricted the breathing of the engine, which partly explains the low BHP per litre (specific output) of these massive engines. In Rigolly's case it was only 8hp per litre as compared to any modern, self-respecting hatchback that commonly produces 50hp per litre. Likewise the more efficient-looking bodywork above the chassis was at odds with the exposed collection of mechanical components below, which created plenty of turbulent airflow.

Eugène Brillié had left the company at the end of 1903 and Automobiles Gobron went bankrupt in 1930. Little is known of Louis Rigolly's fate.

DARRACQ • PAUL BARAS

In 1896 Alexandre Darracq founded his automobile company, A Darracq et Cie, and in 1903 sold it to a privately held English concern named A Darracq and Company Limited, retaining substantial shares and a directorship. To promote the Darracq product, Alexandre motivated his designer, Paul Ribeyrolles, to construct a car that would outdo Louis Rigolly's headline-grabbing feat. The result of his

SPECIFICATIONS

Vehicle	Darracq
Origin	France
Weight	2,204lb (1,000kg)
Length	–
Width	–
Height	–
Transmission	Four-speed gearbox
Powerplant	Four-cylinder in-line
Engine capacity	11,259cc
Horsepower	100hp
BHP per litre	8.8/1
Power/weight ratio	1/22
Venue	Ostend
Speed	104.52mph

efforts was the 11,259cc 100hp Darracq.

Like many of his contemporaries, works driver Paul Baras had competed in cycling events before switching to automobile racing and he now took the wheel of Alexandre Darracq's aspiration. On 6 November 1904, just four months after Rigolly's run, Baras powered through the flying kilometre at Ostend to record a speed of 104.52mph and win acclaim for the emerging Darracq marque.

From what little is known, the Darracq's power-to-weight ratio was not as efficient as that of the Gobron-Brillié as its motor's rating was 10hp less, but engine ratings are open to interpretation if they are not precisely measured.

Other variables came into play within the regulations created by the newly formed Association Internationale des Automobile Clubs Reconnus (AIACR). These

allowed a one-way run. Since few roads are perfectly flat, participants could choose a slight gradient or wait for favourable wind conditions, but not both.

These rules were to change and to claim the record a speed of more than one per cent faster had to be registered. The marginal improvement by the Darracq, one fifth of a second faster than the Gobron-Brillié, was enough to make Baras, with his particular combination, the latest holder of the world record.

There were to be further changes in the regulations. These made a two-way run mandatory, with the added stipulations

that the second attempt should take place within half an hour, later changed to one hour, and that the runs should be timed electronically.

The chosen method for ignition in these early cars was to create a spark to ignite the fuel. This was achieved with a system known as make-and-break ignition that consisted of a battery, induction coil and a contact switch inside the combustion chamber. A current from a battery that is run through an induction coil will produce a strong spark when the circuit is interrupted. The large combustion chambers of the cars allowed room for the simple switch that was mechanically timed to operate just before the piston reached the top of its stroke, known as top dead centre (TDC). This fixed timing was another restriction to engine revolutions. Modern cars have an advance mechanism that creates the spark

SCHEMATIC OF MAKE-AND-BREAK IGNITION

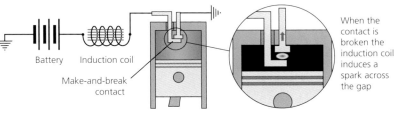

Battery   Induction coil

Make-and-break contact

When the contact is broken the induction coil induces a spark across the gap

progressively earlier as engine RPM increases. The make-and-break contact switches were much more difficult to maintain and clean as compared to the removable spark plugs that were gradually being adopted. This single-contact switch in such large cylinders did not encourage

complete combustion, resulting in flames from open exhausts as fuel continued to burn in the exhaust to complement the fearsome noise. Continual improvements to ignition systems were to help push the boundaries in the relentless quest for speed.

The intense competition in 1904 had seen the record change hands six times, with Paul Baras finishing ahead. Within another 12 months Darracq could claim to hold a total of six automobile records as the company experienced a period of glorious sporting success.

From this high point Darracq's fortunes fluctuated and by 1922 the name and famous badge had disappeared from motor vehicles. Paul Baras also faded from the scene after a brief period in racing, including participation in the first French Grand Prix of 1906.

NAPIER L48 • ARTHUR MACDONALD

Montague Napier began building cars in 1900 and his friend Selwyn Francis Edge formed the Motor Vehicle Company Ltd to sell them to the public. S. F. Edge was a firm believer in creating publicity to help market the product. Edge himself took the wheel in many motor races, including three Gordon Bennett Cups, before deciding to take a Napier L48 to the speed trials at Daytona Beach and challenge for the one-mile record with Napier employee Arthur MacDonald at the controls.

On 25 January 1905 MacDonald drove the Napier, sometimes referred to as *Samson*, along the sand to a record speed of 104.65mph. This beat the Baras

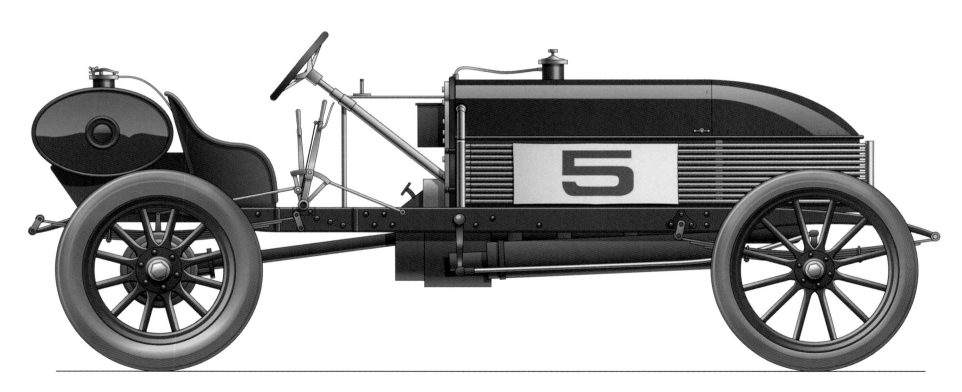

Darracq by just 0.1mph and marked the first time the 'ton' had been topped in America. But the Napier L48 was the fastest car only very briefly. Just an hour later Herbert Bowden went quicker in his twin-engine Mercedes.

By the vagaries of the regulations, however, neither record was recognised by the French AIACR because the organisation did not oversee the timing

SPECIFICATIONS

Vehicle	Napier L48
Origin	England
Weight	2,200lb (998kg)
Length	151in (3.83m)
Width	–
Height	50in (1.27m)
Transmission	Two-speed gearbox
Powerplant	Six-cylinder in-line
Engine capacity	14,328cc
Horsepower	100hp
BHP per litre	7/1
Power/weight ratio	1/22
Venue	Daytona
Speed	104.65mph

equipment and Bowden was disqualified anyway for being over the weight limit. It is interesting that when the mandatory two-way run and the one-per-cent rule came into effect in later years, neither car would have qualified anyway. Conversely, if the regulations in 1905 had remained unchanged, some future heart-breaking failures would have claimed the glory.

The Napier L48 employed a two-speed gearbox with shaft drive and was fitted with a 14,328cc engine that was typically large but had six cylinders. This effectively reduced the weight of each piston and connecting rod, which, together with a short-stroke design, was conducive to higher rpm. The engine was rated at around 100hp and, as the speed indicates, was close to the Darracq's specification.

On the subject of engine outputs, it is worth noting that in

1910 a horsepower rating was devised by Britain's Royal Automobile Club (RAC) for taxation and licensing purposes. The calculation included cylinder diameter but not the engine stroke or rpm, resulting in meaningless figures.

SCHEMATIC OF COOLING SYSTEMS

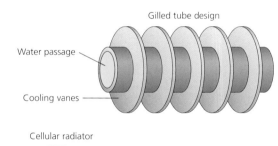

Gilled tube design

Water passage

Cooling vanes

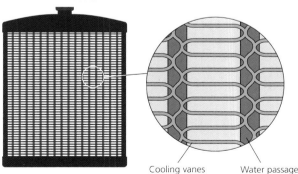

Cellular radiator

Cooling vanes   Water passage

With these large engines, water-filled radiators were used to dissipate the heat generated. An earlier arrangement of pipes known as gilled tubes were used on the Mors, Ford *999* and Gobron-Brillié. The Mercedes and Darracq both featured a cellular flat radiator that became the standard for almost all cars and was placed in front of the engine where it was most efficient. At the same time, though, this presented an unwanted flat frontal area. The L48 demonstrated another system, a series of copper pipes wrapped around the side of its wind-cheating bonnet to give it a unique appearance.

A reconstruction of the Napier L48 exists in Australia. It is fitted with the original engine and new components made from surviving drawings. The car has since roared at the Goodwood Festival of Speed.

THE FLYING DUTCHMAN • HERBERT BOWDEN

Massachusetts man Herbert Bowden's approach to the record-breaking challenge was to follow the logic of the day and use a bigger powerplant. His solution was to extend the chassis of his Mercedes 60hp car to accommodate a second Mercedes 60hp engine taken from his speedboat.

This also involved strengthening the front axle and reportedly machining a nickel-steel straight-eight crankshaft, the work carried out by his mechanics Charlie Basle and Charles Meyer.

The two engines combined to give an overall cubic capacity of 18.5 litres with make-and-break ignition and overhead atmospheric intake valves. The result was dubbed *The Flying Dutchman*.

It is fair to consider the car as an example of the brute-force school of thought with sheer power the key element. Yet based on the maxim that we cannot get the one result we want to the exclusion of all others, the additional engine and lengthened chassis brought extra weight. In fact, although *The Flying Dutchman* had 20hp more than the Napier L48, the power-to-weight ratios of the two cars were similar.

On 25 January 1905, Bowden aimed

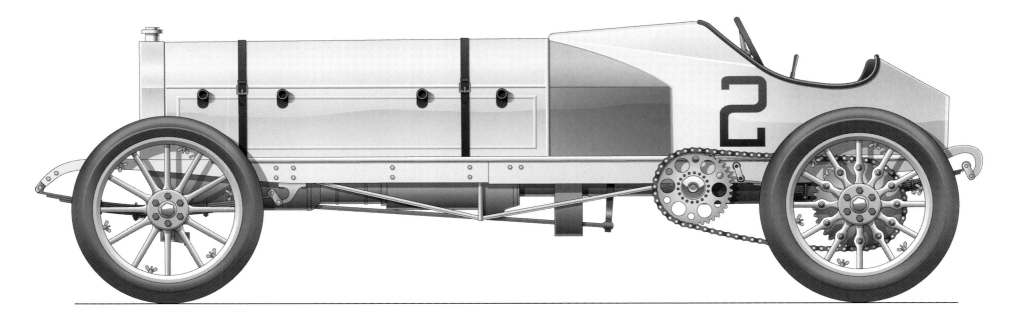

his twin-engine creation's impressively long bonnet down the Ormond Beach at Daytona and, just an hour after Arthur MacDonald's run, smashed the record with a speed of 109.65mph.

All this time, effort and courage

doubt the owner of the world's fastest automobile. In later years, the regulations regarding vehicle weight were changed with anything up to seven tons being allowed for record breaking.

The hard, flat sands of Ormond Beach

potential hazard for *The Flying Dutchman* as its four wheels had not been designed for the car's added weight and length.

Although Bowden's Mercedes car and its engines were built in Germany, his motivation was very probably patriotic as well as personal. When told that his speed would not be officially recognised as a new record, Bowden walked away with no apparent concern. What some authorities at home or 4,500 miles away in Paris thought was

slightly towards the rear and with the driving position nearly over the rear axle this helped to put more bias on the rear tyres, where it was more effective. This may have been only a small improvement but in this highly competitive activity, where one per cent could make a difference, every advantage was welcome.

Like streamlining, weight transfer became food for serious thought.

SCHEMATIC OF WEIGHT TRANSFER

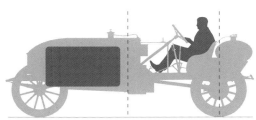

Napier L48 – weight bias of at least 70% on the front wheels and only 30% on the rear wheels

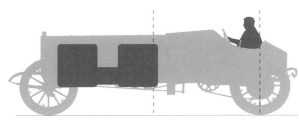

Flying Dutchman – position of engines and driver put approx.10% more weight on rear wheels

came to nought as neither the American (AAA) nor the French (AIACR) regulators acknowledged the feat because *The Flying Dutchman* did not conform to the agreed weight restrictions. Bowden's name does not appear on any record list even though his significantly faster time was registered by six stopwatches, making him without

might have been expected to make the activity safer but the rising speeds brought both known risks and hidden dangers. Punctures were a common occurrence at the time and we cannot know how much thought Bowden gave to the dire consequences of a tyre blow-out at over 100mph. This was a particularly significant

of no consequence to him.

It is possible that slightly better traction contributed to the outcome on the sandy surface. In the diagram it can be seen that, like most cars of the day, the Napier engine configuration put most of the weight bias on the front tyres. The twin engines of *The Flying Dutchman* moved the extra weight

SPECIFICATIONS

Vehicle	Mercedes
Origin	Germany
Weight	2,780lb (1,261kg)
Length	156in (3.96kg)
Width	–
Height	48in (1.22m)
Transmission	Four-speed gearbox
Powerplant	Eight-cylinder in-line
Engine capacity	18.5 litres
Horsepower	120hp
BHP per litre	6.5/1
Power/weight ratio	1/23
Venue	Daytona
Speed	109.65mph

NAPIER K5 • DOROTHY LEVITT

Dorothy Levitt's story is part of the fabric of this epic saga. It began when Selwyn Edge noticed an attractive secretary working in the Napier offices in London. Always on the alert for captivating headlines to help the sale of his cars, he proposed that this 20-year-old woman should become a racing driver. Simple really: all he had to do was teach her to drive. He arranged lessons and then sent her to France where she learned

SPECIFICATIONS

Vehicle	Napier
Origin	England
Weight	2,200lb (998kg)
Length	149in (3.78kg)
Width	–
Height	48in (1.22m)
Transmission	Three-speed gearbox
Powerplant	Four-cylinder in-line
Engine capacity	13 litres
Horsepower	80hp
BHP per litre	6.1/1
Power/weight ratio	1/27
Venue	Brighton
Speed	79.75mph

all about the building and maintenance of cars as racing drivers had to attend to their own vehicles during a race. On her return Levitt became the first British female racing driver to win trophies and set distance records in direct competition with men. She also quickly made her mark on water, setting the first world water speed record and winning numerous events.

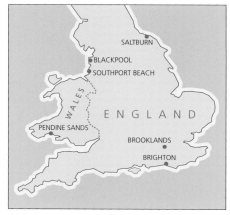

For further diversion in her racing career, Levitt taught Queen Alexandra and the Royal Princesses how to drive and found time to write a book entitled *The Woman and the Car* for those who wished to take up the pastime. Edge's protégé had become a valuable asset in gaining publicity and increasing sales of his cars.

In July 1905 this intrepid member of the so-called weaker sex, who was not yet entitled to vote, entered the Brighton Speed Trials and recorded a speed of 79.75mph to set the women's land speed

record in the four-cylinder 80hp Napier K5. In October the following year Levitt added to this success by driving the Napier L48 to a speed of 90.88mph at the Blackpool Speed Trial, earning her the title 'The Fastest Girl on Earth'. Such fame was yet to be claimed by any man driving an automobile as they had not caught up with the AEG electric railcar.

Levitt's description of the experience informs us that the slightest touch of the hand caused the car to swerve, half the time the wheels did not touch the ground, and the hardest thing was to stay in the driving seat. The land speed saga is full of ifs and buts, yet one cannot help wondering what speed Levitt might have achieved on the long flat sands of Daytona.

The Napier K5 was the precursor to the L48 six-cylinder engine. It consisted of four cylinders of up to 165mm bore and 152mm stroke, giving a capacity of 13

litres. It produced 80hp at 1,200rpm and power was transmitted via a three-speed gearbox and shaft drive. Montague Napier favoured atmospheric inlet valves and the K5 featured four to each cylinder together with make-and-break ignition. A front-mounted flat cellular radiator took care of engine-cooling duties.

Locations in England and Wales where record attempts were made

Although Napier continued to have an effective presence in motor racing, the cars used by Arthur MacDonald and Dorothy

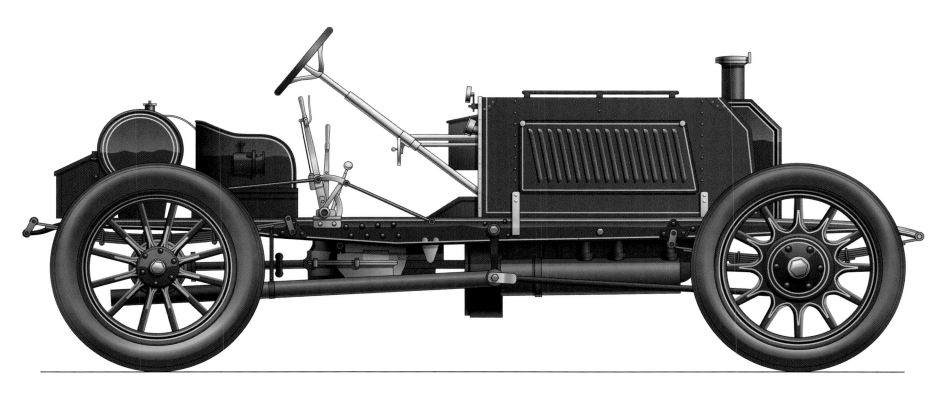

Levitt were the only Napiers to succeed in outright speed records.

In 1914 car manufacturers converted to war production and Napier was contracted to build aircraft engines designed by others. As these engines proved to be sub-standard, Montague Napier designed his own, resulting in the excellent Lion V12 engine, also known as the Broad Arrow. As car sales waned, Montague Napier ended participation in speed trials and finally ceased motor vehicle manufacture in 1924. Production of aero engines, however, continued to expand and the Lion unit powered dozens of different aircraft. Yet Montague Napier could have had little idea that his advanced aero engine would provide the heartbeat and propel future challengers to so many absolute land speed records, more in fact than any other engine manufacturer.

Dorothy Levitt's notable life in the fast lane ended in 1910 when she disappeared from public life. The inequality women faced did not prevent Levitt from leaving an indelible mark on motor sport. She died alone in 1922 at just 40 years old. Women got the vote four years later.

DARRACQ V8 • VICTOR HÉMERY, LOUIS CHEVROLET & VICTOR DEMOGEOT

The success of the Paul Baras Darracq stimulated Alexandre Darracq to go one better, instructing his designer Paul Ribeyrolles to build a car that would exceed the record by a significant amount. The result was the fearsome fire-breathing Darracq V8. Ribeyrolles knew that if he simply imitated *The Flying Dutchman* and added a second four-cylinder engine, he

SPECIFICATIONS

Vehicle	Darracq
Origin	France
Weight	1,982lb (899kg)
Length	140in (3.56m)
Width	–
Height	45in (1.14m)
Transmission	Two-speed gearbox
Powerplant	Eight-cylinder 90° V
Engine capacity	25.4 litres
Horsepower	200hp
BHP per litre	7.9/1
Power/weight ratio	1/10
Venue	Arles-Salon & Daytona
Speeds	109.65mph, 117.64mph & 120.40mph

would also exceed the weight limit. His solution was instead to create one of the first V8 engines by mating together two four-cylinder engine blocks at a 90-degree angle. These were equipped with pushrod-operated overhead valves and fired by spark plugs activated by a Nieuport magneto. Fuel was supplied to the carburettor by pressurising the fuel tank with a pump

SCHEMATIC OF PRESSURISED FUEL TANK

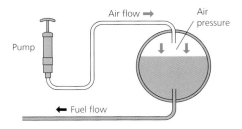

worked by the riding mechanic, who also pumped oil to the engine. Stripped of all unnecessary weight, the powerful Darracq looked like it meant business, albeit with a fairly heavy weight bias towards the front.

Works driver Victor Hémery put himself in the record books with an

official speed of 109.65 mph on the Arles-Salon dirt road in France on 30 December 1905. This was a disappointment as the Darracq developed 200hp and had a much better power-to-weight ratio than *The Flying Dutchman*, yet could only equal its unofficial speed. Hémery blamed this on poor weather conditions and the car was quickly shipped across the Atlantic to prove its real potential on the long stretch at Daytona.

Hémery's abrasive and argumentative nature had already seen him banished from events in Italy and now he found himself disqualified at Daytona before he had hardly begun. Louis Chevrolet was hired instead to drive with Victor Demogeot as riding mechanic, resulting in a record of 117.64mph. When Chevrolet was asked to make another run, he declined and the opportunity was given to Demogeot, with Louis Vivet as his mechanic. The switch helped to realise the car's potential with a speed of 120.40mph.

All this effort came to nought as Fred

Marriott in a quaintly named *Stanley Steamer* (see overleaf) recorded a speed of 121.57mph for the flying kilometre and 127.66mph for the flying mile at the same meeting. As these were the top speeds achieved at the meeting, the efforts of Chevrolet and Demogeot did not make the record books.

Although the Automobile Club de France only recognised the Steamer's slower speed of 121.57mph, this was nonetheless the first American record it had ratified. So the Darracq was the fastest petrol-engine vehicle in the world and the *Stanley Steamer* was the fastest automobile in the world. But neither of the drivers could, as yet, claim to be the fastest man in the world.

Simple arithmetic shows that the Darracq's power increase of 60 per cent gave only a nine per cent increase in speed. The V8 engine was significantly over-square with a bore of 170mm and a stroke of 140mm. Its huge 7in diameter pistons were made of cast iron, as were the connecting rods and crankshaft, all built to an industrial scale. All these heavy parts had to rotate, which was a significant factor in limiting engine speed to 1,200rpm. In time cast-iron pistons were replaced by cast or forged-aluminium alloy versions and as advances were made in metallurgy every part of the engines became lighter, stronger and more efficient.

After Daytona the car was bought by Algernon Lee Guinness and successfully raced by him in Britain. Swiss-born Chevrolet pursued a racing career in America and went on to co-found the Chevrolet company. Demogeot continued as a mechanic and driver before turning to different business interests. Hémery continued road racing and set another record at Brooklands driving for Benz.

The mighty Darracq, now in private ownership, has been rebuilt, using the original engine and many authentic parts. It occasionally emerges to frighten the public with its fiery exhausts.

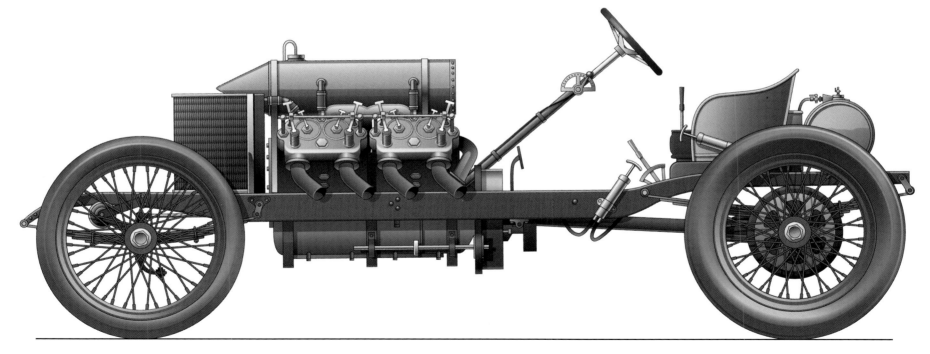

STANLEY STEAMER • FRED MARRIOTT

Twins Francis Edgar and Freelan O. Stanley became interested in steam automobiles in 1897. By 1902 they had formed their own Stanley Motor Carriage Company. To promote steam-powered vehicles they entered the speed contest four years later with racer Fred Marriott at the tiller of their *Stanley Steamer*.

On 26 January 1906 the Steamer eclipsed its nearest rival, the Darracq V8, with runs of 121.57mph over the measured kilometre and 127.66mph over

SPECIFICATIONS

Vehicle	Stanley Steamer
Origin	America
Weight	1,680lb (762kg)
Length	192in (4.88m)
Width	64in (1.63m)
Height	36 (0.91m)
Transmission	Direct drive
Powerplant	Twin-piston steam engine
Engine capacity	3.1 litres
Horsepower	20hp nominal
Venue	Daytona
Speeds	121.57mph & 127.66mph

the measured mile. The previous eight years had seen the record change hands a score of times, by quite small increments, if all claims are included. The Steamer represented a quantum leap. Its historic speed for an automobile over the mile stood for five years and was not exceeded by an AIACR-ratified run until 1922. The true significance of this achievement is that it lasted as a steam-powered record until the Barber-Nichols Engineering car did 147.6mph on a one-way pass at Bonneville in 1985. It was not officially exceeded until 2009 and then only by 21mph.

The Stanley car was nominally rated at 20hp but this related to the boiler not the steam engine itself so it has little real meaning. The only method of measuring an engine's true output was to connect it to some form of brake and calibrate the amount of force required to limit the rpm. The earliest example is the Prony brake invented in 1821. Later versions, known as dynamometers (dynos), involved connection to an electric generator or some form of hydraulic or water brake.

SCHEMATIC OF PRONY BRAKE

Engine / Braking strap / Calibrated tensioning spring

But there is no record that these devices were ever used by the Stanley brothers.

It is reasonable to deduce, given the performance of the Steamer, that it delivered substantially more than 20hp. The standard engines were regulated to a maximum pressure of 550psi (pounds per square inch) whereas Marriott referred to pressures of 1,300psi. It is possible that outputs of 100hp or more were feasible for short periods. Together with lighter weight, better weight distribution (for better traction), smaller frontal area, an aerodynamic body, narrow 3in tyres, a low driver position and a fearless pilot, this made for the best possible combination. The wood and canvas body shell, which was reminiscent of the *Electric Torpedo*, looked like an upturned canoe, which in effect it was having been built by The

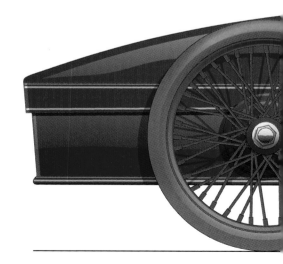

Robertson Canoe Company. The Stanleys understood the principles involved and improvised their own canoe dyno, which was implemented by towing different hull shapes at speed, connected by a calibrated spring to measure wind resistance.

The Steamer's performance was the zenith, but also proved to be the grand finale for steam as a contender for absolute automobile records. An even more powerful version of the car, known as the *Rocket*, made a second attempt that emphasised the terrifying potential of such machines. It reached a claimed speed in excess of 150mph before it hit a rut, took off like a kite and was destroyed. Marriott suffered several broken ribs, a hole in his upper jaw and a cracked breastbone. The top of his scalp was sliced open and his right eye was left hanging from its socket. Neither the Stanley brothers nor Marriott contested the record again.

The one factor that let Marriott down was the track itself. He recovered but nothing survives of the historic cars. The disastrous outcome turned attention away from what some perceived as suicidal attention to aerodynamics.

CURTISS MOTORCYCLE • GLENN CURTISS

Glenn Hammond Curtiss began his steep learning curve building and racing bicycles. He moved on to motorcycles before eventually fulfilling his engineering destiny as a pioneer of American aviation. He made the first officially witnessed flight in North America, won a race at the world's inaugural international air meeting in France and made the first long-distance flight in the United States. His work designing and building aircraft led to the formation of the Curtiss Aeroplane Company.

The approach to building aircraft engines was different from that of cars. Wilbur and Orville Wright had proved the principles of powered flight in 1903 and now that this genie was out of the bottle the contest for engineers was to produce engines that were light and reliable. The powerplants that were appearing in land speed cars were producing only about 8hp per litre and their heavy weight made them

unsuitable for flight. For aircraft designers the priority was not speed but sustained flight. With this aim, Curtiss designed a prototype aircraft engine that he put into a motorcycle frame to prove its capability. This was the genesis of the startling effect that aviation engineering was to have on the future of the land speed saga.

The Curtiss engine was an air-cooled 90-degree V8 with a bore of 92.1mm and

SPECIFICATIONS

Vehicle	Curtiss
Origin	America
Weight	275lb (125kg)
Length	94in (2.39m)
Width	27in (0.69m)
Height	36in (0.91m)
Transmission	Direct drive
Powerplant	V8
Engine capacity	4.4 litres
Horsepower	40hp
BHP per litre	9/1
Power/weight ratio	1/10.6
Venue	Daytona
Speed	136.36mph

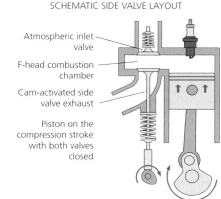

SCHEMATIC SIDE VALVE LAYOUT

Atmospheric inlet valve

F-head combustion chamber

Cam-activated side valve exhaust

Piston on the compression stroke with both valves closed

a stroke of 82.6mm, giving a displacement of 4.4 litres. It was equipped with cam-operated exhaust side valves and atmospheric inlet valves that necessitated an offset combustion chamber known as an F head.

Spark plugs with battery trembler-coil ignition, which produced multiple sparks, had made an early appearance on the Ford *999*. These gradually replaced the make-and-break system, especially where internal cylinder head space was at a premium, such as on the Curtiss V8.

With an output of 40hp at 1,800rpm, this V8 engine was fitted to a modified motorcycle frame and, dispensing with both clutch and gearbox, drove the rear wheel by means of a simple ring-and-pinion gear.

The machine weighed only 275lb and with the rider's weight factored in at a nominal 150lb the total was 425lb. This gave a power-to-weight ratio of 1hp to every 10.6lb. Even though this was a very light machine and 40hp was a huge output for a motorcycle, the Curtiss had only approximately the same power-to-weight ratio as the Darracq V8. So why was it dramatically faster? The answer lies in the minimal frontal area, which was little more than the rider's body shape. This was about as small as could be obtained without the rider lying in the prone or reclining position that was adopted later in the century.

At Daytona on 24 January 1907 Glenn Curtiss was push-started as he sat astride

CURTISS FRONTAL AREA

his creation with miles of open beach ahead for him to build up speed with his single gear. Using tyres that were liable to puncture, burst or shred away from the wheel rims at any moment, he powered his machine through the measured mile to record a speed of 136.36mph. Before he came to a halt, the stresses had broken the universal joint of the driveshaft and bent the bike's frame.

Nothing had ever gone faster yet back in France the AIACR declined to ratify the record because the vehicle had only two wheels. The record was broken unofficially in 1911 but not exceeded officially until 1924. A motorcycle did not improve it until 1930.

Curtiss drove the only motorcycle ever to hold the absolute record and earned the indisputable title of the fastest man on the planet. This historic machine is now on display in the Smithsonian National Air and Space Museum.

BLITZEN BENZ • HEMÉRY, OLDFIELD, BURMAN & TETZLAFF

Motor racing had existed since the car had been invented and was quickly regulated in Europe by the AIACR. Races were usually from city to city and, with little in the way of safety precautions, spectators as well as participants were fatally injured. This led, in 1906, to the first Grand Prix to be staged on a closed circuit, at Le Mans in France, marking the end of racing on public

SPECIFICATIONS

Vehicle	Benz
Origin	Germany
Weight	3,197lb (1,450kg)
Length	161in (4.09m)
Width	63in (1.60m)
Height	50.4in (1.28m)
Transmission	Four-speed, chain drive
Powerplant	Four-cylinder in-line
Engine capacity	21.5 litres
Horsepower	200hp
BHP per litre	9.3/1
Power/weight ratio	1/16
Venues	Brooklands & Daytona
Speeds	125.95mph, 131.27mph, 141.37mph & 142.80mph

roads. Competition was fierce between manufacturers to build winning cars and from this crucible of creativity came a thing of great beauty.

In 1909 Benz designer Julius Ganss was encouraged to create a car for an assault on the speed records. The *Blitzen Benz* was based on a Grand Prix car and designated the Benz 200hp as per normal factory practice. Engine capacity was increased by the practised method of boring out the cylinders to produce 21.5 litres.

The bodywork was made as narrow as possible with the rear end given a theoretically aerodynamic pointed tail that would appear on many Grand Prix cars. Under the bonnet was a beautifully constructed engine featuring pushrod-activated overhead valves, two spark plugs per cylinder and a compression ratio of 5.8 to 1. This improved both breathing and combustion, giving an engine rating of 200hp at 1,600rpm. As AIACR weight restrictions for Grand Prix cars had been eased, the Benz weighed in at 3,197lb,

which was more than 50 per cent heavier than the Darracq V8.

The *Blitzen Benz* made its first impact on 8 November 1909 at Brooklands, the speed bowl in Surrey, south-west of London, that had opened in 1907. In the hands of Victor Hémery, it recorded an AIACR-recognised speed of 125.95mph. With

SCHEMATIC OVERHEAD VALVE LAYOUT

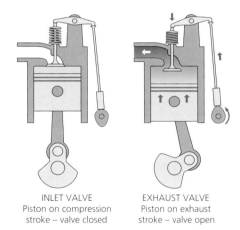

INLET VALVE
Piston on compression
stroke – valve closed

EXHAUST VALVE
Piston on exhaust
stroke – valve open

that, Hémery also passed the landmark of 200kph but even the banked curves at Brooklands did not allow the car to achieve

its full potential. The following January the *Blitzen Benz* was shipped to America, where the opportunist race event manager Ernie Moross acquired the car, dubbed it the *Lightning Benz* and hired Henry Ford's old associate, Barney Oldfield, to imperil his life on the beach at Daytona.

On 16 April 1910, Oldfield notched up 131.27mph but later in the year found himself banned by the American Automobile Association. Bob Burman replaced him and the car was renamed the *Blitzen Benz* of legend. Returning to the sand on 23 April 1911, Burman achieved a speed of 141.37mph. This was faster than a speeding train, twice as fast as any aircraft and, unofficially, even faster than Glenn Curtiss.

The *Blitzen Benz* displays an anomaly because, if specifications are taken in good faith, its power-to-weight ratio is inferior to that of the skeletal Darracq V8. Its performance could be explained by a favourable combination of better tyres, slimline bodywork, a following wind and

optimal gearing. More likely, in Burman's case, the intervening year gave time to modify the engine for more power. Fitting larger valves, machining a new camshaft to give more lift and duration, increasing the compression ratio and improving carburation would all have been within the capabilities of the times. As a result the *Blitzen Benz* was rumoured to produce up to 300hp.

Showman Ernie Moross acquired a second Benz, which was also named *Blitzen Benz*. Always looking for ways to promote his money-making exhibition races, he hired the renowned American racer Teddy Tetzlaff to drive the car on the Bonneville Salt Flats where it recorded an unofficial 142.8mph in 1914.

The story of the *Blitzen Benz* had now become folklore and Oldfield, Burman and Tetzlaff were household names in America. Oldfield made movies and continued barnstorming the country, competing against all-comers, including biplanes, before retiring from competition in 1918. For a while the AAA suspended his

licence because of his 'outlaw' racing but after it was reinstated he appeared twice in the Indy 500, in 1914 and 1916, finishing fifth both times. Burman and Tetzlaff also raced on, the former perishing in a crash in 1916, the latter going on to make several silent movies.

Of the six mighty *Blitzens* originally built, two survive, owned by Mercedes-Benz and an American collector.

THE BEAST OF TURIN • FELICE NAZZARO, PIETRO BORDINO & ARTHUR DURAY

If the Benz 200hp was a thing of beauty then enter the Fiat S76, the 'Beast of Turin'. This monster 28-litre car was conceived in 1910 with the objective of stealing the *Blitzen Benz*'s thunder. The intention of the car, it seemed, was to terminate the careers of its drivers. Although Victor Hémery's official record with the Benz was 125.95mph, the higher 'unofficial'

SPECIFICATIONS

Vehicle	Fiat S76
Origin	Italy
Weight	3,638lb (1,650kg)
Length	180in (4.57m)
Width	51in (1.30m)
Height	60in (1.52m)
Transmission	Four-speed
Powerplant	Four-cylinder in-line
Engine capacity	28.35 litres
Horsepower	290hp
BHP per litre	10.2/1
Power/weight ratio	1/12.5
Venue	Ostend, Belgium
Speeds	115mph, 124mph & 131.5mph

speeds achieved in America did not pass unnoticed and at Fiat drastic measures were taken.

The result was a massive in-line four-cylinder engine with a bore of 7.5in and a stroke of 9.8in. Each cylinder displaced seven litres! An overhead camshaft actuated three valves per cylinder, each cylinder having three spark plugs to ignite the mixture in the big

PISTON COMPARISON SCHEMATIC

1-litre hatchback

Fiat S76

combustion chambers that vented to large stub exhausts. The resultant 290hp in a car weighing 1.6 tons was optimistically supposed to be restrained by inefficient brakes fitted only to the rear wheels.

Two of these cars were built. The

first driver to try to tame the Beast was Felice Nazzaro, a successful Grand Prix racer and works driver for Fiat. On a road near Turin Nazzaro pushed the car to 115mph but deemed it to be uncontrollable.

At a loss what to do next, Fiat shipped the car to England in 1911, to the Brooklands race track near Weybridge in Surrey. Here Pietro Bordino, a rising Grand Prix star and one-time riding mechanic for Nazzaro, found it unstable on the banked circuit and refused to drive it at more than 90mph. It later startled onlookers when Bordino drove it on public roads to Saltburn in North Yorkshire. Along the way the Beast spat fire, belched smoke and sent tremors through the ground. After

a few setbacks Bordino registered 124mph on the beach at Saltburn but was hand-timed only, which meant the speed was not ratified.

The sister car was sold to Russian Prince Boris Soukhanov, who scared himself sufficiently to hire a professional to drive it. The experienced Arthur Duray accepted the challenge in 1913 and the car was sent

to Brooklands for a try-out with the Prince as riding mechanic. Duray recalled that two laps at around 120mph nearly caused them to go over the banking and risk killing themselves, so they looked for another venue. Meanwhile, the Beast was improved with a radiator cowling that narrowed to a 2in vertical slit at the front.

By the time Ostend in Belgium had been chosen for the Beast's next outing, in December 1913, the AIACR had complicated matters by making two-way runs mandatory. Timing cables were laid along the road and Duray made several runs, recording an average speed of 139.6mph. The timing equipment, however, could not verify this speed and the best official figure was 131.5mph.

Duray maintained that the course was too short to build up to full speed. He vividly described the car trying to leave the road when he changed into fourth gear and attempting to turn sideways when the throttle was cut. Simultaneously it poured oil over his riding mechanic, Prince Soukhanov, while occasionally being airborne. To compound things it was

barely able to stop with its limited brakes.

Was the Fiat S76 with its massive engine, the largest ever produced for an automobile, an heroic failure? Or did the combination of faulty timing, weather conditions and an unsuitable track deny the Beast its due? Duncan Pittaway's rebuilt Fiat S76 lives on but the Beast will not be found in any official record books.

BENZ 200hp • LYDSTON HORNSTED

Lydston Granville Hornsted, known as Cupid or simply L.G., was a British-based Benz dealer who raced older Benz vehicles with some success. He went to Germany with the intention of acquiring something with more potential and set his sights on a Benz 200hp that was a variant of the *Blitzen Benz*. A narrowed radiator cowl was fitted to help clean up the frontal area together with a modified exhaust and an elongated, pointed tail.

Starting in November 1913, Hornsted began setting a series of new standing-start speed records. But he called off an attempt at the one-hour endurance record when a front tyre came off and hit him on the arm at more than 100mph. He decided to attempt the flying mile instead.

Hornsted's efforts culminated at Brooklands on 24 June 1914 when he established the AIACR-ratified world record with an average of 124.10mph. This was the first successful attempt to comply with the new mandate that runs had to be made in both directions, within one hour, to negate any wind or gradient advantage, with the average speed calculated as the record. Hornsted's two runs were 120.28mph and 128.16mph. The first was slower than Hémery's best, the second was faster.

L.G.'s experience with the high-speed blow-out highlighted the deficiencies of the tyres available. Early versions used inner tubes to contain air within smooth tyres made from vulcanised rubber. As well

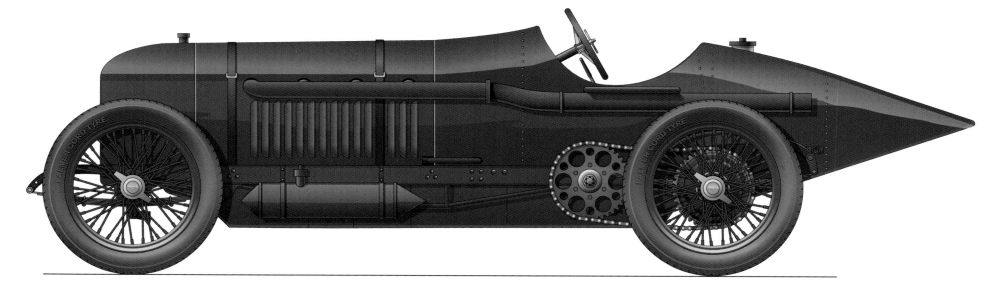

as being subject to regular punctures, tyre rubber would also heat up when running

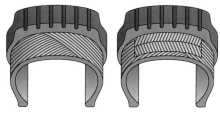

Bias-ply tyre   Belted bias-ply tyre

SPECIFICATIONS

Vehicle	Benz 200hp
Origin	Germany
Weight	3,197lb (1,450kg)
Length	189.8in (4.82m)
Width	63.0in (1.60m)
Height	50.4in (1.28m)
Transmission	Four-speed
Powerplant	Four-cylinder in-line
Engine capacity	21.5 litres
Horsepower	200hp
BHP per litre	9.3/1
Power/weight ratio	1/16
Venue	Brooklands
Speed	124.10mph

at high speed and in turn cause air pressure inside the inner tube to rise, increasing the possibility of sudden failure. By 1910 tyre designers were embedding layers of cotton cord in the vulcanised rubber to strengthen the tyre. This evolved into the bias-ply design, which then added belt plies directly beneath the tread and became standard for the next 50 years.

The 2.75-mile Brooklands track featured two long, banked bends that theoretically allowed drivers to keep the throttle pedal flat to the floor as they built up to maximum speed. Victor Hémery had already made his mark at the circuit in 1909 but Pietro Bordino, driving the 'Beast of Turin', found the experience too dangerous as centrifugal force took the big Fiat S76 — with its notably high centre of gravity — within inches of going over the top of the banking. Many other cars did

come to grief, with 17 fatalities occurring in the 28-year history of the track. Twelve of these were drivers, plus three spectators

BROOKLANDS
RACE TRACK

HOME BANKING

PIT AREA

RAILWAY STRAIGHT

River Wey

FINISHING STRAIGHT

THE FORK

BYFLEET BANKING

Opened in 1907

and two riding mechanics.

In practice Brooklands had its limitations as far as land speed records went. Although

times were ratified, they were always slower than those set elsewhere. The track was simply not as conducive to speed as long stretches of beach.

Although Hornsted's record was still not as fast as the AEG electric railcar had gone in 1903, or the speeds achieved by Glenn Curtiss and Bob Burman, it was the new official land speed record under the AIACR's rules.

Only a few weeks later the European powers blundered into the abyss of the First World War.

Hornsted's Benz 200hp continued to appear in motor races until it was wrecked in 1922, when it did go over the top of the Brooklands banking with Canadian John Duff at the wheel. Although Captain Duff survived the 125mph crash, it again highlighted the shortcomings and dangers of the Brooklands track as far as outright speed records were concerned.

PACKARD • RALPH DePALMA

Raffaele 'Ralph' DePalma was born in Italy and emigrated to America to become famous as a racing driver who never gave up. Blow-outs, mechanical failure and engine fires all failed to extinguish an indomitable spirit that saw him come from way down the field to beat the likes of Barney Oldfield.

DePalma, a truly great driver, is said to have won well over 2,000 motor races,

including the Indianapolis 500 in 1915. His experience and success with many different makes of car led to an approach from Packard to make an attempt at the land speed record with the company's 905 cubic inch (14.8-litre) V12 engine.

Motor racing in Europe ceased during the Great War, when industry, even in America, turned to military production and high-performance vehicle engines were no longer required. The Fiat S76 marked the high tide for big-displacement, purpose-built car engines and it remains the largest ever made. The research and development to create such engines ceased to be financially viable for their limited use.

The aircraft industry was a different proposition altogether. Rapidly increasing demand for improved aircraft led to competition from car companies to supply engines. Aero engines had to meet government requirements in weight and output, which meant considerable amounts of time, effort and money were invested even to have a chip on the table in pursuit

of lucrative government contracts.

Packard had already produced a revolutionary side-valve, 4.9-litre, 60-degree V12 engine that had potential as an aircraft engine and was put into the company's 'Twin Six' production cars with some success. This engine was also one of the first to feature aluminium pistons. The company then developed the 45-degree 905 V12 specifically as an aero engine, changing the set-up from side valves to overhead valves with a single overhead camshaft for each bank of cylinders. This 285hp design was a quantum leap from the four, six or even eight cylinders of previous configurations.

Of Packard's three prototype engines, one was installed in a single-seat car prepared for DePalma with a multiple-disc clutch, three-speed gearbox, aluminium bodywork and a belly pan to clean up the airflow underneath. At Daytona on 12 February 1919, DePalma drove this creation to a record speed of 149.87mph on a one-way run.

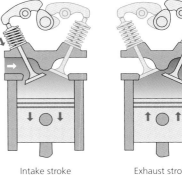

OVERHEAD CAM SCHEMATIC

Intake stroke
Exhaust valve closed

Exhaust stroke
Intake valve closed

The 905 V12 remained an experimental engine but paved the way for its bigger counterpart, the 27-litre Liberty L12 aircraft engine. The Liberty engine shared the same 45-degree vee angle and overhead-camshaft design and proved an excellent unit with over 20,000 manufactured. With 450hp available at 2,000rpm, this weight-efficient engine attracted attention from record breakers and found itself installed in two of the fastest land speed cars. From its conception in 1917 the Liberty engine powered many aircraft and over 20 years

SPECIFICATIONS

Vehicle	Packard
Origin	America
Weight	3,000lb (1,361kg)
Length	208in (5.28m)
Width	–
Height	62in (1.57m)
Transmission	Three-speed
Powerplant	V12
Engine capacity	14.8 litres
Horsepower	285hp
BHP per litre	19/1
Power/weight ratio	1/10.5
Venue	Daytona
Speed	149.87mph

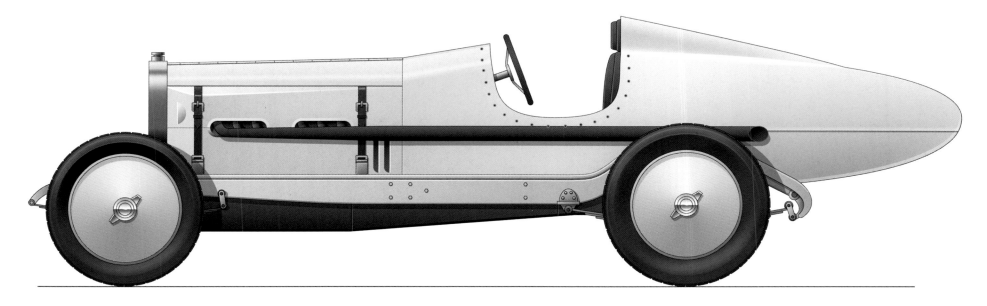

later provided the motive force for the British Crusader tank during the Second World War.

Packard's 905 was the first aero engine to be installed in a land speed car but after the war many other engines became surplus to requirements. This led to powerful aero units gradually becoming predominant in the quest for speed

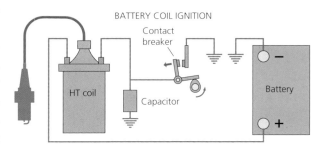

BATTERY COIL IGNITION

over the next two decades.

Mechanically operated valves had now replaced the atmospheric type and a new ignition system had arrived. Charles Kettering had devised a spark plug, coil and external contact-breaker ignition system that was introduced on Cadillac cars in 1910. This became standard equipment on nearly all engines. Voltage was supplied either by a magneto on aircraft or usually a battery on road vehicles and the timing could be easily adjusted. These advances opened up avenues in potential performance. Atmospheric valves and make-and-break ignition were consigned to history.

A surviving example of the 905 engine stands sentinel today in the Smithsonian National Air and Space Museum.

DUESENBERG • TOMMY MILTON

Tommy Milton was an American race driver who made his mark in 1917 and went on to become a dominant figure in the sport. Despite being blind in one eye, he was the first two-time winner of the Indianapolis 500.

Milton started driving for Duesenberg in 1919 with great success in a car powered by the company's straight-eight racing engine. Fred and Augie Duesenberg had designed this 297 cubic inch (4.86-litre) engine to conform to racing regulations. The engine block and cylinder heads were cast iron but the new design featured two exhaust valves and one inlet valve actuated by a single overhead camshaft and could spin up to 3,800rpm. The output of this engine is open to conjecture but the Duesenberg brothers had already produced a 496 cubic inch (8.13-litre) four-cylinder engine capable of 140hp in 1916. It is a reasonable assumption that the straight-eight, at 3,800rpm, was an improvement on this figure as that was the object of the exercise.

Of all the variables concerned, at least two were certain: Milton knew how to drive a race car and the Duesenberg brothers knew how to build engines. But there were mishaps along the way. In 1919 in a race at the Uniontown Speedway in Pennsylvania,

Milton ended up in hospital after being severely burned by an engine fire. He put his convalescence to good use, though, by formulating a plan to capture the land speed record from Ralph DePalma.

When the racing regulations restricted engines to a smaller size, the straight-eights were rendered obsolete. But Milton's plan was to mount two of these units side by side in a land speed car. The Duesenbergs agreed to build the vehicle to Milton's specification if he provided a share of the funding. Each engine drove directly through a clutch to the solid axle through

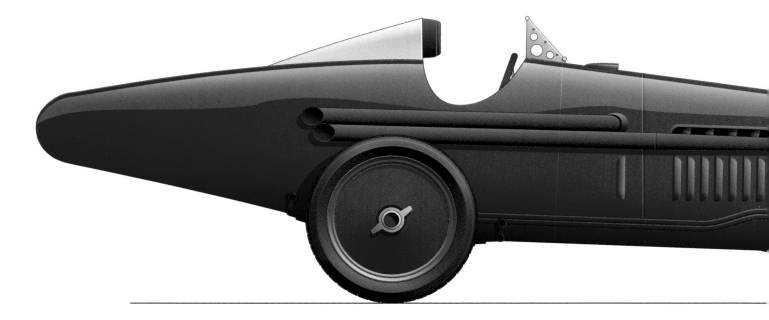

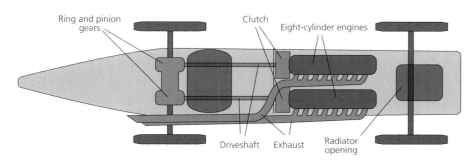

Ring and pinion gears
Clutch
Eight-cylinder engines
Driveshaft
Exhaust
Radiator opening

separate ring-and-pinion gears. The exhaust pipe from the left-hand engine

UNDER VEHICLE AIRFLOW SCHEMATIC

Smooth belly pan helping laminar flow

passed through the bodywork to exit on the same side as the right-hand engine exhaust. Total displacement of the 16 cylinders in the twin-engine set-up was 9.72 litres.

The car had a stance that angled the pointed nose down to reduce the amount of air flowing beneath and incorporated a full belly pan to cover all the irregular shapes and encourage smooth passage of air known as laminar flow. The idea

of reducing airflow beneath the car took decades before it was fully embraced with zero being the theoretical optimal figure. Practical considerations, however, governed the minimum possible ground clearance. Everything was coming together and the harmonious partnership was working well.

The car was taken to Daytona but while Milton was away making demonstration runs in nearby Havana with Oldfield and DePalma, Fred Duesenberg asked his other works driver, Jimmy Murphy, to make a test run. Unbeknown to them a reporter was present and timed the run at 153mph. Understandably, this infuriated Milton when he returned and read about it in a newspaper. He had left express instructions that no record runs should be made in his absence.

After sorting out problems with the car, Milton took his place behind the wheel of the so-called 'Double Duesy' and on 27 April 1920 made progressively faster runs on his way to a record of 156.046mph, as timed by the AAA. This beat DePalma's record by 6mph even though the car suffered another engine fire in the process.

However, the row over Murphy's test run still rankled with Milton. His relationship with Murphy and the Duesenbergs never recovered and they parted company. Murphy died four years later in a racing accident while Milton went on to survive an illustrious career.

SPECIFICATIONS

Vehicle	Duesenberg
Origin	America
Weight	3,000lb (1,361kg)
Length	–
Width	–
Height	–
Transmission	Direct drive
Powerplant	Eight-cylinders in-line x2
Engine capacity	9.72 litres
Horsepower	290hp
BHP per litre	29/1
Power/weight ratio	1/10.3
Venue	Daytona
Speed	156.046mph

SUNBEAM • KENELM LEE GUINNESS

Of Irish descent, Kenelm Lee Guinness — also known as 'KLG' — was a member of the brewing family but found his own fulfilment in the world of speed. His prowess on the track led to his employment as official works driver for the Sunbeam Motor Car Company alongside Henry Segrave, an American-born British national who was raised in Ireland.

Also part of this story is Louis Coatalen. Born in Brittany, he moved across the channel and took British nationality. After working as a successful automotive engineer for several companies, Coatalen joined Sunbeam at the age of 30. His interest in racing and high-performance vehicles led to the construction of land speed contenders. One of these was the

350hp Sunbeam with KLG as the driver.

The motive power for this one-off car was provided by a variation of the Sunbeam V12 Manitou aero engine. With two exhaust valves and one inlet valve per cylinder, twin plugs, one single overhead camshaft to each bank, two magnetos and two carburettors, its 18.2-litre displacement developed 350hp at 2,100rpm. This healthy

output had to haul a 3,417lb car giving a power-to-weight ratio of 1/9.8.

It proved healthy enough at Brooklands on 17 May 1922 to propel KLG, who had waited all day for suitable conditions, to an official two-way run over the kilometre at an average speed of 133.75mph. This is said to be the last land speed record set at Brooklands but that is not strictly true.

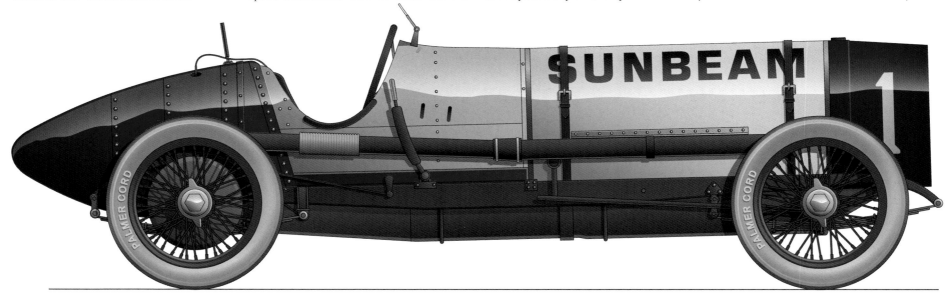

Both Kay Petre and Gwenda Stewart set women's records in excess of KLG's speed a decade later.

What did become obvious, yet again, was that Brooklands had limitations as far as pursuit of the absolute record was concerned. The Sunbeam's power-to-weight ratio was well matched with that of American contenders yet, as the chart on this page shows, speeds recorded at

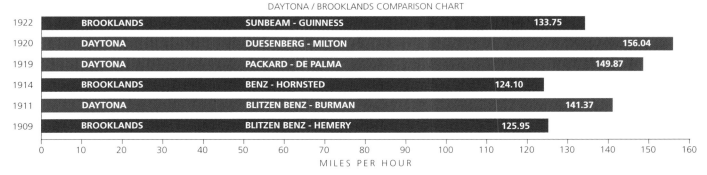

DAYTONA / BROOKLANDS COMPARISON CHART

Year	Venue	Car	Speed
1922	BROOKLANDS	SUNBEAM - GUINNESS	133.75
1920	DAYTONA	DUESENBERG - MILTON	156.04
1919	DAYTONA	PACKARD - DE PALMA	149.87
1914	BROOKLANDS	BENZ - HORNSTED	124.10
1911	DAYTONA	BLITZEN BENZ - BURMAN	141.37
1909	BROOKLANDS	BLITZEN BENZ - HEMERY	125.95

MILES PER HOUR

SPECIFICATIONS

Vehicle	Sunbeam
Origin	England
Weight	3,417lb (1,550kg)
Length	192in (4.88m)
Width	54in (1.37m)
Height	56in (1.42m)
Transmission	Four-speed
Powerplant	Manitou V12
Engine capacity	18.3 litres
Horsepower	350hp
BHP per litre	19/1
Power/weight ratio	1/9.8
Venue	Brooklands
Speed	133.75mph

Daytona were rather higher than those at Brooklands even when a car of the same type, such as the *Blitzen Benz*, was used.

The efforts of Burman, DePalma and Milton in setting records in America owed much to the expanse of beach and the opportunity to have a long run-in to build up speed. When the Brits switched to beaches in England they gained similar benefits and the gap closed. And then when they crossed to Daytona they exceeded American efforts. When the seemingly endless space of the Bonneville Salt Flats eventually beckoned, record breaking there became a largely British affair.

Due to personal experience with faulty spark plugs, KLG developed his own design using mica in place of the unreliable

EARLY SPARK PLUG   KLG SPARK PLUG

Layers of mica

Porcelain insulator

KLG

insulation of the porcelain of the time. These spark plugs were in great demand for performance engines and their brand name, KLG, survives today.

Kenelm Lee Guinness continued winning races until suffering severe injuries in an accident in 1924 that caused the death of riding mechanic Tom Barrett. KLG did not fully recover and never raced again. Riding mechanics were banned.

The Sunbeam went on to greater feats with Malcolm Campbell and now quietly resides, in full working order, at the National Motor Museum at Beaulieu, awaiting its next thunderous day out.

WISCONSIN SPECIAL • SIG HAUGDAHL

Sigurd Olson 'Sig' Haugdahl was born in Norway and moved to America. He started racing with motorcycles then graduated to cars, proving he had the courage, determination and know-how to succeed by winning six International Motor Contest Association (IMCA) championships in a row. Before this he set his mind to outrunning Tommy Miller's record of 156.046mph. It was a daunting

SPECIFICATIONS

Vehicle	Wisconsin Special
Origin	America
Weight	2,250lb (1,021kg)
Length	192in (4.88m)
Width	–
Height	58in (1.47m)
Transmission	Direct drive
Powerplant	Six-cylinder in-line
Engine capacity	13.9 litres
Horsepower	250hp
BHP per litre	18/1
Power/weight ratio	1/9
Venue	Daytona
Speed	180.3mph

task but one for which he had a plan that had at its heart a certain powerplant.

The unit he chose for his *Wisconsin Special* was a straight-six aero engine that displaced 13.9 litres and developed 250hp at 2,600rpm. At first this appears to be just another large engine but its all-aluminium construction with magnesium-alloy pistons reduced its weight to a modest 610lb. This was 30 per cent less than the Blitzen, Packard and Double Duesy motors. The six cylinders allowed smaller bores than a four-cylinder engine of the same displacement and the stroke was almost half that of the Fiat S76. This made it a very compact unit that allowed the *Wisconsin Special* to be declared the narrowest car ever built. It was only 20in wide at the front, significantly less than the Double Duesy.

Haugdahl also used direct drive. By dispensing with a clutch and gearbox, he further reduced weight, giving greater insight into his train of thought.

Haugdahl's concept continued to take shape with a full belly pan, angled stance, low centre of gravity, faired-in radiator cowl, ultra-short exhaust stubs, covered rear wheels, and streamlining at the rear (including behind the driver's head). Showing further attention to detail, he accurately balanced the wheels and tyres,

FRONTAL AREA COMPARISON

Double Duesy   Wisconsin Special

reduced the windshield to a minimum and taped over all bodywork seams to smooth the airflow. The car did not suddenly appear in its finished form but was developed over a period of time.

Finally, on 7 April 1922, the *Wisconsin Special* scorched across the Daytona sand

on its way to a timed run for a mile of 19.97 seconds, a speed of 180.03mph.

But that was far from the end of the story. Although the IMCA had timed the run, the American authorities were not impressed. The AAA did not verify it because Haugdahl was not a member of their association at the time, while the AIACR simply treated the staggering improvement of 24mph with disdain. In Europe it led to controversy that continues to simmer today.

Haugdahl's side of the story is that he put together a near-perfect combination with careful thought and steady development. It is reasonable to deduce that the car may have weighed as little as 2,250lb, giving it a credible 1/9 power-to-weight ratio that was arguably better than previous cars. A reduced frontal area was also very beneficial, as proved later in the century. If the car was only capable of 150mph, as some claimed,

SIG HAUGDAHL'S ROCKET CAR

then either the course was shortened by some 350 yards or the stopwatches were four seconds out.

The case against is that Alex Sloan, founder of the IMCA, and Haugdahl were close associates and the claim of three miles a minute was too good a slogan to pass up. It would help to promote dirt-track events in which Haugdahl made demonstration runs.

Haugdahl went on to build the first manned rocket car. Using 32 solid-fuel rockets, he would blaze around an oval dirt track for a lap and a half until the motors burned out. Amid the noise and flames the modest speed achieved seemed much greater than it was. Gullible crowds were suitably amazed.

The fact that Sig Haugdahl was a champion race driver and also a great showman, who built a spectacular fire-breathing rocket car to attract the crowds and sell tickets, does not prove anything. But science does not rule out that perhaps Haugdahl had considered and met certain criteria, was that darned smart and was the fastest man on earth.

The car is still in existence and makes the occasional appearance at events such as the Goodwood Festival of Speed.

DELAGE • RENÉ THOMAS & KAY PETRE

The status that René Thomas had earned as an aviator, motor racing champion and winner of the Indianapolis 500 at the first attempt, driving a Delage, gave him enough kudos to persuade Louis Delage to build an aero engine and test it in a car.

Delage designer Charles Planchon drew up plans for a 60-degree V12 engine of 10.69 litres. Twelve separate cylinders were mounted on a large common crankcase,

SPECIFICATIONS

Vehicle	Delage
Origin	France
Weight	3,000lb (1,361kg)
Length	168in (4.27m)
Width	56in (1.42m)
Height	54in (1.37m)
Transmission	Four/five-speed
Powerplant	V12
Engine capacity	10.69 litres
Horsepower	280hp
BHP per litre	26/1
Power/weight ratio	1/10.7
Venue	Arpajon, France
Speed	143.31mph

each cylinder featuring two valves actuated by pushrods from a central camshaft. This heavy unit, squeezed into an orthodox chassis, had an estimated output of around 280hp at 3,200rpm. Instantly successful in sprints and hill climbs, the reliable Delage V12 enjoyed a long successful career.

The high point came on 6 July 1924 when Thomas recorded an average speed of 143.31mph in two runs over the kilometre at Arpajon in northern France. This fell short of American claims but was good enough for the AIACR, who recognised it, albeit briefly, as the official land speed record. Ernest Eldridge broke it in *Mephistopheles* the following week, again at Arpajon.

The big Delage did not present any novel technological breakthroughs apart from front-wheel brakes, a rarity at the time even on the world's fastest cars. Five years later, in the hands of British

racer John Cobb, it continued to perform at the highest level at Brooklands. It was there in August 1935, when ten years old and about to be pensioned off, that Louis Delage's creation claimed another record.

This time the driver was Canadian-born Kay Petre and her speed of 134.75mph was the highest yet achieved by a woman. Petre's effort, however, was surpassed only three days later. Gwenda Stewart, a British woman who had been an ambulance driver during the First World War, reached 135.95mph in the highly efficient 1.6-litre Derby-Miller, the handiwork of American engine builder Harry Miller.

These two members of the allegedly weaker sex were just 9mph slower than the all-time Brooklands lap record of 143.44mph that Cobb set two months later in his Napier-Railton and yet their cars had only half the power. Stewart

Kay Petre

and Petre succeeded as competitive race drivers who were as courageous and skilful as any of the male contestants. And unlike the muddle over who was the quickest man on the planet, there was no such uncertainty on the women's side: Stewart and Petre reigned supreme. At only four feet ten inches tall, Petre was so diminutive that her feet did not even reach the controls of the big Delage, so wooden blocks were fitted to the pedals.

But it was the men who continued to dominate the top speeds even if there was no consensus about who was swiftest of all, as illustrated by the Europeans backing René Thomas's claim over that of Ralph DePalma.

Thomas's Delage was broadly similar to DePalma's V12 Packard with a flat-fronted radiator and comparable power-to-weight ratio. His mark of 143.31mph was over the measured kilometre, not the mile, which suggests that it may have been getting difficult to find a long enough stretch of road in good condition to accommodate the rising speeds. Even though roads in France were better than those in Britain, they were reaching their limit.

Other less visible reasons causing variations in performance were clutch slip and inadequate traction, the latter partly a consequence of the accepted paradigm of car construction with the engine, and therefore most of the weight, on the front wheels. Although these problems were not always easy to identify and resolve, improvements were steadily realised.

During the Second World War the Delage suffered neglect but after restoration it was entered into historic events and won its class at Silverstone in 1950. After further damage by an accident and fire it was again brought back to life and attained an impressive speed of 138mph in 1966. It still appears at events such as the Goodwood Festival of Speed.

The career of Louis Delage did not endure as long as his famous car. The effects of the Great Depression of the 1930s caused the eventual bankruptcy of his company. By the time Petre set her record Louis Delage could not afford a car and was reduced to riding a bicycle. Penniless and forgotten, he died in 1947 aged 73.

Delage's story overlaps with that of Ernest Eldridge who in 1924 had been waiting in the wings at Arpajon to unleash what would prove to be the last successful record attempt on a public highway.

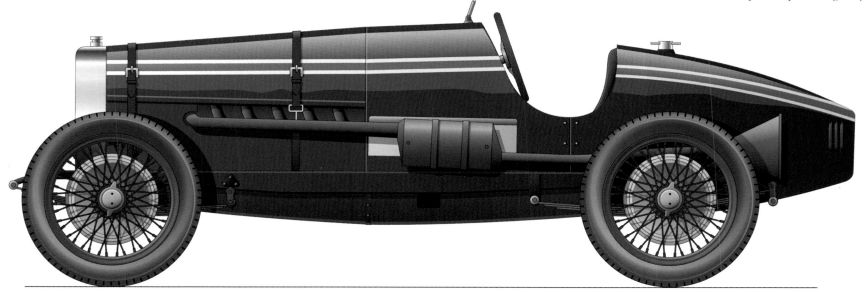

MEPHISTOPHELES • ERNEST ELDRIDGE

Ernest Arthur Douglas Eldridge, born to a wealthy English family, began racing in 1921. He made a tentative start at Brooklands in an Isotta-Fraschini before upgrading it with a 23-litre Maybach aero engine. Next came a 10-litre Fiat, which Eldridge drove with enough success to harden his ambition to contest the land speed record.

To this end he bought the remains of the 1908 Fiat SB4 that Felice Nazarro had driven with such distinction 16 years earlier. It had suffered an engine disintegration in the hands of John Duff at Brooklands in 1922 and it was for its chassis that Eldridge bought it, knowing he needed to fit a bigger engine with more horsepower.

This was resolved by obtaining a 21.7-litre A12 aero engine from Fiat that was only slightly heavier than the previous Maybach unit but produced 30 per cent more power. This straight-six had a single overhead camshaft with four valves and four spark plugs per cylinder. Fitted with two carburettors, it developed 320hp at 1,800rpm. The aged SB4 chassis fortuitously retained the original chain drive but was lengthened by 18in to accommodate the big engine, which was enclosed by a compact bonnet tapered in at the top.

To most onlookers the car, with its impressively long bonnet, looked every inch the image of what a record breaker should be. After being tested to a Brooklands maximum of 124mph, it was taken to Arpajon in northern France. There it was dubbed *Mephistopheles* due to the infernal noise, smoke and flames that this terrifying devil of a contraption produced.

As we have already seen, René Thomas was also at the Arpajon meeting for his attempt with the modern Delage, but the

SPECIFICATIONS

Vehicle	Fiat
Origin	Italy
Weight	4480lb (2,032kg)
Length	208in (5.28m)
Width	–
Height	54in (1.37m)
Transmission	Four-speed
Powerplant	Six-cylinder in-line
Engine capacity	21.7 litres
Horsepower	320hp
BHP per litre	15/1
Power/weight ratio	1/14
Venue	Arpajon, France
Speed	146.01mph

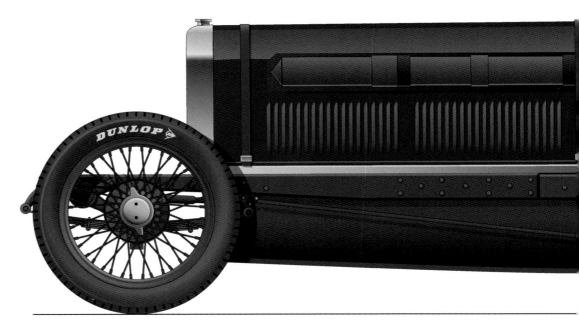

mighty *Mephistopheles* ran first to a record speed of 143.3mph. Thomas lodged an immediate objection, complaining that Eldridge's monster did not comply with the regulation that stipulated the requirement for a reverse gear. The objection was upheld and the Delage went on to take the laurels.

Eldridge responded decisively. He and his mechanic John Ames took the car to Paris to get it equipped with a means to reverse it. Six days later, on 12 July 1924,

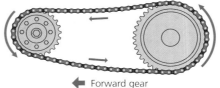

ELDRIDGE REVERSE GEAR SOLUTION

← Forward gear

Reverse gear →

they returned, having fitted a longer chain in a figure-of-eight. This meant they could reverse the rotation of the drive to move the car backwards a sufficient distance, just a few metres, to satisfy the AIACR. Reverting to normal drive, Eldridge curtailed the celebrations of Thomas's camp by thundering his car, in its black livery, to a new record average speed of 146.01mph.

The AIACR, and particularly the French contingent, were justifiably proud of their heritage in the pursuit of absolute speed. This activity had its genesis in France and European machines set most of the early records on French soil.

Inexorably this began to change as the vehicles involved ceased to be adapted from ordinary cars or Grand Prix racers. The automobile engine was to be superseded by aero engines that had almost no application in road-going vehicles.

So it was that Ernest Eldridge would be the last driver to break a land speed record on a public highway. Long, flat beaches in England became the focus as they were the only alternative to expensive trans-Atlantic trips to Daytona.

Eldridge sold *Mephistopheles* but continued to power his way through motorsport driving cars of his own design, Eldridge Specials, and many others. And he kept going despite an accident at the Montlhéry circuit near Paris that caused a serious head injury and the loss of one eye.

SUNBEAM 350hp BLUE BIRD • MALCOLM CAMPBELL

At this point in the saga, sizeable multi-cylinder aero engines, although not as massive as the Fiat S76, were superseding the large, heavy automobile engines. The motivation had come mostly from talented designers and drivers who also had the technical ability to optimise the machines. One of these was someone with a different perspective who would become central in this quest for speed.

Malcolm Campbell, son of a diamond broker, started racing with motorcycles. He went on to compete at Brooklands and twice won the Boulogne Grand Prix in France. But he is best remembered for his exploits in the pursuit of sheer speed.

The fact that Campbell was neither a designer nor a skilful mechanic did not matter. What counted was his ability to envision possibilities and organise the means to attain them.

When Kenelm Lee Guinness set his ratified two-way run, Campbell took note and organised the 'loan' of the car. He recognised the limitations of Brooklands and was proved right when he drove the car at the Saltburn Speed Trials on 17 June 1922 to a speed of 138.08mph only to find that the stopwatch timing was not accepted. Louis Coatalen was persuaded to sell him the car, which he then took to a

speed meeting at Fanø Beach, Denmark, where he recorded 137.72mph. But timing issues foiled him once again.

Disappointed but not discouraged, Campbell arranged for wind-tunnel trials at aircraft manufacturers Boulton & Paul Limited over the winter months.

These rudimentary tests resulted in a new streamlined tail and fairings over the rear suspension as well as in front of the driver and behind him. Modifications were also made to improve the engine with higher-compression pistons, which increased compression ratio and thereby enhanced thermal efficiency. This benefit, which had been restricted hitherto by low-octane petrol, became possible with the addition of tetraethyl lead, which raised the octane rating and enabled more power to be produced with higher compression ratios. Campbell's car was renamed *Blue Bird*.

After testing, Campbell returned to Fanø with the upgraded car in the summer but his efforts suffered from poor crowd control and a sub-standard surface. Both rear tyres came off on the first run and on the second a young spectator was killed after a front tyre detached. Campbell's protests about the poor safety arrangements had gone largely unheeded.

Following this disastrous outcome the car was taken to Pendine Sands in South Wales and on 24 September 1924 Malcolm Campbell recorded his first officially ratified speed of 146.16mph, a mere 0.15mph better than *Mephistopheles* had achieved two months earlier. The one-per-cent rule had not yet come into effect so Campbell took the record.

Knowing the car was near its limit,

HIGH-COMPRESSION SCHEMATIC
Pistons at top of compression stroke

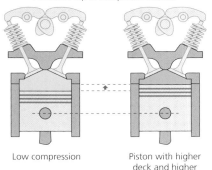

Low compression   Piston with higher deck and higher compression

Campbell decided to sell it but changed his mind on hearing that John Parry-Thomas planned a challenge. Returning to Pendine, Campbell was the first man in Europe to exceed 150mph, officially timed on 21 July 1925 at 150.76mph, thereby beating his own record.

Campbell had managed to combine all the factors required for success: motivation, courage, determination, perseverance, technology, venue, official timing equipment and clement conditions. He had also gained valuable experience that was to pay dividends as he continued on his own very personal quest for speed.

SPECIFICATIONS

Vehicle	Sunbeam
Origin	England
Weight	3,417lb (1,550kg)
Length	232in (5.89m)
Width	54in (1.37m)
Height	56in (1.42m)
Transmission	Four-speed
Powerplant	Manitou V12
Engine capacity	18.3 litres
Horsepower	360hp
BHP per litre	19.5/1
Power/weight ratio	1/9.5
Venue	Pendine, Wales
Speeds	146.16mph & 150.76mph

SUNBEAM LADYBIRD • HENRY SEGRAVE

After serving in the Royal Flying Corps in the First World War, Henry Segrave distinguished himself as a talented racing driver who, among his many successes, was the first Briton, as works driver for Sunbeam, to win a Grand Prix in a British car. In 1924 he retired from racing and turned his full attention to contesting the land speed record.

Enter once more the designer Louis

SPECIFICATIONS

Vehicle	Sunbeam
Origin	England
Weight	2,016lb (914kg)
Length	159in (4.04m)
Width	–
Height	42in (1.07m)
Transmission	Four-speed
Powerplant	V12
Engine capacity	3.976 litres
Horsepower	306hp
BHP per litre	77/1
Power/weight ratio	1/6.6
Venue	Southport, Lancashire
Speed	152.33mph

Coatalen. He was receptive to the idea of designing a new land speed car and conceived another right way of doing it. Having seen his Sunbeam 350hp reach its potential in the hands of Guinness and Campbell, Coatalen reasoned that although Britain's longest beaches were now too short for the heavyweight cars to break records, lighter cars with a higher power-to-weight ratio should be able to manage. This would save the cost of crossing the Atlantic to Daytona and gain valuable publicity at home.

To this end a pair of 2-litre six-cylinder engine blocks were mated to a common crankcase. The result was a high-output 75-degree V12 powerplant with twin double overhead camshafts and four valves per cylinder. It was additionally equipped with a front-mounted Roots-type supercharger,

delivering air at 7lb per square inch, driven off the crankshaft. Each six-cylinder unit was capable of over 100hp, which together with the supercharger makes the claimed

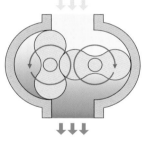

Roots type for larger auto engines

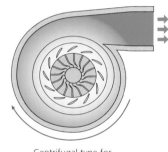

Centrifugal type for auto and aero engines

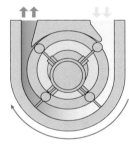

Vane type for smaller auto engines

306hp at 5,300rpm look feasible. With all in place the car was named *Ladybird*.

At initial tests on Southport Sands in north-west England the supercharger gave endless problems. It cracked six casings, causing a retreat to the factory to find a solution. On his return to Southport, on 16 March 1926, Segrave nursed the car through the first run. On the second run

he cast caution to the wind and let the car out to set a record average speed of 152.33mph for the flying kilometre just before the supercharger expired.

The mystery of superchargers is easily explained. The name is simply an evocative description of a pump that delivers air under pressure. The more air pumped into an engine, the more petrol it burns and the more power it produces. Some of that power is used to drive the pump and there are some efficiency losses, but gains in the order of 50 to 75 per cent are not unusual.

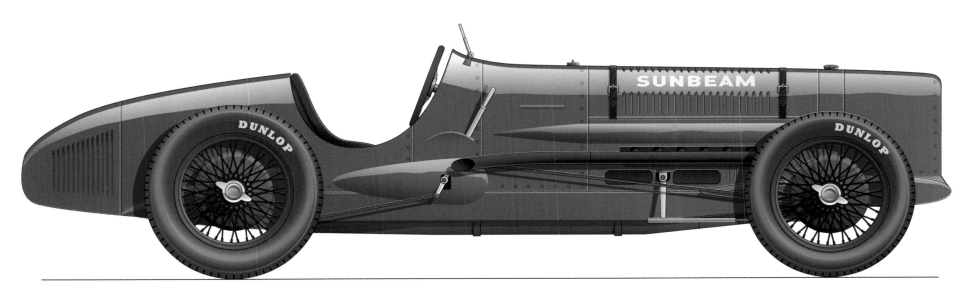

Supercharging contributed to the claimed output of 306hp for *Ladybird* and with its trim 2,016lb gave it a power-to-weight ratio of 1/6.6, which, if genuine, was the most efficient yet.

Superchargers began to appear more often: the vane type for smaller engines, the centrifugal type often found on aero engines and the Roots type becoming almost *de rigueur* on V8 engines. In later years the turbocharger reappeared with dramatic effect.

By narrowly beating Campbell's first hard-won record, Segrave's achievement marked the beginning of a contest for piston engines that was almost entirely a British affair for the next 21 years — with Britain retaining the wheel-driven record for 36 years. Conversely, the light, powerful and efficient concept of *Ladybird* proved to be the last time an adapted Grand Prix car would appear on the elevated stage of the quest for absolute speed. The manufacturers' famous names began to fade from the cars, which took on a unique identity all of their own.

The AIACR ratified Segrave's run with the smallest-ever engine to hold the record. These attempts had now ceased in France and within a year beaches in England and Wales would also no longer provide sufficient space. Hereafter, American venues would enjoy a monopoly. To retain any influence, the AIACR would have to change its outlook and pay more attention to events across the Atlantic.

THE HIGHAM SPECIAL • JOHN PARRY-THOMAS

The story of the *Higham Special* began with Count Louis Zborowski, an Englishman of independent wealth who lived at Higham Park near Canterbury. He began his active role in motor racing at Brooklands and Grand Prix events before going on to construct a series of his own cars. The fourth, named the *Higham Special*, utilised the gearbox and chain drive from a pre-war *Blitzen Benz* and a 27-litre Liberty

aero engine. While still developing his cars, Zborowski died when the Mercedes he was driving in the 1924 Italian Grand Prix at Monza hit a tree.

The *Higham Special* passed to racing driver John Godfrey Parry-Thomas, who purchased it from Zborowski's estate for £125. The Welshman was the

chief engineer at Leyland Motors with Reid Railton as his assistant. Having once convinced the Leyland directors to participate in racing, he later resigned to take up the occupation full-time. And as an inventor he filed many patents. If that was not enough, he founded the Thomas Inventions Development Company in

partnership with Major Ken Thomson. The company operated from premises at Brooklands circuit.

There Parry-Thomas turned his attention to the land speed record using the *Higham Special* as the basis for this effort. The Liberty aero engine and the old Benz

SPECIFICATIONS

Vehicle	Higham Special
Origin	England
Weight	3,920lb (1,778kg)
Length	220in (5.59m)
Width	–
Height	48in (1.22m)
Transmission	Four-speed
Powerplant	Liberty V12
Engine capacity	27.03 litres
Horsepower	500hp
BHP per litre	18.5/1
Power/weight ratio	1/7.8
Venue	Pendine, Wales
Speeds	169.30mph & 171.02mph

gearbox and chain drive were retained. Parry-Thomas applied his considerable talents to the creation of aerodynamic bodywork and increasing the output of the engine. After two years of constantly modifying the car, which he had renamed *Babs*, his hard work paid off on 27 April 1926. This was the day *Babs* rumbled onto Pendine Sands and with its creator at the wheel set a new record average speed of 169.30mph.

But Parry-Thomas was under pressure. He knew that Malcolm Campbell was planning an attempt at the 180mph mark with a new car and the following day the Welshman increased his average speed to 171.02mph with Campbell on hand to congratulate him.

The rivalry between the two men intensified with Pendine Sands their battleground. On 4 February 1927, Campbell took the record up to 174.883mph, a challenge that Parry-Thomas could not resist. Having made further modifications to *Babs*, he attempted to wrest the record back a month later. But his overstressed equipment failed him down the measured mile when a rear wheel collapsed, causing the car to roll over and slide for 400 yards. Parry-Thomas died instantly. He was buried in a churchyard near Brooklands while, for the moment at least, the dunes at Pendine were chosen as the *Higham Special*'s unlikely burial ground.

Comparing the Liberty and Delage engines provides a good illustration of the effect of rpm on specific output. The Delage produced 280hp at 3,200rpm from 10.6 litres whereas the 27-litre Liberty engine generated 450hp at only 2,000rpm. For a direct comparison of efficiency, the Delage produced 26hp per litre and the stock factory Liberty only 16.6hp per litre. It was well understood that more rpm equalled more power yet aero engines were the only units able to provide power

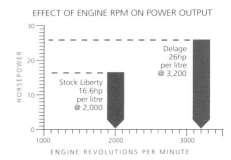

in abundance. Reliability being a prime factor, large-capacity aero engines were not designed to reach the giddy heights of 5,000rpm, like *Ladybird*, but would respond well to the alternative of supercharging.

Parry-Thomas carried out numerous modifications to increase the output of his engine to an estimated 500hp, including adding two more carburettors and increasing the compression ratio with raised-crown pistons of his own design.

The *Higham Special* was disinterred from Pendine Sands in 1969 by Owen Wyn Owen and completely restored. It can now be seen at the Brooklands and Pendine museums at different times of the year.

NAPIER-CAMPBELL BLUE BIRD (1927) • MALCOLM CAMPBELL

When Malcolm Campbell witnessed Parry-Thomas raising the bar by breaking the record at Pendine Sands, he knew that his 350hp Sunbeam was no longer up to the task. But by then he had already started to create a new *Blue Bird*. Designed by C. Amherst Villiers and Joseph Maina and with no expense spared, the purpose-built car was to have only one function.

The chosen powerplant was the

SPECIFICATIONS

Vehicle	Blue Bird
Origin	England
Weight	6,720lb (3,048kg)
Length	226in (5.74m)
Width	–
Height	54in (1.37m)
Transmission	Three-speed
Powerplant	Napier Lion VIIA
Engine capacity	22,299cc
Horsepower	800hp
BHP per litre	35/1
Power/weight ratio	1/8.4
Venue	Pendine, Wales
Speed	174.883mph

12-cylinder Napier Lion, designated a 'broad-arrow' engine because of its three banks of cylinders. With four valves per cylinder and double overhead camshafts for each bank, this remarkable piece of engineering delivered 500hp in production form and more when developed for racing.

The rest of the car was built from scratch to a very high standard. Its nickel-steel chassis with four tubular cross members was of exceptional strength and eliminated any flexing that the engine's massive torque could exert. There was a 16-plate clutch to avoid speed-reducing slip and a three-speed gearbox complete with the mandatory reverse gear. After careful thought regarding streamlining, the businesslike bodywork was tailored to closely cover the front suspension, the small front-mounted radiator and the enormous Napier engine.

This new *Blue Bird* was not a conceptual leap but rather the meticulous result of

Campbell's experience so far, including his observations of other contenders. More of the weight was still over the front wheels and, as usual, the tyres were barely adequate, just 6in wide. The efficient engine weighed only 915lb but the overall weight of the car was 6,720lb,

ENGINE BLOCK CONFIGURATIONS

 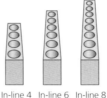

In-line 4 In-line 6 In-line 8   60° V8   45° V12   12-cylinder Broad Arrow

substantially more than the *Higham Special*, which strongly suggests that the engine was capable of 800hp. This would give a power-to-weight ratio similar to that of the *Higham Special* that was so essential if *Blue Bird* were to compete.

The result of Campbell's attention to detail was a car that met all the known requirements for success. It was very stable, which improved its chance of

traversing an unpredictable tidal beach. It was reliable and likely to last the course. It had the requisite power-to-weight ratio and a proficient shape.

Knowing that Parry-Thomas felt that more speed could be extracted from his *Higham Special*, Campbell took the Napier-

Campbell to Pendine Sands on 4 February 1927 to find out whether his new creation could be a serious challenger.

With the official timekeepers recording him, he set an average speed of 174.883mph, 3mph faster than Parry-Thomas's record. Yet this was perceived as a disappointment because the car had run at 195mph in one direction but only 154mph the other way. This spelled the end for British beaches as venues for successful absolute speed records, the tragic attempt by Parry-Thomas the following month sealing their fate.

Even though these beaches — Pendine Sands and Southport Beach — were as much as seven miles long, they were too short to accelerate up to top speed and the surfaces were often dangerously inconsistent. The ever-advancing speed and technology of the new vehicles had made European sites too small for the task.

As the fearsome roar of Henry Segrave's twin engines firing up sounded in the distance, Campbell cast his eyes to the far horizons. He had already broken the record three times but was not satisfied. Enthusiasm was turning into obsession.

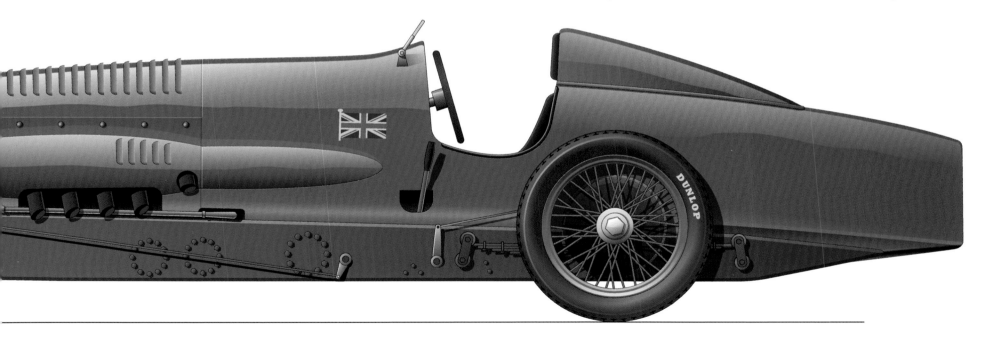

MYSTERY SUNBEAM • HENRY SEGRAVE

Sunbeam had by now put its proud name on four ratified records. Although the company had withdrawn from expensive Grand Prix racing, its designer, Louis Coatalen, was still interested in the land speed record, with its welcome publicity, if something could be done on a reasonable budget. Having studied the possibilities, he instructed John Samuel Irving to build a car for Eton-educated Henry Segrave with the aim of reaching 200mph on the longer beach at Daytona.

The final design was a conceptual leap that departed from the conventional layouts, creating a new paradigm, another right way to do something. It was to use two redundant Sunbeam Matabele aero engines that had been salvaged from a powerboat, one placed in front of the driver's central position and the other behind, directly over the rear axle.

The streamlined aluminium bodywork, developed after wind-tunnel tests at the Aviation Department of Vickers, was fabricated to enclose the whole machine, taking the wheels out of the airstream. This simplified shape offended the eye of purists accustomed to the accepted version of what a car should look like but diverted attention from the now-obsolete

chain drive that was retained to reduce cost. Tyres were supplied by the Dunlop Rubber Company, designed to last for three minutes at 200mph and therefore requiring replacement after each run.

Each Matabele engine was a V12 of 22.4 litres with four valves per cylinder and twin overhead camshafts. Power output was around 450hp each at 2,000rpm,

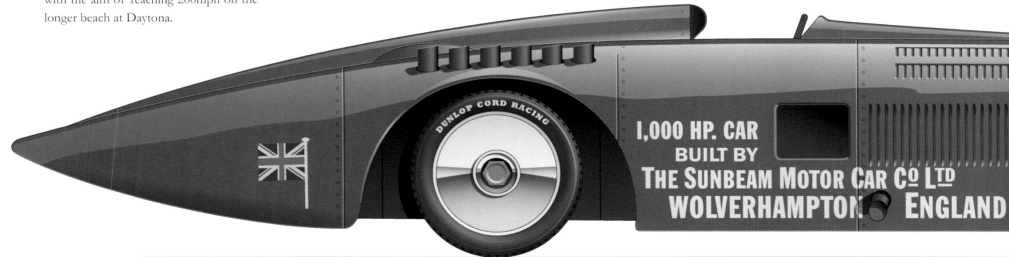

with the potential for 500hp given enough distance to allow 2,200rpm to be reached. Safety precautions had increased the weight of the car to about 8,500lb. This was substantially heavier than Campbell's *Blue Bird* and its power-to-weight ratio was only comparable.

Because the car was built in secret it was dubbed the 'Mystery Sunbeam' by the press, who quickly renamed it the 'Slug'

when it was unveiled, with '1,000 HP' painted large on its side.

Segrave had now retired from other forms of racing to concentrate solely on speed records. He managed to convince the AIACR to recognise his attempt at

On 29 March 1927 Segrave made his two runs at an average of 203.793mph, nearly 30mph faster than the previous ratified record. This magnificent performance marked the first success for either a British driver or a British car at Daytona and

in 1934. The 'Mystery Sunbeam' had recorded its fifth and last record in the quest for speed. The car's slab-like, fully enclosed bodywork had been vindicated. It marked the beginning of a new awareness of aerodynamics.

Today, awaiting a rebuild and no longer able to run, the 'Mystery Sunbeam' still impresses visitors to the National Motor Museum at Beaulieu.

WEIGHT TRANSFER SCHEMATIC

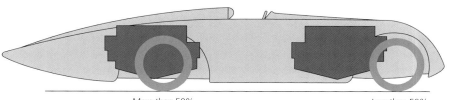

More than 50%   Less than 50%

Daytona, which would be timed by the AAA. This proved to be a wise decision by the AIACR: had this body not recognised Segrave's effort, surely its influence would have withered given America's rise in hosting record-breaking attempts.

With Parry-Thomas gone, the scene was now set for Campbell and Segrave to continue the twentieth-century version of single combat with the American Ray Keech making only a brief appearance.

began a period of dominance.

The power-to-weight ratio of the 'Mystery Sunbeam' was no better than that of Campbell's *Blue Bird*. Instead the car relied on efficient streamlining and improved weight distribution, with more than half of its weight at the rear giving better traction.

The Sunbeam Motor Company ran into financial difficulties during the Great Depression and went into receivership

SPECIFICATIONS

Vehicle	Sunbeam
Origin	England
Weight	8,518lb (3,864kg)
Length	260in (6.60m)
Width	–
Height	48in (1.22m)
Transmission	Three-speed, chain drive
Powerplant	Matabele V12 x 2
Engine capacity	44.8 litres
Horsepower	1,000hp
BHP per litre	22/1
Power/weight ratio	1/8.5
Venue	Daytona
Speed	203.793mph

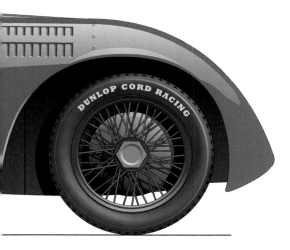

NAPIER-CAMPBELL BLUE BIRD (1928) • MALCOLM CAMPBELL

Henry Segrave had not only beaten Malcolm Campbell's record by a large margin but had also exceeded the spellbinding 200mph mark, beaten the Americans on their own sand and set a record that was ratified on both sides of the Atlantic. He was, indisputably, the fastest man in the world and had created a benchmark for future attempts.

Campbell was not about to accept

SPECIFICATIONS

Vehicle	Blue Bird
Origin	England
Weight	6,720lb (3,048kg)
Length	228in (5.79m)
Width	–
Height	54in (1.37m)
Transmission	Three-speed
Powerplant	Napier Lion Sprint
Engine capacity	23,944cc
Horsepower	900hp
BHP per litre	37.5/1
Power/weight ratio	1/7.5
Venue	Daytona
Speed	206.956mph

second best, though, and set to work modifying his *Blue Bird*. Using his skills of persuasion, he arranged the loan of a Schneider Trophy-tuned Napier Lion Sprint engine, as fitted to the Supermarine S.5 seaplane. Then, after wind-tunnel testing at Vickers, new bodywork was devised, produced by Mulliner, to enclose all but the wheels, and a vertical tail fin was fitted to aid directional stability. Fairings were added beside the wheels to reduce drag and external radiators, made by Fairey Aviation, were mounted at the rear to allow the car to have a smoother front without an opening for cooling air. Beneath these improvements, the structure of the car remained the same.

Now with a genuine 900hp available and every possible improvement in place, *Blue Bird* made the Atlantic crossing to the scene of Segrave's triumph. There on 19 February 1928, after trial runs, Campbell pushed the record to 206.956mph, 3mph faster than the 'Mystery Sunbeam'. An advantageous power-to-weight ratio of

1/7.5 and improved streamlining proved to be enough for the record — but not for Campbell. Nor was it enough to prevent the American Ray Keech from retaking the honours just two months later in his *White Triplex*.

The fact that the benefits of the long track at Daytona were now confirmed did not stop Campbell from looking for somewhere better than a tidal beach. In 1929 this quest led him to another continent and ultimately to the dry salt pan at Verneukpan in South Africa. The expedition had a mixed outcome.

Having twice broken the record, the car was rebuilt a third time. The chassis,

engine and transmission were retained but the bodywork was replaced by a new design fabricated by Arrol-Aster. It was lower over the engine compartment, swept up to the driver's position and reverted to a front-mounted radiator.

After the monumental task of shipping the remodelled car, spares and team to Cape Town and then travelling 450 rugged miles to Verneukpan to clear ten miles of

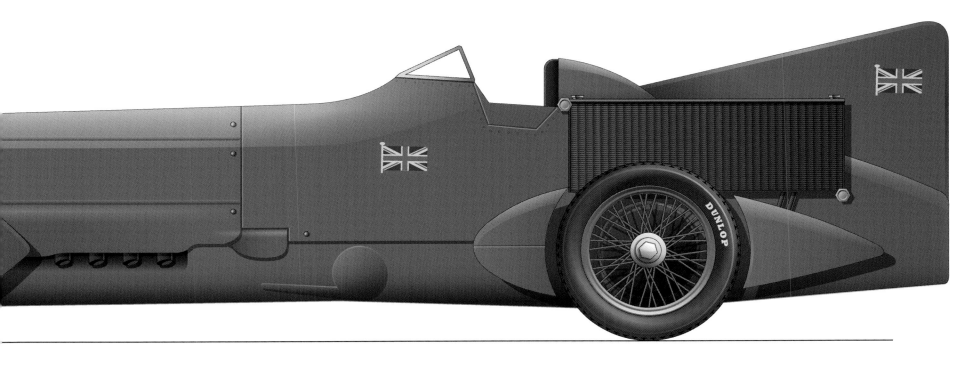

track, it poured with rain at a place that had suffered a five-year drought. Proceedings were delayed and the record attempt was scuppered. Campbell had bounced back from such disappointments before but on his 44th birthday he received a crushing blow when he learned that Segrave had returned to Daytona with a new car and without much ado had powered to 231.44mph.

Campbell knew *Blue Bird* was outclassed and had to be satisfied with distance records at lower speeds on the unsuitable Verneukpan track. Far from being discouraged, his resolve simply hardened. Even the lessons of running at 2,923ft above sea level at Verneukpan were useful and filed for future reference.

Small increments of improvement were not enough and Campbell's now obsessive quest for speed demanded the construction of a car that would represent the sum of all his experience. He knew that a fresh approach was necessary. For that he needed a designer with new ideas who could translate his aspirations into reality.

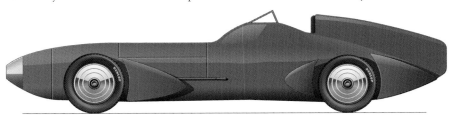

REBUILT BLUE BIRD

TRIPLEX • RAY KEECH

Americans had paid little attention to achievements across the divide that paled by comparison with the deeds of Ralph DePalma, Tommy Milton and Sig Haugdahl. They were just European records adjudicated by the fussy AIACR. The advent of Henry Segrave and Malcolm Campbell changed this when they made their two-way runs at Daytona, timed and ratified by the AAA, and won the laurels for Britain. This crystallised American attention and wealthy patriot J. W. White stepped up to commission a car that would win back the title.

White reasoned that the solution was overwhelming power. Since no engine was available to compete with the Napier Lion, he decided to use three Liberty V12 aero engines totalling 81 litres and producing 1,500hp. One engine was in front of the driver, the other two side by side behind him. Each engine drove directly to the rear axle through a ring-and-pinion gear similar to that on the Ford *999* and there was no clutch, gearbox or differential, either to save weight or cost or both. The driver was in an exposed position without the benefit of a crash helmet, roll bar or safety harness, although at the time the lesser of two evils was to be flung from the machine rather than trapped in

SPECIFICATIONS

Vehicle	Triplex
Origin	America
Weight	8,960lb (4,064kg)
Length	232in (5.89m)
Width	–
Height	62in (1.57m)
Transmission	None
Powerplant	Liberty V12 x 3
Engine capacity	81.09 litres
Horsepower	1,500hp
BHP per litre	18.5/1
Power/weight ratio	1/6
Venue	Daytona
Speed	207.55mph

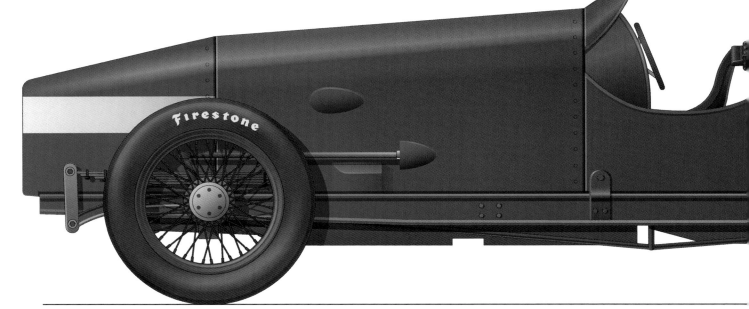

hurtling wreckage. Little heed was paid to aerodynamics. The front engine had a chiselled nose cover reminiscent of the Jeantaud Profilé but the rear engines and wheels were left exposed. The chassis was high off the ground and there was no belly pan. This concept of brute force reprised the Fiat S76 on a massive scale.

The overall weight of 8,960lb, with each engine weighing 845lb, put excessive strain on wire wheels not designed for such a high load.

Once push-started the only way to stop the car was to switch off the ignition and use the engine compression together with the inadequate drum brakes on the rear wheels. If one drive wheel lost traction when moving at speed the other wheel would push the car off course and

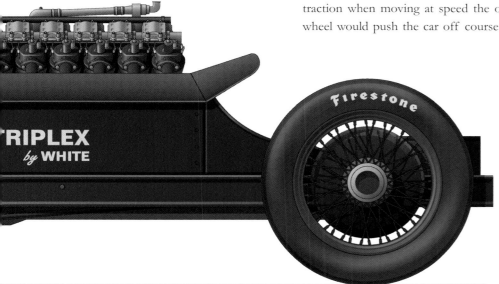

without a clutch or differential to help compensate the car could become very difficult to control. To astute designers such as Irving, Villiers and Maina, it must have seemed like the automotive version of Frankenstein's monster.

With the help of a substantial fee, J. W. White persuaded experienced racing driver Ray Keech to take control of *Triplex*, named for its three engines. On arrival at Daytona it was found that, to challenge Campbell's official two-way record, the new contender would require a reverse gear. This was accomplished by incorporating a second rear axle, with its own drive, which could be lowered into position while the drive axle was raised from the ground. This farcical contraption met the requirement and was removed before the record attempt.

Keech was now free to risk his life in the monster and, on 22 April 1928, he bludgeoned his way down the track, first

TRIPLEX ENGINE AND DRIVE SCHEMATIC

scalded by a burst hose and then burned by exhaust flames. With 50 per cent more horsepower than Campbell, he averaged 207.55mph to edge the Englishman's speed by less than 0.5 per cent. Regardless, the record was Keech's and appeared to prove that White's mammoth creation was the right way to do it.

One experience of this behemoth was enough for Keech. He returned to 'safer' competition, winning the Indianapolis 500 in May the following year. But his luck ran out 16 days later when he was killed in a crash on the Altoona speedway at Tipton, Pennsylvania, midway through a 200-mile event.

The story of White's *Triplex* also ended in tragedy, in March 1929, during an attempt to regain the record that Segrave now held. Its inexperienced driver, Lee Bible, and a watching cameraman were killed in what was a futile effort to compete with a better-designed machine.

STUTZ BLACK HAWK • FRANK LOCKHART

Until 1928 all the protagonists in this drama had been born in the 1800s. There now appeared a young man of the twentieth century by the name of Frank Lockhart who scorched his way to fame and fortune behind the wheel. He first made his mark in 1926 when, aged 23, he became the youngest winner of the Indianapolis 500 driving a Miller Special. The following year he led the race for its first 81 laps, a feat

SPECIFICATIONS

Vehicle	Stutz Black Hawk
Origin	America
Weight	2,700lb (1,225kg)
Length	189in (4.80m)
Width	60in (1.52m)
Height	44in (1.12m)
Transmission	Three-speed
Powerplant	Miller eight-cylinder x 2
Engine capacity	2.98 litres
Horsepower	380hp+
BHP per litre	128/1
Power/weight ratio	1/7
Venue	Daytona
Speed	200mph+

that would be unequalled for 64 years. He won 44 per cent of his races and at Atlantic City he posted a lap record of 147.7mph that would not be beaten for 33 years.

Lockhart was also a gifted engineer and innovator. Realising that the centrifugal

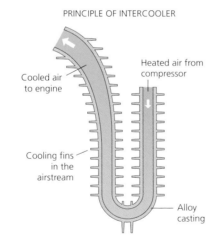

PRINCIPLE OF INTERCOOLER

Cooled air to engine

Heated air from compressor

Cooling fins in the airstream

Alloy casting

supercharger, as fitted to the Miller engine, heated the air as it was compressed, he deduced that cooling it by some means would increase power output. With his team, brothers Zenas and John Weisel and

Ernie Olsen, he developed an intercooler that gave his car an advantage.

In 1927 Lockhart took his 91 cubic inch (1,500cc) supercharged straight-eight Miller to the Muroc dry lake where he pushed the engine to over 8,000rpm and set a class record of 164mph. He decided to challenge for the absolute record.

Together with the Weisel brothers, he devised a car that followed the Haugdahl school of thought with close attention to every detail. Lockhart's high profile helped to secure half the necessary funding from the Stutz Motor Car Company on condition that the car carried the Stutz name for publicity purposes. It would incorporate two of Miller's supercharged 91 cubic inch engines running on their own crankshafts but geared to a central drive. This unusual layout is described as a U16. The original idea for bodywork that enclosed the wheels was discarded in order to reduce frontal area and weight.

Scale models were tested at the Curtiss and Army Air Services wind tunnels

and the narrow body (only 2ft wide) and streamlined wheel covers proved the efficiency of the design. Even the exposed parts of the axles were covered with fairings. The small 2in diameter pistons and correspondingly light rotational parts

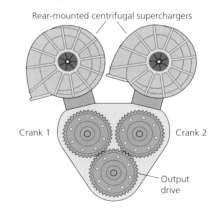

BLACK HAWK ENGINE SCHEMATIC

Rear-mounted centrifugal superchargers

Crank 1

Crank 2

Output drive

allowed the engine to reach very high revs. Together with Lockhart's intercooler and internal modifications, the two Miller engines, supercharged up to 30psi, produced well over 380hp. Even at that conservative figure, the power-to-weight

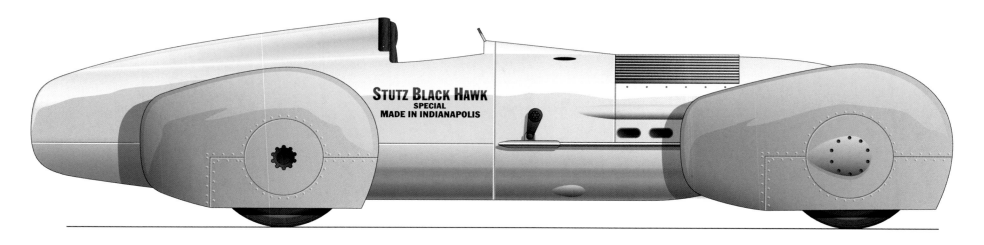

ratio was better than those of British rivals.

The finished car made its début at Daytona to challenge the 203.793mph achieved by the 'Mystery Sunbeam'. The occasion was hotly contested with events unfolding as follows. On 19 February Campbell took the record at 206.956mph. The next day Lockhart made a promising run but withdrew with clutch problems. In adverse weather on 28 February Lockhart crashed into the sea and was injured. After recovery, he returned to Daytona

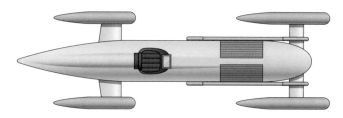

with his repaired Stutz on 20 April only to experience carburation problems. Two days later Ray Keech in the *Triplex* edged the record with 207.552mph. Having made his car reliable at over 200mph, Lockhart

went for the record on 25 April. At a claimed speed of 220mph, disaster struck when a rear tyre burst. The car skidded and rolled for hundreds of yards, ending 26-year-old Lockhart's life.

Although the displacement of the 16-cylinder Stutz Black Hawk was even less than that of the V12 *Ladybird*, it had pushed the boundaries and represented a

very sophisticated design. However, tyre technology remained the Achilles' heel for the pioneering daredevils challenging the frontiers of speed. Had Lockhart succeeded, perhaps the age of the aero engine would have ended sooner, to be superseded by a trend towards smaller, higher-revving engines.

Did Lockhart take a chance on, reportedly, a previously damaged tyre? Or perhaps this brightest of flames just ran out of luck?

OPEL RAK 2 • FRITZ VON OPEL

Fritz Adam Hermann von Opel was the son of Wilhelm von Opel, the founder of Germany's Opel Motor Company. From a wealthy background, Fritz von Opel could have idled his life away in harmless pursuits but when he became director of testing and publicity for Opel he chose to involve himself in the unstable world of rocket propulsion.

This he did to the benefit of the Opel company together with personal recognition that included his being dubbed 'Rocket Fritz'. His success owed a great deal to two important collaborators, Max Valier and Friedrich Sander. Valier was an Austrian rocket pioneer and science writer who predicted space travel. His motivation to work with Fritz was to raise public awareness of rocket propulsion's possibilities. To help with the practical side, Valier enlisted Sander, who manufactured black-powder motors for signal rockets.

The triumvirate began experimenting by fitting two rockets to an Opel road car that travelled 500ft at 3mph — an unimpressive start. Technology can evolve rapidly,

however, once principles are grasped and this duly happened. Next came an Opel race car fitted with 12 rockets that achieved a speed of 47mph.

This was enough encouragement to create *Rak 2*, a purpose-built car, this time with 24 rocket motors. The chassis from an Opel 10/40 production vehicle, minus engine and running gear, was encased in aerodynamic bodywork equipped with two stub wings behind the front wheels that generated downforce to prevent the lightweight nose from lifting. Weighing

SPECIFICATIONS

Vehicle	Opel RAK 1
Origin	Germany
Weight	1,234lb (560kg)
Length	192in (4.88m)
Width	–
Height	47in (1.19m)
Powerplant	24 Sander rockets
Thrust	1,320lbf
Thrust/weight	1.06/1
Venue	Avus, Berlin
Speed	143mph

only 1,234lb, including a rapidly diminishing 264lb payload of black powder, *Rak 2* had a maximum potential of 1,320lb of thrust but for a very limited duration.

On 23 May 1928, only two months into the programme, *Rak 2* made a spectacular run at the Avus track in Berlin. In front of 3,000 spectators it caused a sensation by clocking 143mph, which also generated priceless publicity for Opel. Although *Rak 2* did not break any records, it did break the boundaries of public perception and gave a glimpse of a new era.

The odd mismatch of cutting-edge aerodynamics and gunpowder technology, developed by the Chinese in the ninth

BASIC BLACK POWDER SIGNAL ROCKET

Mixture of sulphur, saltpetre & charcoal

century and largely unchanged, had many repercussions. *Rak 2*'s streamlined bodywork pre-dated similarly shaped

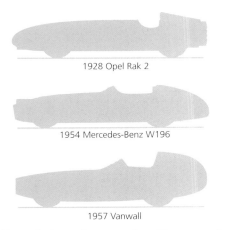

1928 Opel Rak 2

1954 Mercedes-Benz W196

1957 Vanwall

Formula 1 cars by more than 20 years and the absence of a radiator opening made it more efficient. The car's motive power helped spark the beginning of manned rocket vehicles.

As the Great Depression bit into Europe, General Motors took full control of the Opel company and extravagant experiments were curtailed.

The fates of the triumvirate varied dramatically. Fritz von Opel continued demonstrations with railcars and aircraft, which crashed or exploded as often as

not, before leaving Opel and Germany in 1930 and eventually heading for America in 1940. The prophet Valier met his maker when a liquid-fuel rocket engine exploded on his test bench in 1930. Sander continued to develop rocket motors, including for military purposes, until he was denounced as a traitor by the Nazi regime and eventually put in prison, where he died in 1938.

Once liquid propellant replaced low-energy gunpowder, rocket innovation accelerated inexorably. In 1947 the US airman Chuck Yeager, piloting the Bell X-1, was the first person to punch a hole in the sound barrier. And then in 1969,

OPEL ROCKET-POWERED GLIDER

just 41 years after Opel's blistering 3mph experiment, rocket propulsion put man on the moon.

IRVING NAPIER 'GOLDEN ARROW' • HENRY SEGRAVE

Within a year Henry Segrave's 'Mystery Sunbeam' record of 203.792mph was surpassed first by Malcolm Campbell's *Blue Bird* in February 1928 and then, two months later, by Ray Keech in the *Triplex*. The twin-engine 'Mystery Sunbeam', with only 74 miles on the clock, had been consigned to history and Segrave and designer John Samuel Irving had left the company — but not the world of fast cars.

To finance his next attempt, Segrave set about raising backing from Portland Cement, his new employer, and previous sponsors. Having done this he engaged Irving to design a new car. Very soon the Irving Napier Special or *Golden Arrow* began to take shape on the drawing board.

Irving's masterwork evolved around the acquisition of a Napier Lion VIIA engine, as used in Schneider Trophy aircraft. Running on alcohol-based fuel supplied by British Petroleum and with a compression ratio of 10:1, it developed 930hp at 3,300rpm and could spin up to 3,600rpm.

Unlike the *Triplex*, great attention was paid to every detail of the bespoke component parts. Conscious of safety in this dangerous activity, measures were taken at the expense of critical weight. Massive frame rails were constructed to eliminate flexing and the cockpit was encased in steel plate. Each wheel was provided with 17in drum brakes with servo assistance. The multi-plate clutch with one-and-a-half-ton clamping pressure, to prevent slip, was also servo-assisted. The engine was placed in a

conventional position just behind the front wheels and a low central driving position was achieved at the expense of the added complexity of a three-speed transmission driving twin shafts either side of the cockpit. Ground clearance was reduced to just 7in.

Irving used extensive wind-tunnel testing to create the bodywork, which swept up from the nose to generate 450lb of downforce. It was closely tailored to fit around the engine and blended into an

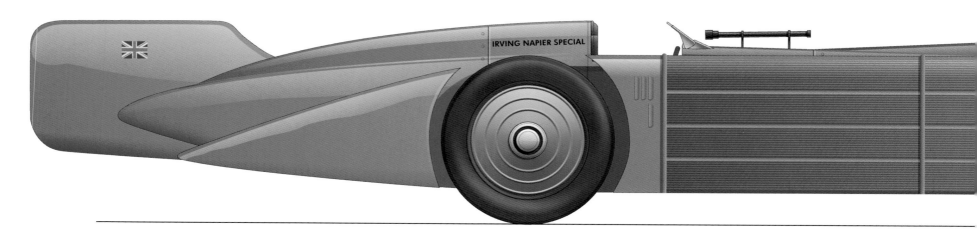

extended tail fin to aid directional stability. The surface radiators were positioned in the 'dead' area between the wheels, helping to clean up airflow. In this configuration *Golden Arrow* presented an efficient frontal area of only 11.6sq ft. The Dunlop Rubber Company provided tyres that were guaranteed to last for 25 seconds at 240mph. The carefully conceived car was built at Kenelm Lee Guinness's Robinhood Engineering Works.

Arriving at Daytona with the untested car, Segrave waited several weeks until weather conditions allowed him a practice run. Satisfied that everything was optimal, he donned a rudimentary crash helmet and

GOLDEN ARROW FRONTAL AREA

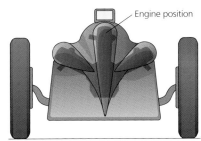

Engine position

Cowlings closely fit the Napier Lion engine

made his first run on 11 March 1929. Despite being sprayed with hot water, he then turned around and the car, true to its name, arrowed back down the beach to return an average speed of 231.446mph, smashing the record by over 23mph.

The *Triplex* was also present at Daytona but Keech decided that the car was too dangerous and declined to drive it. This was when the luckless Lee Bible all too briefly entered our story. He was a mechanic who had limited experience of driving at high speeds and the decision to let him take Keech's place was reckless in the extreme. Segrave knew that *Golden Arrow* was capable of more and was prepared to respond if Bible was successful. He did not have to. *Triplex* went out of control, killing Bible and a photographer as it careered to destruction.

As a result Segrave switched his efforts and became the first person to hold the land and water speed records simultaneously. But he had no time to savour his double triumph, which he clinched on

Windermere in the Lake District on Friday 13 June 1930. Within hours of setting the record at 98.76mph, he perished trying to better it when his boat *Miss England II* hit an object in the water.

As for *Golden Arrow*, it never ran again. With a recorded mileage of only 40, it now resides in Britain's National Motor Museum at Beaulieu next to its equally low-mileage predecessor, the 'Mystery Sunbeam'.

SPECIFICATIONS

Vehicle	Irving Napier
Origin	England
Weight	7,694lb (3,490kg)
Length	330in (8.38m)
Width	72in (1.83m)
Height	44in (1.12m)
Transmission	Three-speed
Powerplant	Napier Lion VIIA
Engine capacity	23.94 litres
Horsepower	930hp
BHP per litre	39/1
Power/weight ratio	1/8.3
Venue	Daytona
Speed	231.446mph

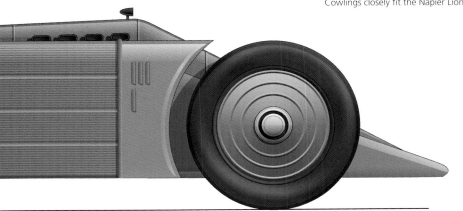

NAPIER-RAILTON BLUE BIRD • MALCOLM CAMPBELL

When confronting the fates in South Africa, Malcolm Campbell learned that *Golden Arrow* had increased the record by 23mph and knew he would have to reassess his own strategy. *Golden Arrow* had the same Napier engine as his own car and, with 260lb of lead ballast over the rear end, weighed slightly more. The great advantage was the superior aerodynamics with a smaller frontal area, longer length and lower height than any aero-engined predecessor.

After Henry Segrave's death, however, Campbell was left to contest the land speed record alone. Having already broken the record four times, he went on to make it his sole property for the next four years.

The key to Campbell's further success was Reid Railton. At Leyland Motors, Railton had been assistant to John Parry-Thomas, who also became a close friend. After Parry-Thomas's death at Pendine Sands, Railton joined Thomson & Taylor, the company that Parry-Thomas had founded, as chief engineer. It was here that Campbell came to commission the redesign and construction of a new car at his own expense.

Railton, like John Irving, demonstrated his ability to break records on the drawing board with the business of construction, transportation and driving taken care of by others. As it was difficult to improve on

the aerodynamics of *Golden Arrow*, another advantage had to be found. This led to the selection of a centrifugally supercharged Napier Lion VIID as the power source. This unit developed 1,450hp at 3,600rpm, representing a huge 55 per cent increase on the previous *Blue Bird* engine.

Taking note of *Golden Arrow*'s efficiency, Railton set to work designing a drive shaft and an offset gearbox, built by KLG Sparking Plugs Ltd, that also allowed a lower driving position. The radiator was kept in the conventional place but within its own pod to prevent turbulent air passing into the engine compartment. Bodywork contours and the vertical stabilising fin were conceived after wind-tunnel testing with models.

Reid Railton

The extra power available allowed a focus on safety and stability at the expense of weight. Although the revised *Blue Bird* was heavier than *Golden Arrow*, it had a greatly improved power-to-weight ratio of

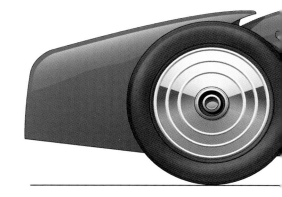

1/5.5. The finished article, with a length of 25ft, was rightly described as a behemoth when compared with the modest four-seater 20hp saloon cars available on the British market at that time.

Campbell broke Segrave's record when he achieved a two-way average of 246.09mph at Daytona on 5 February 1931. After some modifications he returned the following year and on 24 February 1932 he registered an average of 253.97mph to claim a sixth title for himself and Britain.

SPECIFICATIONS

Vehicle	Blue Bird
Origin	England
Weight	7,952lb (3,607kg)
Length	300in (7.62m)
Width	64in (1.63m)
Height	63in (1.60m)
Transmission	Three-speed
Powerplant	Napier Lion VIID
Engine capacity	23.94 litres
Horsepower	1,450hp
BHP per litre	60/1
Power/weight ratio	1/5.5
Venue	Daytona
Speeds	246.09mph & 253.97mph

Campbell had drawn upon all his experience to make the challenge and to survive the attempts. In earlier years he had experienced several burst and shredded tyres, the same element of risk that had cost Frank Lockhart his life. Luck had played its part in propelling him into the realms of legend but still he pursued his obsession.

THE AGE OF THE BEHEMOTH

1931 24-litre Napier-Railton Bluebird (length 300in)   1931 800cc Morris Minor (length 120in)

As the man who risked all, Campbell won world renown and a knighthood.

The Napier-Railton design was the first to use supercharging on a large aero engine and this would now become standard practice for record breaking.

Although this *Blue Bird* was at the cutting edge of design and had shown that length in itself was not detrimental to speed as long as airflow was smooth, its weight bias was still over the front wheels and with the large amount of power now available traction was not optimal, leaving room for improvement.

Reid Railton was just the man to extract this improvement. Like no other designer before him, he was beginning to understand how to achieve greater speeds and would carry on pushing the boundaries in the highly specialised world of creating super-fast vehicles.

Sir Malcolm Campbell could now continue with his obsession with a target of 300mph a real possibility.

CAMPBELL-RAILTON BLUE BIRD • MALCOLM CAMPBELL

Malcolm Campbell was the first man past 250mph and with this sixth record consolidated his position at the top of the pyramid in the quest for speed. Having no serious competition, he simply set his sights on the mind-boggling peak of 300mph. The formidable 24-litre Napier broad-arrow engine was at its limit in a single-engine configuration and more power was

SPECIFICATIONS

Vehicle	Blue Bird
Origin	England
Weight	10,640lb (4,826kg)
Length	324in (8.23m)
Width	63in (1.60m)
Height	58in (1.47m)
Transmission	Three-speed
Powerplant	Rolls-Royce R V12
Engine capacity	36.7 litres
Horsepower	2,500hp
BHP per litre	68/1
Power/weight ratio	1/4.2
Venue	Daytona & Bonneville
Speeds	272.46mph, 276.82mph & 301.129mph

essential. After negotiations with the Air Ministry, Campbell received permission to use the supercharged Rolls-Royce R V12 engine that had been designed for Schneider Trophy aircraft.

Reid Railton was given the task of making modifications to the 1931 car to accommodate the massive 36.7-litre engine and redesign all of the running gear. Supercharged at 18lb per square inch (psi) and running on a mix of 30 per cent benzole, 60 per cent methanol and 10 per cent acetone, an output of 2,500hp was feasible at 3,200rpm.

This reincarnation of *Blue Bird* returned to Daytona on 22 February 1933 and set a record of 272.46mph. It is no surprise that Campbell was not satisfied as the large increase in power was not reflected in the speed at peak rpm. A 60 per cent increase in power had only resulted in a nine per cent increase in speed.

Railton, knowing the wheel diameter, gear ratios and engine rpm, had calculated that the car was capable of 300mph and

deduced that wheelspin was responsible for the loss in performance. Campbell provided the funds and Railton undertook the major modifications needed to solve this problem. The drive was separated into two shafts, one to each side, driving double rear wheels through ring-and-pinion gears.

This arrangement involved shortening the wheelbase on one side by 1.5in. All-new bodywork was created to the width of the wheels but not enclosing them. A flap was fitted so the rectangular front radiator intake could be closed for the short period in the measured mile.

Back at Daytona on 7 March 1933,

Campbell raised the record by 4mph to an average speed of 276.82mph. The car was still experiencing wheelspin and he realised that competing on the famous sandy beach had reached an impasse.

American racer Ab Jenkins had been making a habit of breaking endurance records on the Bonneville Salt Flats in north-west Utah. The surface was perfectly level and after the summer, given the right conditions, the salt became hard-packed, giving much better traction than sand.

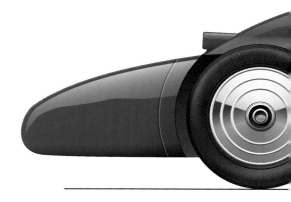

Also, there was enough space for an extended run to build up to speed. At more than 4,000ft above sea level Bonneville's oxygen was reduced, causing a loss of power, but this is what supercharged aircraft engines were designed for when operating at altitude.

When Campbell decided to switch operations to Bonneville, he effectively consigned Daytona to history as far as absolute records were concerned. His

1935 CAMPBELL-RAILTON BLUE BIRD WHEEL LAYOUT

previous experience running above sea level at Verneukpan helped to set up the huge supercharged Rolls-Royce R V12 engine and on 3 September 1935 in this last beautiful metamorphosis of *Blue Bird* he realised his ambition to break

the 300mph barrier with an average speed of 301.129mph. This was his ninth and last record to be set on land.

The critical factor was the venue. Bonneville's firm salt gave the double rear wheels a chance to convert *Blue Bird*'s 2,500hp into speed and prove Railton's calculations to be correct. It posed the question of how fast some of the Daytona cars or even Ford's *999*

might have gone on the salt flats but that page had now been turned. The new era of record breaking in Utah would see new contenders, ever-increasing speeds and more drama than ever before.

Satisfied at last, Sir Malcolm Campbell turned from land to water. He set three records with his *K3* hydroplane and one final record with *K4*, designed by Railton, before retiring with his luck and life intact.

THUNDERBOLT • GEORGE EYSTON

The life of George Eyston MC OBE was immersed in a world of speed. Behind the wheel of famous marques such as Bugatti, MG, Sunbeam, Bentley, Hotchkiss, Singer, Riley, Panhard-Lavassor, Alfa Romeo, Lea-Francis, Maserati, OM, Halford Special and Chrysler, he registered success on the track and amassed more than 200 endurance records. With his friend and

SPECIFICATIONS

Vehicle	Thunderbolt
Origin	England
Weight	15,680lb (7,112kg)
Length	365in (9.27m)
Width	85.5in (2.17m)
Height	53in (1.35m)
Transmission	Three-speed
Powerplant	Rolls-Royce R V12 x2
Engine capacity	73.4 litres
Horsepower	5,000hp
BHP per litre	68/1
Power/weight ratio	1/3.1
Venue	Bonneville
Speeds	312.00mph, 345.50mph & 357.50mph

colleague Ernest Eldridge he designed *Speed of the Wind* to successfully contest the 24- and 48-hour records achieved by Ab Jenkins at Bonneville.

Eyston studied engineering at Cambridge University either side of the First World War, in which he served as an army officer. When, in later life, he was not searing his name into the land speed record books, he served as a director of the Burmah and Castrol oil companies and was engineering consultant to Chrysler. He also made his mark as an engineer with other record-breaking cars, high-

performance gearboxes and invented the Powerplus supercharger that made the MG record-breakers world famous.

It was in 1937 that he turned his attention to the ultimate accolade. In doing so he reasoned that he would need to integrate more power, adequate traction and an efficient shape with a sturdy chassis that included the transmission, steering and suspension necessary to create a stable platform for the highest speeds.

The result was a car of epic proportions powered by two Rolls-Royce R V12 engines mounted side by side in a massive chassis.

They were coupled through a water-cooled gearbox, of Eyston's own design, to drive the rear axle through a single shaft and ring-and-pinion gear. The rear wheels were

THUNDERBOLT WHEEL LAYOUT

doubled up and the steering comprised four wheels on two axles with the second pair set outside the track of the first so they did not run in the same wheel ruts. The aerodynamic bodyshell with a large

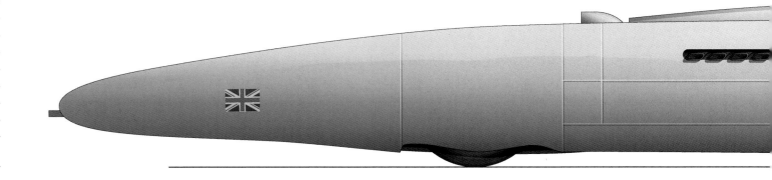

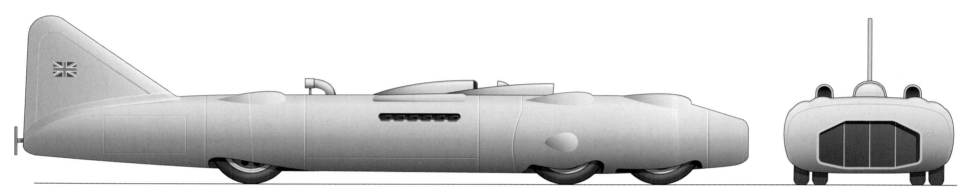

FIRST CONFIGURATION OF THUNDERBOLT

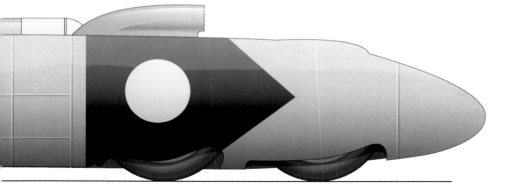

stabilising rear fin brought the weight to seven tons but with an output of 5,000hp this gave the car a power-to-weight ratio of 1/3.1. The downsides of the design were its large frontal area of approximately 24sq ft, with a gaping octagonal hole for the radiator, and also increased rolling resistance roughly double that of previous four-wheel cars.

Eyston arrived at Bonneville in October 1937. What followed is an example of the trials and tribulations involved in the evolution of a land speed car. First, bad weather caused delays and then clutch problems held things up further before the car broke the record on 19 November with an average of 312mph — but this was just four per cent faster than Campbell's *Blue Bird* despite having twice the horsepower.

After improving the streamlining, reducing the radiator opening and enclosing the cockpit, Eyston returned in 1938 to share the salt with fellow Briton John Cobb in a mighty combat to be King of Speed. Eyston's first attempt was thwarted because the silver car did not register on the timing system. A black arrow with a yellow disc painted on the car's flank resolved this problem and Eyston sped to 345.50mph on 27 August.

The following month, on 15 September, Cobb broke the 350mph barrier, but by less than 1mph. Within 24 hours Eyston reclaimed the record with a speed of 357.50mph. He did it in what was to be the final version of *Thunderbolt* with tail fin removed, radiator replaced by water tanks and its nose fully enclosed.

With a displacement of 73.4 litres and weighing seven tons, Eyston's car represented the high tide for land speed leviathans, which would soon be made extinct by Cobb's smaller, less powerful car. *Thunderbolt* never ran again and ended up in New Zealand, where it was exhibited before being destroyed in a fire.

RAILTON MOBIL SPECIAL • JOHN COBB

Englishman John Cobb was wealthy enough to indulge in his passion for motor racing. He enjoyed a long spell of success driving a variety of cars including the old V12 Delage used by René Thomas, often vying with Malcolm Campbell and George Eyston. In 1933 he commissioned Reid Railton to build the Napier-Railton racing car powered by the broad-arrow engine. He drove it to 47 speed and endurance records, including the fastest ever lap of Brooklands at an average speed of 143.44mph.

Turning his attention to the absolute record in 1935, Cobb again commissioned Reid Railton to design the car. Given a clean slate, this brilliant designer created a masterpiece that defied convention. At its heart was an S-shaped chassis that carried two supercharged Napier Lion VIID engines. They were set at an angle that allowed separate drives to both front and rear wheels with the driving position placed ahead of the front axle. The entire structure, including wheels, was enclosed within a one-piece aerodynamic shell.

As we have already seen, Eyston's *Thunderbolt* had appeared first at Bonneville in 1937. It had been constructed in just eight months and set a record of 312mph. Eyston returned the following year to compete against the now-finished *Railton* and upped his speed to 345.50mph. Cobb responded on 15 September 1938 to claim his first record with 350.20mph but within 24 hours Eyston ended proceedings for the year when he regained the laurels with 357.50mph.

Thunderbolt was close to its limit. The

Railton, on the other hand, had a better power-to-weight ratio, a more efficient frontal area and streamlining, and better weight distribution with traction improved by four-wheel drive. With the engines available, Railton had put together a near-perfect combination. This was borne out a year later when on 23 August 1939 Cobb pushed the record up to 369.70mph, putting him at the pinnacle of speed.

Some sections of the public questioned the sense of achieving ever-higher speeds simply for the sake of it. But it was this

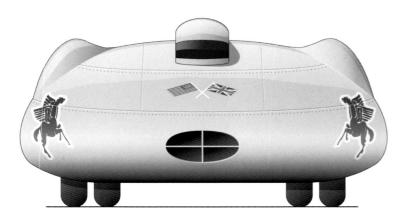

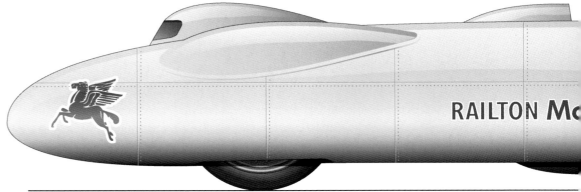

freedom of individuals to express themselves in whatever way they chose that was under threat as the Second World War plunged mankind into a period of human destruction on an unprecedented scale.

As the world slowly recovered, Cobb and Railton returned to the salt with the same car, now named *Railton Mobil Special*. Changes had been made by paring excess weight from the engines, which were also

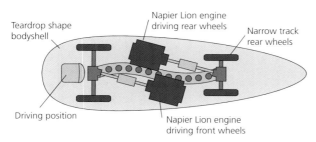

Teardrop shape
bodyshell

Napier Lion engine
driving rear wheels

Narrow track
rear wheels

Driving position

Napier Lion engine
driving front wheels

modified to spin up to 4,000rpm (to the consternation of Napier engineers) and now ran on an alcohol-based fuel that increased the power. On 16 September 1947 Cobb smashed the 400mph barrier with a second run of 403mph. This followed a first run of 385mph and

established a new record of 394.194mph. A piston-engine car would not officially exceed this mark until 1964, ending a British reign of 36 years.

In this grand finale the *Railton Mobil Special* was the last piston-engine car to hold the absolute record. The Napier Lion engine, designed in 1917, passed into legend, having powered Segrave, Campbell and Cobb to eight absolute records.

Cobb died in 1952 in an attempt at the water speed record on Loch Ness, piloting the Railton-designed *Crusader*. A distraught Railton, whose ability is hard to overstate, had left his watermark on eight absolute records but took no further part in land speed challenges.

The *Railton Mobil Special* survives.

It can be seen in the Thinktank science museum in Birmingham.

British drivers, who wore a shirt and tie at the wheel, raised the land speed record by nearly 170mph in just 18 years. It would be another 18 years before the Summers brothers officially edged it up by just 15mph with a different way of doing things.

SPECIFICATIONS

Vehicle	Railton Mobil Special
Origin	England
Weight	6,720lb (3,048kg)
Length	344in (8.74m)
Width	96in (2.43m)
Height	51in (1.30m)
Transmission	Three-speed
Powerplant	2 x Napier Lion VIID
Engine capacity	47.87 litres
Horsepower	3,000hp
BHP per litre	62/1
Power/weight ratio	1/2.2
Venue	Bonneville
Speeds	350.20mph, 369.70mph & 394.194mph

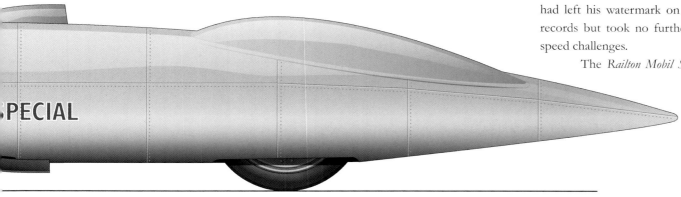

SPECIAL

BELLY TANK • BILL BURKE

The post-war years in America were a time of prosperity. Many young men had returned from military service and wished to indulge in the pursuit of speed. The scrapyards were full of Model T Fords and other cars, with a plentiful supply of Ford V8 engines. The Southern California Timing Association (SCTA), which came into being in 1937, had extended its operations at the El Mirage and Muroc dry lakes to include Bonneville, where all-comers could test their machines.

It was the dawn of a new era in which the term 'hot rod' became common currency. The origin of the name is unclear but its meaning is the installation of a powerful engine in a small, lightened jalopy in its most basic form. Without the private wealth and heavy sponsorship of the British Speed Kings, these young men resorted to the qualities essential to any hot rodder: ingenuity and improvisation.

Californian Bill Burke was one such hot rodder. Remembering the aircraft 'drop' tanks he saw during the war, Burke bought a surplus 165-gallon P-51 Mustang fuel tank. Then, using chassis rails and components from a Model T and an early Ford flathead V8, he put together the first 'belly tank' racer, which was so rudimentary it had a bicycle seat for the driver.

By powering down the dry lakes to 131.96mph, Burke caused quite a stir that in 1950 resulted in the SCTA introducing the Lakester class to cover such vehicles. Although he fell short of Bob Rufi's 140mph pre-war record, Burke inspired many hot rodders to emulate and improve on his early pioneering effort. The efficient shape of the belly tank was obviously offset by the aerodynamic drag caused by the driver's exposed upper body.

The natural progression was Burke's next car, which he named *Sweet 16*. For this he acquired a larger 315-gallon tank from a P-38 Lightning, situated the engine to the rear, enclosed the driver and hit 151.085mph. Next came a modified Bantam Coupe followed by *Super Shaker*, a tiny streamlined vehicle weighing only

604lb that achieved 151.38mph with a V-twin Harley-Davidson engine. The indefatigable Burke, who would live to the age of 97, then partnered with Mickey Thompson to build the *Swallow*, a glass-fibre sports car that set another record at 167mph.

Burke's relentless endeavour continued with the *Pumpkin Seed*, a fully enclosed streamliner powered by a Ford Falcon

SPECIFICATIONS

Vehicle	Belly Tank
Origin	America
Weight	850lb (386kg)
Length	144in (3.66in)
Width	–
Height	31in (0.79m)
Transmission	Three-speed
Powerplant	Flathead V8
Engine capacity	2.6 litres
Horsepower	75hp
BHP per litre	28/1
Power/weight ratio	1/11
Venue	Muroc
Speed	131.96mph

six-cylinder engine. This car earned him admission to the 200mph club with a speed of 205.949mph. After an approach by Studebaker in 1962 his attentions focused

PUMPKIN SEED

on breaking records with the Studebaker Avanti. This car was campaigned for 30 years with different engine combinations and two generations of Burkes involved. They set 30 records with a one-way best of 252mph.

The engine of choice for most contenders in the early days was the compact Ford Flathead V8. In 1932 this was the first V8 engine to go into mass production and it remained in use until 1953 in various sizes from 2.2 to 5.5 litres. Paradoxically the engine was not designed for high-

performance applications as its side-valve configuration had long been surpassed by overhead valves and overhead camshafts. The reason Ford mass-produced this engine was its simple design. And the reason the hot rodders liked it was its abundance. Although it offered only 65–125hp in stock form, some self-taught engine maestros eventually squeezed

SO-CAL LAKESTER

700hp or more from this modest unit.

After seeing Burke's belly tank, Alex Xydias, owner of the So-Cal Speed Shop,

was motivated to compete in the new open-wheel Lakester class. With help from Bill Burke and using the larger P-38 tank, the rear engine *So-Cal Lakester*, sporting the original bronze and white colours, was born.

Several class records were set at Bonneville by this legendary car, powered by various flatheads: a 156 cu in (2.6-litre), built with Vic Edelbrock Sr, for

COMPARATIVE FRONTAL AREAS

Electric Torpedo   Burke Belly Tank

145.50mph; a 259 cu in (4.3-litre) for 181.085mph; and a 296 cu in (4.9-litre) for 195.77mph, with a one-way speed of 197.88mph. This tiny car ran in the wheel tracks of the pre-war aero-engine monsters and vindicated the concepts of the *Electric Torpedo* and the *Stanley Steamer*. Alex Xydias would return to the salt with more radical cars.

LAMBRETTA • ROMOLO FERRI

In this epic saga, as the era of aero-engine juggernauts came to a close, there now appeared the little motor scooter. The factories, roads and economy in post-war Italy were in ruins. Money and petrol were in short supply, resulting in the need for a cheap form of practical transport. Two companies rose from the rubble to meet this challenge. The Innocenti Company had specialised in steel tube manufacture

SPECIFICATIONS

Vehicle	Lambretta
Origin	Italy
Weight	–
Length	–
Width	–
Height	–
Transmission	Three-speed
Powerplant	Single-cylinder, two-stroke
Engine capacity	125cc
Horsepower	20.6hp
BHP per litre	165/1
Power/weight ratio	–
Venue	Ingolstadt
Speed	124.89mph

but now produced the 125cc Lambretta. Piaggio, after being involved in many industrial products, including aircraft engines, created the 125cc Vespa. The great rivalry that developed between the two companies found expression in breaking endurance records, from one hour to 48 hours. By proving that their products could run at speed non-stop for two days, the two manufacturers built consumer confidence and increased sales.

Unlike the personal ambition and desire for national prestige of the British and the growing American obsession for sheer speed, the Italian motivation was simply to generate publicity to promote the sale of their products. The intense competition for endurance records culminated in a contest between the scooter makers for the outright speed record. This made streamlining a priority.

These modest machines already had a small frontal area but, as the rider was a significant proportion of the overall weight, any additional weight had to be

justified. Pierluigi Torre at Innocenti and Corradino D'Ascanio at Vespa had aeronautical experience and their well-designed, streamlined bodies proved their

1950 Lambretta – the basis for the streamliner

worth as both machines topped 100mph. Piaggio was so intent on the contest that it designed a one-off engine for its campaign with a complex opposed-piston layout. It

was similar in principle to the Gobron-Brillié engine but would never see light of day as a production unit. It had also reached the limit of its potential.

At Innocenti, head engineer Torre, with his team that included Luigi Cassola and Giulio Alfieri, had built an engine dyno and continued to develop the shaft-drive production engine, which Cassola described as a jewel. This was a basic piston-ported two-stroke with only three moving parts. Without the benefits of modern alloy components and with the expansion exhaust not yet invented, it was radical work on the ports that allowed high rpm and pursuit of the unit's potential.

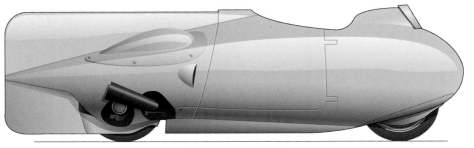

PIAGGIO STREAMLINER

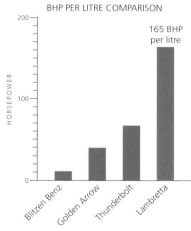

165 BHP
per litre

Although Vespa had retired from the contest, Innocenti felt that 200kph was within its grasp. Torre came up with the idea to use a supercharger driven from the crankshaft. An idiosyncrasy of the piston-ported two-stroke is that the exhaust port is always open after the fuel transfer ports are closed, which means that supercharging cannot be technically applied. However,

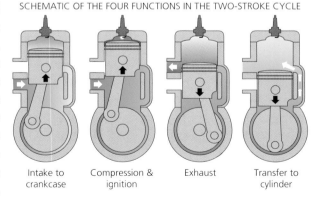

SCHEMATIC OF THE FOUR FUNCTIONS IN THE TWO-STROKE CYCLE

| Intake to crankcase | Compression & ignition | Exhaust | Transfer to cylinder |

pumping fuel mixture through the engine increases cylinder-filling efficiency. After months on the dyno, finding the right combination running on alcohol, power reached 20.675hp at 9,700rpm. This engine's specific output was an impressive 165bhp per litre compared to *Thunderbolt*'s 68bhp per litre.

Motorcycle racer Romolo Ferri's compact size and light weight helped him squeeze into the bright red machine before he broke the 200kph barrier on a stretch of German *Autobahn* between Munich and Ingolstadt on 8 August 1951.

His average speed of 124.89mph achieved with 125cc was once the realm of Victor Hémery's fire-breathing 25-litre Darracq V8. This incredible feat remained unbeaten by a 125cc motorcycle for 16 years and has not, to date, been equalled by any 125cc Lambretta. Furthermore, it has taken 60 years to raise the class record by just 20mph.

THE BEAST III • CHET HERBERT

All the participants in the pursuit of speed accepted the risks, which included being sprayed with hot oil, scalded by boiling water, suffering broken bones and losing their lives. Street racer Chet Herbert looked set for a life confronting these perils until, in 1948 at the age of 20, he was afflicted with polio. After spending six months in an iron lung he emerged to spend the rest of his life in a wheelchair. Although

SPECIFICATIONS

Vehicle	The Beast
Origin	America
Weight	–
Length	240in (6.10m)
Width	66in (1.68m)
Height	42in (1.07m)
Transmission	Direct drive
Powerplant	Chrysler Hemi V8
Engine capacity	5.4 litres
Horsepower	350hp
BHP per litre	60/1
Power/weight ratio	–
Venue	Bonneville
Speed	235.991mph

no longer able to drive, Herbert overcame this devastating setback to make himself a household name.

Herbert started by building a nitro-burning Harley-Davidson motorcycle named *The Beast*, which outran cars to become the fastest-accelerating machine

SCHEMATIC ROLLER TAPPET LAYOUT

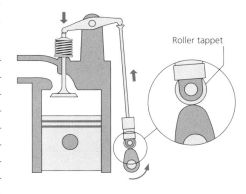

Roller tappet

on the drag strip. Noting the roller tappets used by Harley-Davidson, he then taught himself to grind roller cams and adapt the technology for automobile engines with dramatic results. These roller cams improved valve breathing and went

on to survive in the extremely hostile environment inside the nitro-burning dragster engine.

Breaking records was a good way to advertise his product and after an early learning curve with *The Beast II*, a rudimentary hot rod, he attempted a more serious project. The budget needed to take on the absolute record was beyond the means of hot rodders but class records were a worthwhile target. Herbert, who was aware of the belly tanks at Bonneville, understood the value of streamlining.

He partnered with Rod Schapel, a Cal Tech consultant, to create the first American car to be designed using wind-tunnel tests. With a one-tenth scale model, an efficient shape was developed for speed and stability. The result was a futuristic car that looked like no other.

Herbert started work on the chassis and mechanical parts while Schapel built the glass-fibre body in his back yard. A friend loaned him the Chrysler Firepower V8 engine, the first generation 'Hemi'. This

engine, with its hemispherical cylinder head, had more power and considerably more potential than the flathead V8. The car was put together in a last frantic stint with the help of willing hands who included Art and Lloyd Chrisman and

THE DISTINCTIVE FIREPOWER ROCKER COVER

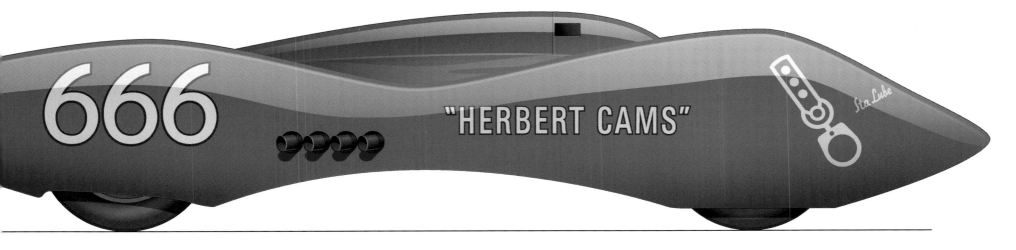

their father, Everett, who had a garage in Compton, California.

Arriving a week into an event at Bonneville, *The Beast III* was entered as D-streamliner and given the number 666. Hired driver George Bentley made some promising runs before missing a shift and destroying the clutch. An all-night effort welding the clutch solid created an improvised direct drive. Bentley failed to show up the next day so Art Chrisman volunteered to drive. With such high gearing, *The Beast III* had to be pushed by

both a Chevrolet coupe and a Ford hot rod to a speed of 130mph just to get it started.

Art Chrisman's first attempt using a percentage of nitro was a promising 219mph but resulted in valve failure. By luck spare valves were located and the next day Chrisman ran progressively faster to power *The Beast III* to a class record of 235.991mph, making it the fastest single-engine car in America.

The inspirational Chet Herbert went

Art Chrisman

on to set diesel records with *The Beast III*, develop and construct *The Beast IV*, and pioneer the first twin-engine dragsters. He developed the 'zoomie' headers that were almost universally adopted by the dragster fraternity. Herbert also helped his sister, Doris, to purchase *Drag News* and turn it into 'the drag racer's bible'.

Rod Schapel went on to design *Spirit of America*, the first successful jet-powered car in which Craig Breedlove

hurtled to three absolute records and Art Chrisman drove to fame on America's drag strips, being the first to 140mph and 180mph.

The genesis of the Chrysler Hemi was to have a major impact as it went through its evolution from 331 cubic inches to 392 and 426 versions. With two valves per cylinder, pushrod-operated by a single central camshaft, it was relatively uncomplicated and its dimensions gave it the strength to absorb a lot of punishment when supercharged on nitro.

SO-CAL COUPE • ALEX XYDIAS

On returning to America after serving in the Second World War, Alex Xydias renewed his interest in cars and opened the So-Cal Speed Shop in Burbank, California. Inspired by Bill Burke, he ran a belly-tanker to record speeds and then a streamliner that was influenced by the Reid Railton bodywork on the record-breaking MG EX135. The So-Cal streamliner set a record of 208.927mph in 1950 that stood the test of time for a non-supercharged flathead engine.

Neither of these cars related directly to the hot rod culture of So-Cal customers but the '34 Ford Coupe, owned by brothers Bob and Dick Pierson, did. Xydias was inspired by this legendary car and as the Southern California Timing Association had just introduced a coupe class he opted to run one himself to promote his business, both on the salt and the drag strip.

The project began with the purchase of a '34 coupe that was built by John 'Cruiser' Quinton, Russell Lanthorne and Jim Gray. Xydias continued to develop it by applying lessons he had learned through experience. These included stretching the wheelbase, lowering the suspension, dropping the body over the chassis (known as channelling), sectioning the bodywork, chopping the roof, gutting the interior and setting the engine back. The way the car

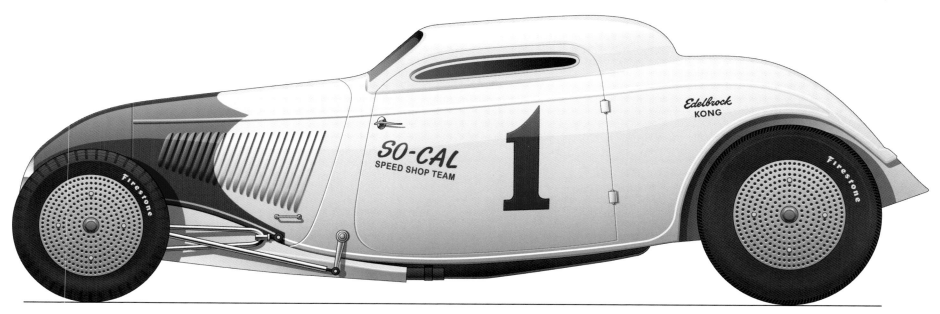

looked was a by-product of form designed to follow function. The end result became the quintessential image of a hot rod coupe. Power was supplied by a 255 cu in (4.2-litre) Mercury flathead fitted with a GMC 4-71 Roots supercharger.

The radical changes to this car were not for the sake of style but rather to achieve a smaller frontal area, reduced weight, efficient weight transfer, improved stability

SPECIFICATIONS

Vehicle	1934 Ford Coupe
Origin	America
Weight	1,500lb (680kg)
Length	164in (4.17m)
Width	–
Height	50in (1.27in)
Transmission	Three-speed
Powerplant	Mercury flathead
Engine capacity	4.2 litres
Horsepower	250hp
BHP per litre	60/1
Power/weight ratio	1/6
Venue	Bonneville
Speed	172.749mph

and a better power-to-weight ratio. The effectiveness of the construction led to a Class C Competition Coupe record of 172.749mph on the salt and a record pass

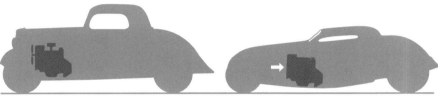

Original stock 1934 Ford   '34 So-Cal coupe with engine set back

of 132.79mph at the drag strip.

After so much accomplishment in just a handful of years, tragedy visited the So-Cal team when the clutch disintegrated on the start line at Pomona drag strip, starting a fire that severely burned driver Dave DeLangton, Xydias's brother-in-law. DeLangton, who was only wearing a T-shirt, did not survive his burns, dying a month later. A devastated Xydias sold the car. Although he remained deeply involved in motorsport, including documenting events on film and working with Mickey Thompson, he never competed again.

The So-Cal Coupe continued setting records in the possession of John Moxley and then Jerry Eisert before Jim Travis bought it. Travis raced it until 1996, setting a record of 236mph at Bonneville with a supercharged Chevrolet engine. Few race cars have ever had such prolonged front-line careers.

There was a multitude of such cars at the salt. Many were backyard constructions using components salvaged from boneyards. As little remains of most of them today, it falls to survivors like the So-Cal Coupe and the Pierson Coupe to represent the genre. The ethos of the lake cars and the ingenuity of the early hot rodders showed what could be done on a limited budget and gave notice of the

feats that might become possible if, for example, any of them ever got their hands on a jet engine.

The So-Cal Coupe has since been restored by its owner, Don Orosco, and appears in concours events where today's generations of spectators are able to admire this classic piece of American tin that rolled off the production line some 80 years ago before being saved from the scrapyard in 1950 and driven into the realm of legend.

Legend also has it that organised drag racing first started on a closed airport service road near Goleta, California, in 1949. As the sport expanded, enthusiasts could test their machines on local disused airstrips at the weekend without making the pilgrimage to the lakes. In the process of remorselessly driving their engines to destruction in their efforts to win with cars like the So-Cal Coupe, the racers learned vital lessons in how to create power with reliability and apply them to the lake cars in a cross-germination of ideas.

MG EX181 • STIRLING MOSS & PHIL HILL

In near-bankrupt Britain the post-war years of austerity were not conducive to extravagant tilts at the absolute land speed record. Most motor companies had little incentive as the specially built vehicles bore no relation to what was rolling off their production lines. Even John Cobb's magnificent effort in 1947 was accomplished with a car built before the war. Few ordinary people owned cars

SPECIFICATIONS

Vehicle	MG EX181
Origin	Britain
Weight	1,911lb (867kg)
Length	181.5in (4.61m)
Width	64.3in (1.63m)
Height	38.3in (0.97m)
Transmission	Four-speed
Powerplant	Four-cylinder in-line
Engine capacity	1,489cc
Horsepower	290hp
BHP per litre	195/1
Power/weight ratio	1/6.5
Venue	Bonneville
Speeds	245.64mph & 254.91mph

in Britain, Bonneville was 5,000 miles away, there were no local drag strips, hardly any V8 engines and no hot rod culture.

Across the Atlantic serious efforts were yet to materialise for the ultimate

GOLDIE GARDNER MG EX135

prize but the lakes were proliferating with all kinds of machinery in the lower classes. As Britain slowly recovered, news of American 'low-buck' teams making headlines with their home-built cars filtered through and the MG Car Company decided to renew its challenge.

MG, originally a sporting Morris derivative developed by Morris Garages in Oxford, was both proud and protective of its extensive catalogue of speed records

set by drivers such as George Eyston and Lieutenant-Colonel Goldie Gardner. They still considered this activity to have enough publicity value to promote sales of their famous sporting marque. Gardner alone had posted more than 100 records in England, Europe and the USA by 1950.

He set one of the last of these in the pre-war MG EX135, which had aerodynamic bodywork designed by Reid Railton and a 1-litre engine. Gardner reached 200mph in this little machine — a staggering feat.

Now a new wind-tunnel-tested vehicle designed by Syd Enever and built by Terry Mitchell appeared on the scene to contest the 1.5-litre class. Railton had

long since left his home country to live in America but his influence is apparent in the creation of MG EX181. Apart from having only rear-wheel drive, it was reminiscent of a small-scale *Railton Mobil Special* with its enclosed teardrop bodyshell, forward driving position, mid-mounted engine and narrowed rear axle.

The engine of EX181 was based on a standard factory 1,489cc four-cylinder block equipped with two valves per cylinder and double overhead camshafts. Fitted with a large Shorrock vane-type supercharger pumping at 32psi, the little engine thought it was three times bigger than it was. It gulped down a mixture of 86 per cent methanol laced with nitrobenzene, acetone and sulphuric ether to produce 290hp at 7,300rpm. This was a specific output of 195bhp per litre as compared to the *Railton Mobil Special*'s 65bhp per litre.

Two racing drivers who knew their business were enlisted for the assault. One was British hero Stirling Moss, who by the end of his career had won 40 per cent

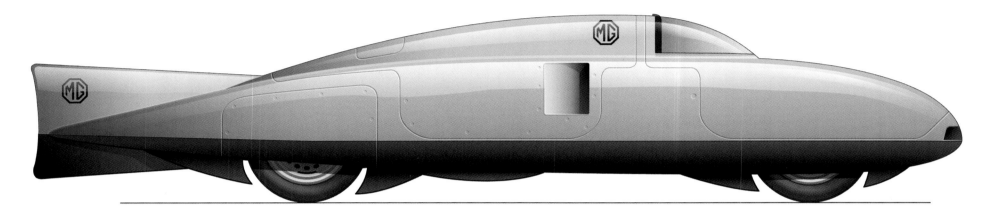

of the races he had entered and collected many endurance records. The other was Phil Hill, still the only American-born driver to have won the Formula 1 World Championship as well as the major endurance races at Le Mans and Sebring.

With George Eyston watching, Moss made the first runs at Bonneville in August 1957. He broke five class F records (up to 1,500cc, supercharged on fuel) including the flying kilometre at 245.64mph. Two years later EX181 returned to the salt with its

Phil Hill

rear stabilising fin removed and the engine bored out to 1,506cc to put the car in class E (up to 2 litres). On 3 October 1959 the MG, with Hill at the wheel, swept up another six records including the flying kilometre at 254.91mph.

MG had proved that British expertise could still make itself felt. By providing the designers, engineers, mechanics and finance, the company had delivered a stunning performance that had a great impact on the early hot rodders who were working with limited resources and second-hand parts.

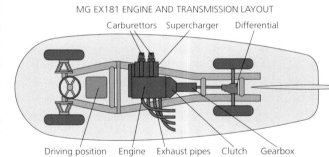

MG EX181 ENGINE AND TRANSMISSION LAYOUT

Carburettors   Supercharger   Differential

Driving position   Engine   Exhaust pipes   Clutch   Gearbox

Yet great changes were already taking place. British dominance was on the wane as a new generation of young pretenders prepared to take centre stage and make piston-engine records almost exclusively their own property.

MG set no more records as the British motor industry drifted into decline and finally met its fate. Only the MG badge is left, on Chinese-made cars, an emotive echo of the extraordinary deeds that caused such a flurry of excitement more than half a century ago.

As for MG's EX181 and EX135 streamliners, they are displayed at the British Motor Museum in proud testament to automotive excellence.

CHALLENGER 1 • MICKEY THOMPSON

The phrase 'Life in the fast lane' was a perfect fit for Marion Lee Thompson. Better known to the world as Mickey Thompson, he involved himself in every facet of motorsport.

At the age of 15 he raced at El Mirage. Later his attention was captured by drag racing, which led to his creating a new paradigm in the shape of the slingshot dragster and becoming manager of the

SPECIFICATIONS

Vehicle	Challenger 1
Origin	America
Weight	7,000lb (3,175kg)
Length	234in (5.94m)
Width	70in (1.78m)
Height	45in (1.14m)
Transmission	Three-speed
Powerplant	Pontiac V8 x 4
Engine capacity	27.1 litres
Horsepower	3,000hp
BHP per litre	108/1
Power/weight ratio	1/2.3
Venue	Bonneville
Speed	406.60mph

legendary Lions Drag Strip. Twin-engine dragsters were followed by success with 'funny' cars before his innovative involvement with racing cars at the Indianapolis 500.

And this was not the end of it. There followed off-road racing, which through the formation of the Mickey Thompson Entertainment Group he made into a spectator sport in stadiums around America. He founded SCORE as a sanctioning body and dabbled in producing racing tyres and performance parts under the MT banner. As driver and designer he won with midgets, sprint cars, off-road vehicles, stock cars, dragsters and sports cars. He gathered 485 national and international speed and endurance records before his untimely death.

It was no surprise that during this hectic career Thompson decided to challenge the British stranglehold on the absolute

record and bring it back to America. Showing typical innovation, he dispensed with suspension and mounted four 398 cubic inch (6.5-litre) Pontiac V8 engines in two parallel pairs, each with its own clutch and gearbox. The front pair were turned

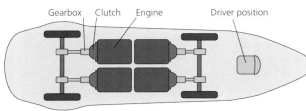

Gearbox   Clutch   Engine   Driver position

SCHEMATIC OF CHALLENGER I ENGINES AND TRANSMISSIONS

around and counter rotated to drive the front wheels while the other pair drove the rear wheels. A single pedal operated all four clutches and a single lever shifted the four gearboxes. Although without the benefit of wind-tunnel testing, the car's smooth bodywork with its small frontal area paid more than a passing nod to the Reid Railton EX135.

Challenger 1's first attempt in August 1959 ended in disappointment with speeds

well short of the record. Fate then lent a hand when Thompson had a chance meeting with George Eyston, the record-breaking supercharger exponent, who was at Bonneville supervising the EX181 campaign. Eyston talked, Thompson listened — and then left to find more horsepower for his engines.

Meanwhile momentum was gathering in America as other contenders and new technology arrived on the scene. The stakes were high and Athol Graham's death in August 1960, driving *City Of Salt Lake*,

ATHOL GRAHAM'S CITY OF SALT LAKE

proved that little more than a bad patch of salt or a failed component lay between the hero and the hereafter.

When Thompson returned to Bonneville the *Challenger I* engines had been enlarged to 414 cubic inches (6.8 litres) and each one had a top-mounted GMC 6-71 supercharger. These improvements raised output to around 3,000hp and gave a power-to-weight ratio of 2.3/1. Now the car was a contender.

On 9 September 1960 Thompson made a run at 406.60mph. Unfortunately the return run was denied by mechanical failure so the record could not be ratified. It was another disappointment but no one could deny that Mickey Thompson had gone faster than anyone else.

When the Summers brothers, Bill and Bob, set a record with the pencil-slim *Goldenrod* in 1965, Thompson knew that *Challenger I* — now in the NHRA Museum — had been made instantly obsolete. He understood the significance of reduced frontal area and returned to Bonneville in 1968 with a second *Challenger*, dubbed the *Autolite Special*. But attempts were rained off and again his car was sidelined.

After surviving such dangerous activities, Thompson and his wife Trudy were tragically shot dead in front of their California home in 1988, a crime that went unsolved until 2001, when a former business partner was implicated. Yet the story did not end there. *Challenger II*, having lain dormant for 40 years, was to run again.

MUNRO SPECIAL • BURT MUNRO

Herbert 'Burt'* James Munro was born in Invercargill, New Zealand, in 1899. In 1920 he bought an imported American-made Indian Scout motorcycle, little knowing that this, the object of his desire, would guide his life.

The original side-valve machine displaced 600cc, put out 18hp and had a

SPECIFICATIONS

Vehicle	Munro Special
Origin	New Zealand
Weight	400lb (181kg), incl rider
Length	152in (3.86m)
Width	24in (0.61m)
Height	34in (0.86m)
Transmission	Three-speed
Powerplant	V-twin
Engine capacity	850/950cc
Horsepower	100hp
BHP per litre	100/1
Power/weight ratio	1/4
Venue	Bonneville
Speeds	178.97mph, 168.07mph & 184.087mph

* Herbert 'Bert' Munro changed his name to 'Burt' because the American press insisted on spelling it that way

top speed of 55mph. After about six years Munro began to modify the Indian Scout for more power and started taking part in every kind of motorcycle race with it, and later a 1936 Velocette MSS, rising to become one of New Zealand's top riders. Gradually an obsession began to take hold that centred on outright speed records.

Divorced in 1945, Munro continued to modify his Indian Scout and earned his first record on the open road in New Zealand at 120.8mph. By 1957 he had captured the beach record at 132.38mph and was running out of room in his native country. This did not discourage him as he continued to develop the Indian engine and considered plans to run on the Australian dry lakes. But after a sightseeing trip to Bonneville in 1957 Munro realised that this was the place to test his machine to the limit.

His work as a maintenance mechanic eventually got in the way of his purpose in life. So he gave it up to devote his entire existence to the god of speed. He built what served as a garage, workshop and living quarters and it was here that he regularly spent 16 hours a day working on the Indian engine. Without factory backing, help from sponsors or any over-the-counter performance components, he developed his own unique way of doing things.

Necessity being the mother of invention, Munro began fabricating everything himself. The side-valve layout was redesigned to incorporate overhead valves with four cams to replace the original two so that the exhaust and inlet timings could be altered independently. He turned cylinder barrels from old cast-iron drainpipes that had matured with age and gradually increased the displacement. Without specialised machinery, he carved connecting rods by hand from old Ford axles, turned cams on his lathe and created the profiles with a hand file. He cast new pistons by melting down more modern scrapped items with better alloys. Flywheel, transmission, lubrication system — all these and other parts he modified as time went on. And he worked in the metal without any technical drawings.

His method of research

1920 INDIAN SCOUT

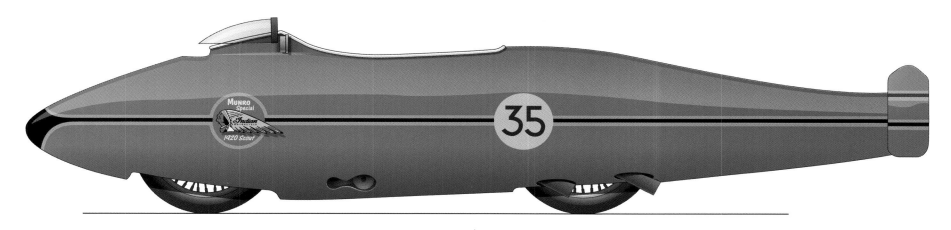

and development was to test the machine to destruction, rebuild and try again. His work ethos was never to give up. There was no obstacle that Munro would not overcome. Blow-ups, lack of funds, logistics, disappointment, accident, injury or illness were all grist to the mill of Munro's indomitable spirit.

Taking the machine he called the *Munro Special* to Bonneville for the first time, he part-funded the trip by working as a ship's cook. He made it to Bonneville only to find that, unlike in New Zealand, he should have pre-registered and was not eligible to run. Other racers found they had an affinity with this man, who had travelled

from the other side of the world to fulfil his ambition of running on the salt. They convinced the authorities to let him run and somehow got the machine through tech inspection with its worn tyres and an engine apparently cobbled together. Yet any idea of patronising the 63-year-old Munro evaporated instantly when he stunned the faithful by setting a record in the 850cc class with a speed of 178.971mph.

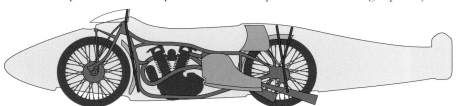

Munro went to Bonneville eight more times, often frustrated by engine failures or poor conditions that did not allow a single run until he set a second record in the 1,000cc class in 1966. He returned the following year with the engine rebuilt and punched out to 950cc and the bike clad in an aluminium body that he had hand-formed himself. It served as the perfect example of the extra weight penalty more

than paying off in improved airflow. He registered an average of 184.087mph that included a one-way run of 190.07mph and a peak speed of 205.67mph. The 48-year-old Indian Scout and Munro passed into land speed folklore.

Munro, who was elected to the AMA Motorcycle Hall of Fame, is honoured today in the annual Burt Munro Challenge, a six-day motorcycle event in Invercargill. He was immortalised in the film *The World's Fastest Indian*. The famous machine, true to the humble nature and wishes of Munro, remains in New Zealand on display in a hardware shop and his record still stands in its class.

SPIRIT OF AMERICA • CRAIG BREEDLOVE

From the moment Craig Breedlove read in a school textbook about John Cobb's land speed record with the *Railton Mobil Special*, he developed an obsession for speed that would dominate his life. He bought his first car at the age of 13, a 1934 Ford coupe, and equipped it with a blown flathead engine. At 16 he was a serious contender at Saugus drag strip and El Mirage. By the time he was 21, in 1958, he had topped 236mph in a belly-tank lakester.

Further inspired by Mickey Thompson,

who had shown what could be done on a limited budget, Breedlove turned to his ultimate ambition. He soon realised that piston-engine cars were nearing their limit but the jet age had progressed so rapidly that surplus engines were readily available. So he bought a General Electric J47 turbojet with 5,970lb of thrust for

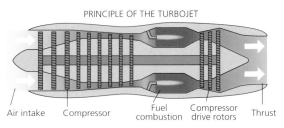

PRINCIPLE OF THE TURBOJET

Air intake   Compressor   Fuel combustion   Compressor drive rotors   Thrust

$500. This engine had seen service with jet fighters such as the North American F86 Sabre. This new technology eliminated all the clutch, transmission and traction problems of normal cars.

Rod Schapel, designer of Chet Herbert's *Beast*, was involved with the wind-tunnel aerodynamics of the bodyshell, paying particular attention to creating negative

lift in order to prevent the vehicle from becoming airborne.

With minimal sponsorship funds, Breedlove extended his father's garage so he could build the car himself with help from many volunteers. This monumental task became obsessive. As time went by it cost Breedlove his marriage, his job, his beloved '34 coupe and, on top of all this, his sponsor pulled out. Down but not out, he named the car *Spirit of America*, put together a presentation and convinced the Shell Oil Company to provide half of the funding he needed. This gave Goodyear the confidence to step forward with the other half and his dream became reality.

Spirit of America looked like a jet plane without wings. Two wheels were outrigged at the rear with a single fixed wheel at the front. Steering was intended by braking each rear

wheel independently in concert with a movable fin under the nose. Long-overdue safety precautions included a crash helmet, safety harness, on-board fire extinguishers and parachutes for braking. The fabulous $250,000 machine was loaded up for the 700-mile trip to Bonneville.

NORTH AMERICAN F86 SABRE

SPECIFICATIONS

Vehicle	Spirit of America
Origin	America
Weight	6,726lb (3,051kg)
Length	456in (11.58m)
Width	138in (3.51m)
Height	131in (3.33m)
Powerplant	J47 Turbojet
Thrust	5,970lbf
Thrust weight ratio	1/1.1
Venue	Bonneville
Speeds	407.45mph, 468.72mph & 526.28mph

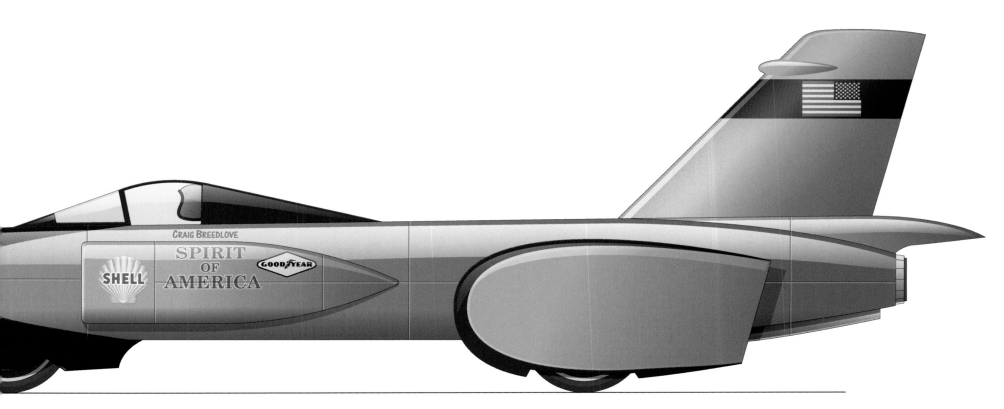

Donald Campbell had crashed on the salt two years earlier, just escaping with his life. *Bluebird* was being extensively rebuilt so the only competition was Glenn Leasher in the unrefined *Infinity* jet car.

Breedlove's first attempt in 1962 ended in abject failure as the car was impossible to steer. After a frustrating two weeks the demoralised crew headed home to California and before arriving they heard news of Leasher's fatal crash with *Infinity*.

The following year Breedlove returned to Bonneville having devised a steering front wheel for the car and added a tail fin. This time everything went smoothly. On 5 August 1963 he posted an average speed of 407.45mph at 85 per cent power to break

INFINITY JET CAR

the record. But he had beaten Cobb's mark by only a small margin and the record was not ratified because his vehicle only had three wheels. This, though, was a nicety that did not matter to Americans. The Stars and Stripes now fluttered at the summit of speed and Craig Breedlove was renowned in his country as the fastest man on earth.

There followed two years of the most dramatic action in the whole saga of speed with almost 200mph added to the top number. Intense competition with the Arfons brothers, Art and Walt, saw Breedlove go to 468.72mph and then with the J47 at maximum power become the first past the 500mph mark.

Piston engines were consigned to history as far as the absolute record was concerned. Conversely, jet-powered cars were in the early stages of their development. There were even more powerful engines to come and Breedlove played a central part in the unfolding drama.

BLUEBIRD-PROTEUS CN7 • DONALD CAMPBELL

Donald Campbell elected to follow his famous father into the world of speed and took the water record seven times in the period 1955–64. From 1956 he began planning an attempt on the land speed record. Eighty British companies backed the project with no expense spared, including Dunlop, BP, Smiths Industries and Lucas Automotive.

Campbell's car, completed in 1960, was a monocoque design created by Ken and Lew Norris. It was powered by a Bristol-Siddeley Proteus turboprop developing 4,450hp. This free-turbine configuration converted the thrust into mechanical power and was adapted to drive a shaft to the giant 52in front and rear wheels. Its power-to-weight ratio was 1hp for every 2lb, an improvement on John Cobb's *Railton Mobil Special*.

Construction of the *Bluebird-Proteus CN7* cost £1 million. With nearly 100 personnel and 40 tons of equipment, it appeared at Bonneville in 1960 to share the salt with the shoestring operations of Mickey Thompson and Art Arfons. It was clear the British had arrived with serious intent but it was not to be. Campbell suffered a high-speed crash when *Bluebird* spun out, rolled over several times and destroyed itself as well as fracturing Campbell's skull.

Displaying the same characteristics of

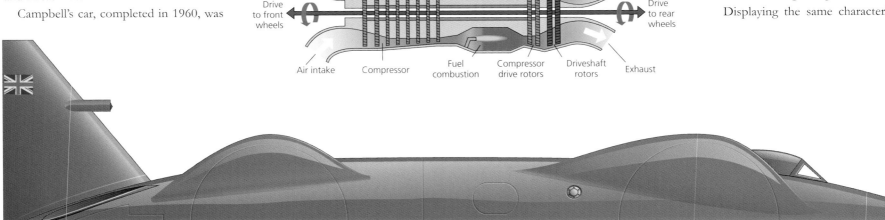

PRINCIPLE OF THE FREE TURBOSHAFT

Drive to front wheels

Drive to rear wheels

Air intake — Compressor — Fuel combustion — Compressor drive rotors — Driveshaft rotors — Exhaust

determination, courage and obsession as his father, Donald resolved to recover and try again even though the Norris brothers had reservations about the gyroscopic effect of the big wheels and fragile tyres.

The course at Bonneville was deemed unsuitable and too short, at 11 miles, so one of the sponsors, British Petroleum, scoured the world for an alternative venue. The salt flats at Lake Eyre in Australia were

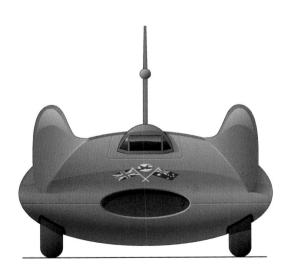

chosen for the next attempt. The whole operation was shipped down-under but at the beginning of tests in 1963 rain fell for the first time in nine years. The lake was flooded to a depth of three inches and the attempt was called off shortly before the team heard the news that Craig Breedlove had achieved 407.45mph at Bonneville.

Persevering to an extraordinary degree, Campbell returned to Lake Eyre the following year. Conditions were not optimal but taking advantage of a dry spell Campbell made two runs on a damp track on 17 July 1964 to bring home an average of 403.10mph with a peak recorded speed of 440mph. By now eight years had passed since the project's conception.

Although Campbell had finally achieved his goal, it was not at the level he had hoped for and he was bitterly disappointed. The French arbitrators, now known as the Fédération Internationale de

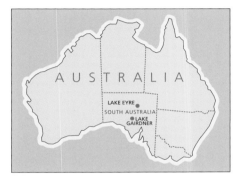

l'Automobile (FIA), ratified *Bluebird*'s runs in the four-wheel category.

With six water speed records already and now a land speed record, Campbell then recorded a last water speed success in December 1964 at Lake Dumbleyung in Australia. In doing so he became the first and, to date, the only person to win the laurels for both water and land in the same year. Yet this all fell short of the ultimate prize. The Fédération Internationale de Motocyclisme (FIM) had recognised Breedlove's three-wheel *Spirit of America* in the motorcycle with sidecar class. Donald Campbell had overcome every conceivable

setback but could not claim to be the world's fastest man.

Putting the car to one side, and while planning a rocket-powered supersonic car for the future, Campbell returned with *Bluebird K7*, his jet-powered hydroplane, to seek an eighth water speed record but died in the attempt at Coniston Water in Britain's Lake District on 4 January 1967.

Bluebird-Proteus CN7 is now on display in Britain's National Motor Museum at Beaulieu, quietly keeping the secret of its true potential.

SPECIFICATIONS

Vehicle	Bluebird-Proteus CN7
Origin	Britain
Weight	8,960lb (4,064kg)
Length	360in (9.14m)
Width	66in (1.68m)
Height	92in (2.34m)
Powerplant	Proteus gas turbine
Horsepower	4,450hp
Thrust/weight ratio	1/2
Venue	Lake Eyre, Australia
Speed	403.10mph

WINGFOOT EXPRESS • WALT ARFONS

Half brothers Walt and Art Arfons, who lived in Ohio, became fascinated with the new sport of drag racing and as a team they started building drag cars. The jet age had made piston-engine fighter planes obsolete, creating a surplus of the 28-litre Allison V12 engines that they favoured. These 1,500hp crowd pleasers were known as *Green Monster*, the colour of the leftover tractor paint in which they were daubed. At some point the brothers' relationship strained and they

ceased to speak to each other. Thereafter, as rivals, they duelled with jet engines on the vast expanse at Bonneville.

A chance meeting with Tom Green, chief engineer for a tool company,

PRINCIPLE OF TURBOJET AFTERBURNER

Additional fuel combusted with residual air — Increased thrust

crystallised Walt's aspiration for a land speed car. Green's interest in aerodynamics complemented Arfons's mechanical skills and the pair successfully approached Goodyear, already sponsoring Breedlove, for funding. They started work with the tight budget of $78,000. To put this in perspective, Donald Campbell's car cost £1,000,000. With close to $3 to the £1 at that time, Walt's outlay was less than three per cent of Campbell's.

An early three-wheel design was

discarded in favour of four to comply with the FIA, which soon had to reconsider its own position regarding reverse gears and modern powerplants to avoid being left on the sidelines by technology. The land of opportunity provided a surplus Westinghouse J46 jet engine complete with an afterburner for extra power. This engine had seen service in the Vought F7U Cutlass, a United States Navy carrier-based jet fighter.

Walt's car resembled a long cylinder with outrigged wheels at the rear and the cockpit situated ahead of the engine's air intake with the driver encased in an acrylic glass canopy. The frontal area was reduced to the minimum with a narrow track and relatively small wheels. The car was not as slippery as *Spirit of America* but Green calculated that its superior thrust-to-weight ratio would be more than sufficient. It was named *Wingfoot Express* after the mythical

winged foot on the Goodyear logo.

Fate then played a part as Walt suffered a heart attack when watching the car crash in testing. Later, while repairing the car, he injured his hand seriously enough to rule out any chance of driving it. Tom Green,

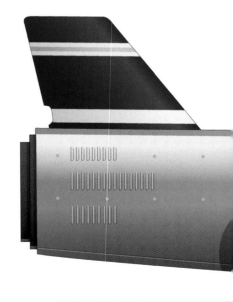

SPECIFICATIONS

Vehicle	Wingfoot Express
Origin	America
Weight	3,773lb (1,711kg)
Length	288in (7.32m)
Height	73in (1.85m)
Powerplant	Westinghouse J46
Thrust	6,000lbf
Thrust weight ratio	1.6/1
Venue	Bonneville
Speed	413.20mph

who had driven stock cars ten years previously, volunteered to take the seat. In 1963 Green made some successful shakedown runs before vacating the salt for Breedlove, who promptly ran his 407.45mph. The following year, on the other side of the world, Campbell edged the wheel-driven record to 403.10mph.

On their return to Bonneville, Walt Arfons and Green could not get the engine up to full power and the situation looked bleak. Fate now dealt a different card as

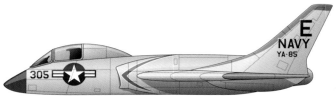

VOUGHT F7U CUTLASS

Art Arfons was also present. Although the brothers were still not normally on speaking terms, Art intervened to show that on the salt all men were brothers. He suggested an adjustment to the tail of the exhaust (clamshells) and cutting away the shroud around the air intake.

These simple modifications made the

difference and on the final day, 2 October 1964, Green made a 406mph run. With one last chance to make a back-up run in the fading daylight, Green saved time by taking a shorter two-mile run-up and registered 420.07mph for an average of 413.20mph — and the record.

Walt Arfons and Green held the record for only three days before Art Arfons returned with his *Green Monster* and double the power to record an average of 434.02mph. In that short passage of time

the *Wingfoot Express* had been left behind in the technology race and it was never to run again.

For Tom Green, one attempt was enough. Walt Arfons, though, came back the following year with yet another way of doing things. Acknowledged as a pioneer of jet-powered vehicles, he would pursue his obsession with speed for another ten years before retiring relatively intact.

Whatever came of *Wingfoot Express* is a mystery. Neither Tom Green nor Walt Arfons ever knew what happened to it.

GREEN MONSTER • ART ARFONS

Art Arfons had already gained valuable experience venturing along the path of John Cobb with an Allison-powered vehicle and then with *Cyclops*, an experimental jet car. Now, transfixed by the salt, he began planning a new campaign.

While his half brother, Walt Arfons, was building the *Wingfoot Express*, Art was making his own ideas a reality in his workshop next door. Horsepower, which cannot be directly calculated as thrust, was valid only in the wheel-driven classes.

SPECIFICATIONS

Vehicle	Green Monster
Origin	America
Weight	6,500lb (2,948kg)
Length	252in (6.40m)
Height	86in (2.18m)
Width	–
Powerplant	General Electric J79
Thrust	17,835lbf
Thrust weight ratio	2.7/1
Venue	Bonneville
Speeds	434.02mph, 536.71mph & 576.553mph

Thrust was now the common currency in the ultimate contest and Art knew he would need a lot of it. The answer was a damaged General Electric J79 Starfighter unit found in a salvage yard and bought for its scrap value of $625. What could anyone want with a written-off jet engine?

After General Electric declined to let him have a handbook, Art countered with his own negative response when a representative from the military came asking if they could have their classified engine back.

Applying himself to the daunting task of constructing the car, he first reasoned that it was not a good idea to place the cockpit in front of the air intakes as was the case with *Cyclops*, *Wingfoot Express* and other cars of the era. From this starting point he displayed the hot rodder's hallmark of ingenuity by removing 60 damaged rotors from the engine and respacing the others to keep it in balance. The removal of that many rotor blades reduced the designed 17,835lbf of thrust but Arfons

figured he still had more than enough. The J79 was then mounted on a fabricated chassis supported by a '37 Lincoln axle at the front and a '47 Ford truck axle at the rear with a pre-war Packard supplying the steering box. The gaping air intake was left unobstructed by hanging a cockpit and fuel tank on either side of the engine.

Then, with a secondhand forming machine, Art created the bodywork himself. Notably, he employed a wing

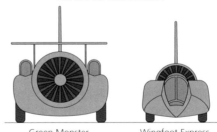

AIR INTAKE COMPARISON

Green Monster   Wingfoot Express

above the front end to generate downforce. Excluding the wheels and tyres, supplied by sponsor Firestone, Art's total outlay was $10,000, a mere fraction of Breedlove's budget, and yet his creation packed a punch

of nearly three times the power. The paint scheme was blue and red but Art retained the name *Green Monster*. Compared with the rapiers of Breedlove and Walt Arfons, *Green Monster* was like a sawn-off shotgun.

It did not take much mental arithmetic for Breedlove to figure that the power of *Green Monster* was enough to overcome any aerodynamic deficiency. And so it proved three days after Tom Green's triumph when, on 5 October 1964, Art howled to 434.02mph, relegating *Spirit of America* to third place in the new order. Breedlove's response just eight days later was to smash the record again with 468.72mph.

Turning the power up to maximum, Breedlove returned yet again for a fearsome run on 15 October that ripped off both braking chutes. The unstoppable machine careered down the course and ended up miles away in a brine lake. Breedlove became, after Frank Lockhart, the second man to nearly drown during a land-speed attempt. He had broken the 500mph mark and shattered his own record by nearly

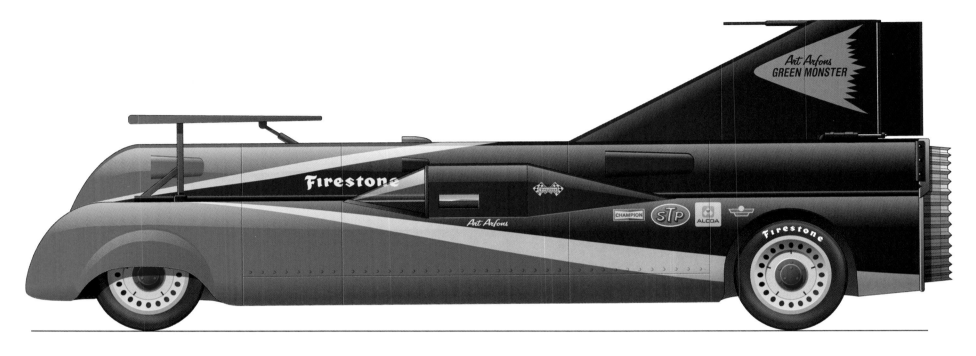

60mph with an average of 526.28mph. Even this was not enough as Art Arfons responded on 27 October with an average of 536.71mph, despite losing a tyre in the process. He closed the year as the new King of Speed.

The duel between Arfons and Breedlove, which resumed with a vengeance the following year, was also part of an intense battle between tyre giants Firestone and Goodyear, who had taken their marketing conflict from the racetracks to the desolate expanse of the salt flats.

On 2 November 1965, Breedlove clocked 555.483mph in a new car. This prompted Arfons to increase his power

LOCKHEED F104 STARFIGHTER

settings and five days later he achieved his last record at 576.553mph, once again riding out a burst tyre. This figure survived

only until 15 November, when Breedlove roared through the 600mph barrier with a speed of 600.601mph.

Art Arfons returned to the salt in 1966 to miraculously survive a devastating crash when a wheel bearing seized and a wheel

was ripped off at 610mph. It took more than a mile for the car to come to a halt and a lucky Arfons to emerge from the wreck with relatively minor injuries.

With British heroes Henry Segrave, John Cobb and Donald Campbell having all lost their lives attempting the water speed record, the land speed record had now become an all-American affair.

Art Arfons did make a return to Bonneville some 20 years later but could not recapture the glory of his days duelling with Craig Breedlove.

SPIRIT OF AMERICA / SONIC 1 • CRAIG & LEE BREEDLOVE

Craig Breedlove was first deposed by Walt Arfons and then edged out by Art Arfons in the high-speed stakes in 1964. Breedlove's *Spirit of America* had ended its last run with the tail sticking out of a brine lake. Knowing that even if he did repair the car the J47 engine would not have the necessary power, Breedlove resolved to build a new car from scratch. Naming it *Spirit of America Sonic 1* did no harm in attracting attention, even if ambitions of sonic speeds were unrealistic. Goodyear again agreed to fund the project together with a number of smaller sponsors.

Sonic 1 was closer in basic design to the *Wingfoot Express* but with a more efficient shape and particular attention paid to the air intake duct that would feed the larger J79 engine. This was the same type of engine that Art Arfons used but came from a McDonnell Douglas F-4 Phantom II Air Force jet. Construction began in March, leaving only six months to build the car in time for proceedings at Bonneville. A difficult task became even tougher when civil unrest complete with burning cars

Lee Breedlove

and buildings broke out in a neighbouring area of Los Angeles. But working under duress was nothing unusual for Breedlove and the car was duly finished in time.

Breedlove was confronted with a new set of problems when, after promising test runs, *Sonic 1* failed to meet expectations on the record attempt. Efforts were made to put things right but further tests resulted in damage to the bodywork and inlet ducts. The car was removed again for repairs. More frustration followed

when the chutes failed on the next run and the brakes melted under the extreme conditions. While the car was undergoing yet more repairs, Breedlove went for a solitary walk and by chance met Art Arfons. Neither man wished to risk his life — both had to overcome raw fear to get into the cockpit — but acknowledged their commitment as the game played out.

The following morning the team's dedicated work paid off as *Sonic 1* ran true and Breedlove reclaimed the world crown with his speed of 555.483mph. Then as he had the salt booked for the

week he decided to make use of it to keep Art Arfons at arm's length, possibly for another year. First he convinced his wife, Lee, to come to Bonneville and try for the women's record in *Sonic 1*. After a few days of practice runs, Lee raised the record to 308.56mph, deposing Betty Skelton, who had previously taken Art Arfons's *Cyclops* jet car to 276mph.

Next came an assault on endurance records with a Cobra Daytona. Walt Arfons had been at the salt making abortive runs with his *Wingfoot Express 2*, a rocket car driven by Bobby Tatroe. Breedlove hired Tatroe as co-driver and between

COBRA DAYTONA

them they set 23 world records just to pass the time and keep a fuming Arfons off the salt. By now the weather had turned and it started to rain. Thinking the season was over, Breedlove headed home believing he had secured the record for a whole year. Art Arfons had other ideas. The weather cleared briefly enough to allow *Green Monster* to make two runs straight off the trailer and pinch the record with an average of 576.553mph.

Back in LA, a devastated Breedlove heard that he had been pipped at the post again only five days after reclaiming the record. He could not resist the momentous decision to return to the salt flats. He oversaw more modifications to prevent the

nose lift experienced on his previous run and then it was his turn to wait patiently for a break in the weather. His chance came on 15 November 1965.

Setting the throttle stop to give just enough power for the record and walk away alive, he came through with 600.601mph, a record that held for five years. Craig and Lee Breedlove were the fastest man and woman on earth while Goodyear collected the kudos in its battle with Firestone.

Craig Breedlove kept occupied with drag racing and endurance records with AMC (American Motors Corporation). However, the salt — always his raison d'être — never lost its attraction and later he undertook the construction of a new car with supersonic potential but it failed to meet expectations.

Sonic 1 never ran again in earnest and is on display at the Indianapolis Motor Speedway Hall of Fame Museum.

SPECIFICATIONS

Vehicle	Sonic 1
Origin	America
Weight	7,991lb (3,625kg)
Length	408in (10.36m)
Height	126in (3.20m)
Powerplant	J79 Turbojet
Thrust	17,835lbf
Thrust/weight ratio	2.2/1
Venue	Bonneville
Speeds	555.483mph & 600.601mph

GOLDENROD • BILL & BOB SUMMERS

The duel of the jets had captured the world's imagination yet few of the general public understood the workings of either a turbojet or a piston engine. What they did understand was the spectacle and big numbers that Art Arfons and Craig Breedlove had provided with an increase of nearly 200mph in just two years. In the shadow of this titanic battle and just three days before Breedlove returned to

SPECIFICATIONS

Vehicle	Goldenrod
Origin	America
Weight	8,450lb (3,833kg)
Length	384in (9.75m)
Width	48in (1.22m)
Height	42in (1.07m)
Transmission	Four-speed
Powerplant	Chrysler V8 x4
Engine capacity	28 litres
Horsepower	2,500hp
BHP per litre	90/1
Power/weight ratio	1/3.4
Venue	Bonneville
Speed	409.277mph

Bonneville to break 600mph, two brothers set a record that would not be seen in its true perspective for several decades.

The purist hot rodders acknowledged the fiery jets but to them this was a different ball game. The Holy Grail was the official piston-powered, wheel-driven record that was held by the late John Cobb and had been in the hands of the Brits for 36 years. Two such advocates were the Summers brothers. After attending regular high school, Bill became a truck driver and Bob a welder. Both were captivated by the hot-rod culture and ran roadsters to success on the dry lakes and at Bonneville, gaining enough experience and confidence to aspire to the ultimate prize.

Both Cobb and Mickey Thompson had cars with engines arranged side by side, creating a wide frontal area. The brothers realised that this format would not give them an edge. So, after priceless advice from racing pioneer Tony Capanna, they

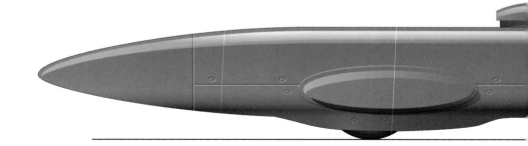

Bill Summers

decided to defy convention by placing four engines in line and have a scale model tested in the wind tunnel at the California Institute of Technology. The results gave the brothers enough belief in the design to start the project in an abandoned fruit shed. Hurst Performance Products helped with funding, Chrysler loaned four Hemi engines, Firestone agreed to provide the wheels and tyres, and Mobil Oil also helped out. Limited funding was enhanced by the Summers brothers' unlimited determination and perseverance.

With Jim Crosby on the team, the brothers contrived to fit the four 7-litre Hemi engines with clutches and gearboxes into a narrow body measuring only 48in wide and 28in high. Together with offset drive shafts, fuel and oil tanks, cockpit, parachutes, wheels, brakes and control linkages, everything was packed in like a cigar in a tube. The two forward engines provided drive to the front wheels and the other two powered the rear, which gave four-wheel drive and added to the already complex engineering.

With space under the bodywork at a premium, mechanical fuel injectors

FRONTAL AREA COMPARISON

Thunderbolt   Mobil Railton Special   Goldenrod

developed by Stuart Hilborn replaced the bulky carburettors. These more compact, uncomplicated units were designed solely for full-power applications. One was fitted to each inlet port with all 32 injectors linked to work in unison.

Named *Goldenrod*, the car was a masterpiece of engineering that created a new paradigm for all future land speed contenders. Its inferior power-to-weight ratio, as compared with the *Railton Mobil Special* and *Challenger*, was more than offset by a frontal area of less than 9sq ft.

Goldenrod first ran in September 1965 but encountered mechanical problems and bad weather for two months. On 13 November, however, Bob Summers made history with an average of 409.277mph on a track that was turning to slush. The following day he made a one-way pass of 425mph but did not make the return run. The brothers had the official record and would keep it for 42 years. They wanted to run the car again but their sponsors were unwilling to fund them just to break their own record. The engines were returned to Chrysler and *Goldenrod* spent decades open to the elements, steadily deteriorating.

Goldenrod was a tough act to follow. Al Teague broke the record in 1991 but in a different class, as did the Burklands' streamliner in 2008. It was not until 2010 when Charlie Nearburg drove to an average of 414.316mph in the same FIA class from which *Goldenrod* was finally deposed after 45 years.

After Bob Summers died in 1991, his widow gave the car to Bill on condition that it would never be fired up again. *Goldenrod* has since been meticulously restored and resides in the Henry Ford Museum in Dearborn, Michigan, as if captured in amber for future generations of visitors to wonder how fast it might have gone in perfect conditions.

WINGFOOT EXPRESS 2 • WALT ARFONS

Walt Arfons had pioneered a jet dragster to one of the first 200mph passes and held the absolute land speed record for three days with the jet-powered *Wingfoot Express* before returning to Bonneville with a different way of doing things.

Chuck Yeager had long since broken the sound barrier in the Bell X-1, a rocket-propelled plane, so why not a car? Always the innovator, Walt constructed his own. Without access to or experience with liquid-fuel rockets, he improvised in typical hot-rodder fashion with a readily available form of motive power known as the JATO (jet assisted take-off) bottle. This type of solid-fuel rocket was originally designed to help heavily laden aircraft take off on short runways and provided 1,000lbf of

SOLID-FUEL JET-ASSISTED TAKE-OFF BOTTLE

thrust for 14 seconds at a cost of $1,000 each. In a case of form following function, accommodating 15 such units in the tail of a car resulted in a conical shape, pointed at the front and bulky at the rear.

The car itself was built with a large structural safety margin that together with the JATO bottles pushed the weight

LIQUID FUEL BELL X-1

to over 6,500lb. Two front wheels were mounted very close together to conform to the rules. The rear wheels were mounted on outriggers. The car also featured two small canard wings and a vertical stabiliser mounted on the nose. Jets had eliminated all the mechanical complications of transmission and now the rocket principle removed the complexity of all the jet engine's multitude of internal components.

SPECIFICATIONS

Vehicle	Wingfoot Express 2
Origin	America
Weight	6,500lb (2,948kg)
Length	372in (9.45m)
Height	114in (2.89m)
Width	196in (4.98m)
Powerplant	JATO units
Thrust	25,000lbf potential
Thrust/weight ratio	3.8/1
Venue	Bonneville
Speed	476mph

JET-POWERED PLYMOUTH BARRACUDA

Nearly 40 years earlier Fritz von Opel had stunned a crowd of 3,000 and harvested valuable publicity in what was essentially an attention-grabbing stunt. Now, in October 1965, with 15,000lbf of thrust *Wingfoot Express 2* appeared to be a serious contender as driver Bobby Tatroe took off on his first run, igniting the motors in sequence. This run recorded a disappointing 385mph and inherent problems began to emerge. Undeterred, Walt decided to fit ten more JATOs overnight, five angled on each side, to give a total of 25,000lbf of thrust. This 66 per cent increase in thrust delivered 476mph the following day, still well short of Art Arfons's 536mph benchmark.

The two runs had used 40 JATOs at a cost of $40,000 compared with the $20 that Craig Breedlove spent on 60 gallons of fuel per run. The high cost precluded any practice runs so the theory was an act of faith. With the JATOs having a burn time of only 14 seconds, a two-mile run-up and then the measured mile itself meant that there was no possibility that all the rockets would deliver thrust throughout, so they had to be fired sequentially to cover the whole course. The sheer bulk of the rear end plus the outrigged wheels also presented over five times the frontal area of *Goldenrod*.

These defects, together with the car's weight, seriously limited its speed, especially when the motors were expended during the timed run. The fact that the car ran straight and its weight actually decreased as 1,800lb of propellant was

Bobby Tatroe

used up could not compensate for the fundamental flaws in the design.

Walt Arfons knew he was beaten and was unwilling to spend another $25,000 to risk the fearless Bobby Tatroe's life on a forlorn hope with a return run. It was small consolation that *Wingfoot Express 2* was the first rocket car at Bonneville.

Walt did not return to the salt flats but was approached by Chrysler to convert a series of its stock models into jet-propelled crowd pleasers to promote the company's wares at dragstrips. He went on to construct several purpose-built glass-fibre jet-powered funny cars for drag racing before retiring.

He lived long enough to see the Brits reclaim the record and break the sound barrier on land before quietly passing away at the age of 96.

Wingfoot Express 2 was later cut up and cannibalised for other projects. Like its predecessor, it has been lost forever.

BLUE FLAME • GARY GABELICH

In 1970 there appeared at Bonneville a car like no other. It was the first, and last, rocket to break the absolute record, and its record of 622.407mph was the last to be achieved at the hallowed salt flats. The car was called *Blue Flame*.

The rocket brethren's first step on the long and bumpy path to righteousness began even before Walt Arfons's JATO experiments when, in 1963, Pete Farnsworth decided that working full-time and maintaining a dragster was no way to live. He decided to build an exhibition car that did not require such constant attention. A chance meeting with Dick Keller, who had built a scaled-down rocket motor with Ray Dausman, led to the formation of Reaction Dynamics Inc. and the team undertook the construction of a rocket dragster in Farnsworth's garage.

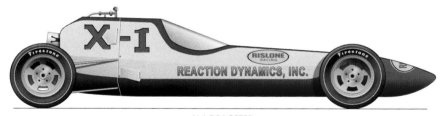

X-1 DRAGSTER

What emerged looked something like a contemporary racing car but tipped the scales at only 750lb.

The motive power was a hydrogen peroxide rocket delivering 2,500lbf of thrust for about four seconds. The rocket motor was simplicity itself with almost no moving parts. It operated by pressurising 97 per cent pure hydrogen peroxide with inert nitrogen gas. Opening a valve passed it through a silver-plated, nickel-mesh catalyst. This caused the hydrogen peroxide to instantly separate into water and oxygen at temperatures of about 1,300 degrees centigrade, which turned the water into steam and produced thrust. The car was named X-1 after the rocket plane that Chuck Yeager had flown through the sound barrier.

The X-1, with hired gun Chuck Suba at the controls, outran everything at the dragstrip and became the first to break into the five-second bracket. Motivated by this success, the team aspired to the biggest prize in speed. The first step was to get a commitment from Goodyear to supply tyres, which in turn helped in raising funding from the AGA (American Gas Association), with technical assistance from the IGT (Institute of Gas Technology). A model was tested in the Ohio State University wind tunnel to theoretical speeds of 850mph and the project became a reality. The X-1 engine design was scaled up and modified to use LNG (liquefied natural gas) as a second propellant. This was ignited with the oxygen produced from the hydrogen peroxide to create a hybrid engine producing 22,000lbf of thrust. To comply with FIA requirements the car also adopted the twin-front-wheel set-up used on *Wingfoot Express 2*.

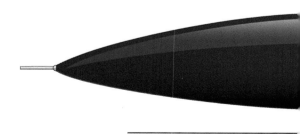

SPECIFICATIONS

Vehicle	Blue Flame
Origin	America
Weight	6,600lb (2,994kg) loaded
Length	449in (11.4m)
Height	98in (2.49m)
Width	92in (2.34m)
Powerplant	Rocket motor
Thrust	22,000lbf
Thrust/weight ratio	3.3/1 potential
Venue	Bonneville
Speed	622.407mph

With construction under way, the team encountered a setback that was to have significant repercussions. Goodyear was in no hurry to help break a record that had already been set by Breedlove using its rubber and did not deliver the promised tyres in time. So the decision was made to use the tyre design from *Sonic 1*. This increased the proportions of the car, which contributed to the project going over budget and Reaction Dynamics losing ownership to the AGA.

After a pause of six months the project restarted with Reaction Dynamics as paid employees and finally came to fruition a year later than planned. It was named *Blue Flame* and adopted the IGT flame logo on the tail fin. Gary Gabelich was hired by the AGA to drive the car. His colourful CV included driving dragsters and funny cars, recording a quarter-mile drag-boat record of 200.44mph and working as a test astronaut for the Apollo project.

Arriving at Bonneville in September 1970, Gabelich spent nearly two months troubled by technical problems until on 23 October the combination came together. With reduced throttle settings, he averaged 622.407mph for the mile and 630.388mph for the kilometre, reaching a peak of 650mph midway through the mile. The record and the car belonged to the AGA.

Blue Flame had more potential and could have been worked up to even greater feats, as Reaction Dynamics had intended, but the AGA had reaped the promotional benefits and had no interest in taking on the expense running costs of breaking its own record. As it turned out, the mile record stood for 13 years and the kilometre record for 26 years until broken by the jet-powered *Thrust SSC* in 1997.

Gabelich went back to drag racing, suffering a severe crash that nearly severed his arm. He recovered and started planning another rocket car before losing his life in a motorcycle accident in 1984.

After finding no takers in America, *Blue Flame* was bought by a private collector and is on permanent display in the Auto & Technik Museum at Sinsheim in Germany.

MOTIVATOR • KITTY O'NEIL

The hot rodders' experience at the drag strip had enabled them to depose the Brits and then tighten America's grip on the absolute record. Now came a challenge from an entirely different facet of American society: Tinseltown. Looking back down the decades this extraordinary chapter in the quest for speed has sometimes been seen through a veil of Hollywood hoopla. The main protagonists did emanate from the dream factory but came from the harsh reality of the stunt industry.

There had always been some element

of hype in the quest for speed, especially when it came to crystallising the attention of sponsors. Craig Breedlove had named his second car *Sonic 1* with no realistic possibility of supersonic speed. The *Blue Flame* scale model had been wind-tunnel tested to 850mph and when the team recorded a peak speed of 650mph at reduced thrust it excited expectation that the speed of sound was within reach. Cost and corporate policy ensured that the attempt was never made.

This new challenge turned into a two-act drama with Bill Fredrick's rocket car in

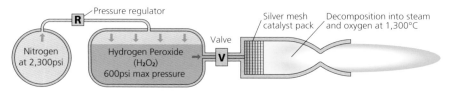

HYDROGEN PEROXIDE ROCKET ENGINE SCHEMATIC

the opening scene. Fredrick was an active enthusiast of high-speed vehicles, building *Valkyrie*, one of the first jet cars, which was driven by a young Gary Gabelich. After

his previous career in meat marketing, Fredrick decided to spend the rest of his life doing things he found more interesting. He made a career in rocketry that involved spectacular stunts such as flinging speeding cars into the air while people like Hal Needham and Kitty O'Neil were driving them. Later he created the *Courage of Australia* hydrogen peroxide rocket car, which Vic Wilson drove in 1971 to the first 300mph pass at a drag strip.

Hal Needham, after serving in the 82nd Airborne Division, wrecked hundreds of cars during a legendary career as the world's highest-paid stuntman. He suffered more than 50 broken bones and demonstrated his fearlessness with a 128ft jump across a gorge in a rocket-propelled pickup truck

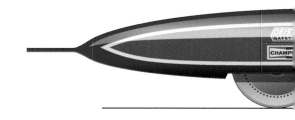

prepared by Fredrick. He progressed to stunt coordinator, second unit director and, ultimately, to film director.

Kitty O'Neil was of Cherokee blood and her petite 5ft 3in stature belied a giant reserve of spirit and determination that few could match. Falling ill with measles, mumps and smallpox at the age of five months cost Kitty her hearing. She learned how to lip read and talk normally. Then, as a teenager, she developed an interest in high-board diving but this was cut short by an attack of spinal meningitis that threatened the use of her legs. Two bouts of cancer followed. She recovered from all of these setbacks and, fascinated by speed, set a water-ski record of 104.85mph. Two of her fingers were severed in a motorcycle

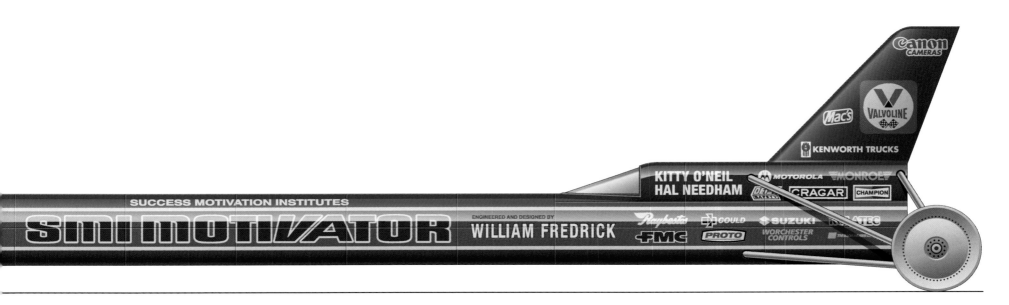

race but were successfully reattached. Then, like any sensible girl, she forged a career as a stuntwoman. By the time she retired O'Neil had become the fastest woman on earth, set a quarter-mile record (as yet unbeaten) in a Ky Michaelson rocket dragster at 3.22 seconds, and made the highest stunt fall by a woman at 105ft. She set a total of 22 different world records.

Bill Fredrick was familiar with the *Blue Flame* project and knew he needed a better combination. He made a quantum leap by discarding outdated tyre technology and adopting solid alloy wheels, which at only 2in wide created less rolling resistance. The car was just 20in wide, presenting a much smaller frontal area than *Blue Flame* while also weighing considerably less. The

hydrogen peroxide motor produced less thrust at 9,000lbf but the maximum thrust-to-weight ratio compared favourably to that of *Blue Flame* on its record run. It was a well-considered concept and O'Neil and Needham were contracted to drive it.

Needham took ownership of the car, which was named *Motivator*, and raised the money from 30 sponsors to complete and run it. Fredrick's rocket-car veteran, John

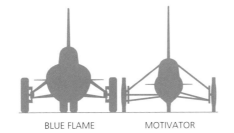

BLUE FLAME   MOTIVATOR

Paxson, gave the car a systematic work-out with four shakedown runs at El Mirage dry lake. But he experienced directional problems at 360mph when making a run at Bonneville. O'Neil then made a pass at 300mph and also had trouble staying on line. After Fredrick had checked over *Motivator* he concluded that the condition of the salt was not suitable for its solid alloy wheels and switched operations to Alvord Desert in Oregon.

Here, over a period of three days, O'Neil made five runs, pushing the speed to over 400mph. On 6 December 1976, still using only 60 per cent of the available power, she set a new record of 512.710mph after reaching a peak speed of 618mph. With enough in reserve to

contest the absolute record, things took a different turn. Conservationists objected to *Motivator* running in the desert and a legal wrangle ensued.

Meanwhile Needham was raising his own objections. O'Neil had been contracted to run for the women's record but not the absolute one. Needham, who wanted to break the absolute record himself, demanded the agreement was upheld. Fredrick knew that time was running out and wished to continue with O'Neil in the seat. By the time the dust began to settle on these disputes, snow had begun to fall, ending the season.

Kitty O'Neil had increased the women's record by over 200mph but was denied the chance to become the fastest of them all.

BUDWEISER ROCKET • STAN BARRETT

The second act in Bill Fredrick's rocket story continued when *Motivator* was taken to the Mud Lake at Tonopah where Hal Needham made two trial runs before his chutes failed during an all-out effort in excess of 600mph. The car kept going for three miles, ran out of track and crashed across gullies and through sagebrush before coming to rest.

The Tonopah episode quenched Needham's desire to drive but not his ambition, which became not only to break the land speed record but go beyond it to

the speed of sound. Accepting that the damaged *Motivator* had run its course, he commissioned Fredrick to construct a new projectile.

Needham and Fredrick realised from the outset that their new car would never make an official FIA run. A fundamental problem with a rocket is that it cannot sustain peak thrust through a run-up and

the measured mile. In addition it cannot make a return run within one hour — and this rocket had only three wheels. Breaching the sound barrier, therefore, became the aim.

The practical application of jets differed from rockets. A jet-powered car had a heavy engine with a relatively light fuel load. It could make a run of four miles to wind up to speed and then maintain full power through the measured mile. A rocket-propelled car had a light engine and a heavy payload of fuel that was expended in only 20 seconds or so. This meant a much shorter run-up but the power came on instantly and the car rapidly reduced in

weight, which enhanced acceleration.

Fredrick, aware of these parameters, created the new car along the same lines as *Motivator*, which had proved its structural and aerodynamic integrity. Based on experience gained, he upgraded the internal equipment to a more sophisticated level. A new hydrogen peroxide engine was designed to burn polybutadiene rings as a second fuel, producing 18,000lbf of thrust. Even this was calculated to be less than needed. So Fredrick purchased six Sidewinder missile solid-fuel rocket motors. These were individually mounted above the hybrid motor to provide five seconds or so of added thrust at 4,000lbf, giving total thrust of 22,000lbf. The rear

SPECIFICATIONS

Vehicle	Budweiser Rocket
Origin	America
Weight	5,320lb (2,413kg) loaded
Length	470in (11.94m)
Height	108in (2.74m)
Width	120in (3.04m)
Powerplant	Rocket motors
Thrust	22,000lbf
Thrust/weight ratio	4/1
Venue	Rogers Dry Lake
Speed	739mph claimed

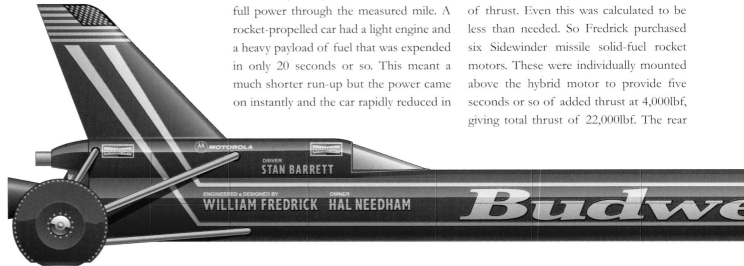

wheels were fitted with uprated brakes and enclosed in fairings. Construction took two years in Fredrick's backyard workshop.

Needham's fellow stuntman Stan Barrett was selected to take the ride. Film star Paul Newman helped broker a sponsorship deal with Budweiser that included a $500,000 bonus for breaking the sound barrier. The vehicle was named the *Budweiser Rocket*. Since the team knew that it could not establish an official record, the venture became a case of boom or bust.

The first trial was made at Bonneville on 4 September 1979 when Barrett squeezed into the 20in-wide cockpit and made a tentative run at 350mph. Five days later more runs pushed the speed

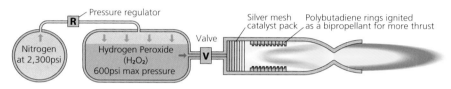

HYDROGEN PEROXIDE BIPROPELLANT ROCKET ENGINE SCHEMATIC

up by increments to 638mph. During this fastest pass Barrett experienced severe vibrations that were caused by the solid wheels alternately cutting through the salt crust and skipping over the surface. It was decided that the track at Bonneville was not suitable and the team relocated to Rogers Dry Lake, site of the USAF Edwards Air Base in California's Mojave Desert.

Testing now continued using hydrogen peroxide alone, then the hybrid motor, and then both power sources alternately with a

Sidewinder solid-fuel rocket. On 3 December a run fuelled only by hydrogen peroxide reached 643mph. More runs followed with the hybrid engine at speeds of 677mph and 714mph. Finally, on its 18th outing on 16 December, the *Budweiser Rocket* broke the sound barrier by igniting the Sidewinder 12 seconds into its run to exert all of the 22,000lbf of thrust at the optimum time. It recorded a speed of 739mph before running out of fuel after 16.8 seconds. The USAF's visual radar tracking and an on-board accelerometer calculated the speed, which was calibrated and checked weeks later.

The supersonic claim was met with suspicion from many quarters and the pendulum of doubt has swung backwards and forwards ever since. The pros and cons

are as follows. No sonic boom was heard above the sound of the rocket motors. Highly efficient shapes do not produce a boom as loud as bulky shapes. Chuck Yeager and some high-ranking USAF officers endorsed the claim but not in an official capacity. The radar tracking was not accurate. The on-board telemetry was not an impartial source of data. Some quarters claimed it was just a publicity stunt. Yet the team pursued its objective with determination for over three months with rocket fuel, payroll and accommodation costs spiralling. Budweiser accepted the claim to enjoy a publicity bonanza.

Science says that the *Budweiser Rocket*'s power-to-weight ratio of around 4/1 was more than enough to get the job done.

All of the above is a matter for debate — and will remain so. The simple facts are that Stan Barrett unofficially risked his life 18 times in the quest for speed and on at least four runs went faster than anyone had gone before. Somehow this got lost in the kerfuffle.

SPIRIT OF '76 • AL TEAGUE

Like many young boys, Al Teague daydreamed of emulating the exploits of George Eyston, John Cobb and Malcolm Campbell. By his late teens he was running a roadster with his older brother Harvey at drag strips around Los Angeles, upgrading it from a six-cylinder engine to a V8 before switching to dragsters. All of this was Teague's education in the black arts of using superchargers and running on nitro.

SPECIFICATIONS

Vehicle	Spirit of '76
Origin	America
Weight	4,600lb (2,087kg)
Length	333in (8.46m)
Width	49in (1.25m)
Height	36in (0.91m)
Transmission	Four-speed
Powerplant	Hemi V8
Engine capacity	8 litres
Horsepower	1,600hp+
BHP per litre	200/1
Power/weight ratio	1/2.9
Venue	Bonneville
Speed	409.978mph

In 1963 Teague's pursuit of speed was put on hold for three years when he was drafted into the army and served in Vietnam. After his return he made his first visit, as a spectator, to Bonneville and there he found his vocation in life. The following year he returned with the Sadd, Teague & Bentley '29 Model A roadster powered by a blown Hemi. This car was campaigned with great success until it made a stunning one-way pass of 268mph in 1972. This speed was almost science fiction for a roadster. It made Teague's name.

With many records already in the book, Teague set his sights higher. The aerodynamic qualities of the roadster were almost nil, which meant any significant improvement would need a different approach. In 1974 Teague began construction of an open-wheel lakester in his mother's garage in Los Angeles. He created bodywork using a motorcycle streamliner mould borrowed from Denis Manning. The chassis was a tubular space frame with torsion-bar suspension up front and a rigid rear end with a four-

SPIRIT OF '76 WHEEL LAYOUT

speed transaxle and rear-wheel drive. The engine was the proven Chrysler 392 Hemi. Inspired by early lakes racer Earl Evans, Al named the car *Spirit of '76* for Evans's lucky number.

Years of constant modification and improvement followed. The original car featured twin turbos and a wheelbase of 160in that was later extended by 18in. Then the decision was made to change the car into a fully enclosed streamliner and the chassis was extended twice more. The two front wheels, unusually, were brought within the narrow 21in-wide nose, in tandem but not quite in line, to conform with four-wheel rules, and the narrowed rear end was enclosed by integral fairings. The engine was upgraded to a supercharged 490 cu in aluminium Hemi manufactured by Keith

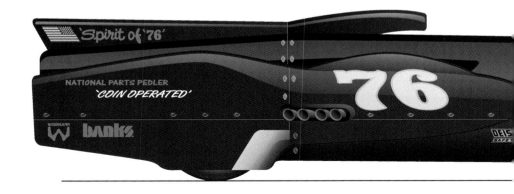

Black and capable of delivering 1,600hp.

Teague worked tirelessly on the car to improve on an early mark of 260mph but was held back by only being able to test at the salt flats once a year. Mechanical failure and a period of two years when conditions prevented a run did little to dampen Teague's enthusiasm. When he achieved progressive increases in speed to 349.695mph, 378.567mph and finally 382mph, he had gone faster than Eyston and the possibility of 400mph appeared on the horizon.

Only Cobb, Donald Campbell, Mickey

AL TEAGUE'S '29 MODEL A ROADSTER

Thompson and Bob Summers had gone that fast in wheel-driven cars, all with more backing and more power than *Spirit of '76*. Even tyres were hard to come by because, with the advent of jets and rockets running on solid alloy wheels, Goodyear and Firestone were no longer interested. Yet Teague had put together a special combination. Compared with previous wheel-driven machines, his uncomplicated single-engine concept was lighter and

aerodynamically more efficient, which compensated for its lower power output.

Teague was beaten to his target in September 1990 by Nolan White's one-way 401mph. But the following year, on 21 August, having sourced some 31-year-old Firestone tyres that had aged to a suitable hardness and running on a mix of alcohol and nitro, Teague set a new record for A/BFS (blown fuel streamliner under 8.2 litres) with an average speed of

409.978mph and a peak speed of 432.692mph. The record with *Spirit of '76* had been 17 years in the making.

Breaking the 26-year-old record set by *Goldenrod* required a speed one per cent higher, but in the record books there is no wheel-driven record in itself; rather there are many records in different classes. So Teague's record was ratified in its class while also being, if only by a whisker, the fastest wheel-driven time ever recorded, 0.701mph better than the 409.277mph reached by *Goldenrod*, which ran in a different class for cars with normally aspirated engines of more than 8.2 litres.

Teague continued running at Bonneville until retiring in 2002, sweeping up many more records at different displacements. The quintessential hot rodder had outrun his boyhood heroes on a limited budget and like Burt Munro had shown what could be done with ingenuity, improvisation and sheer determination. Even today only ten people have officially exceeded 400mph in a piston-engine car.

SPIRIT OF AMERICA FORMULA SHELL LSRV • CRAIG BREEDLOVE

The fires of ambition that drove Craig Breedlove in his early 20s had waned. When Art Arfons returned in 1966 to make a challenge his car was destroyed and Arfons was lucky to escape with his life. Breedlove had no motivation to break his own record and the roar of jets on the salt ceased. Gary Gabelich took the honours four years later in his rocket-propelled *Blue Flame* but at least the record remained in America.

Meanwhile, Breedlove hustled a living with personal appearances, a trucking company, endurance records with AMC cars and forays into drag racing. This was followed by a business in real estate and then a Ford dealership. Even during this period Breedlove came up with the idea of bringing his friend Donald Campbell's *Bluebird CN7* out of retirement to prove its true potential and dallied with designing a rocket-propelled car of his own. But neither of these projects came to fruition.

The success of Richard Noble's *Thrust 2*, which took the record back to Britain, helped to fan the embers of Breedlove's true purpose in life. The man who was first to 400mph, then 500mph and 600mph began to formulate his ideas. In 1992 it happened: Craig Breedlove returned, aiming to be the first to 700mph and possibly beyond.

Knowing what it took, he bought an old tractor dealership, added living quarters and moved in, committed to spending 24 hours a day on the project. Putting in $2 million of his own money, he used his credibility as a true pioneer and the siren call of supersonic speed to attract sponsors.

When Shell renewed its relationship with Breedlove to provide substantial funding, the venture was truly under way.

Meanwhile, news of the construction of a third-generation *Spirit of America* car was enough to motivate Richard Noble to meet the challenge to keep the record in British hands. In christening his new project *Thrust SSC* (Supersonic Car), Noble left no one in any doubt as to his intentions.

Breedlove was not convinced by expensive wind-tunnel testing and modern computational fluid dynamics (CFD)

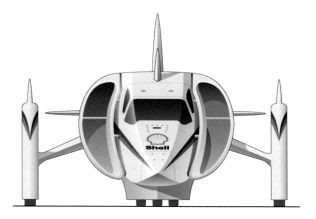

barrel carburettors and running on gasoline to produce 1,182hp. This basic single-engine configuration kept things relatively simple. With less mechanical complexity, there was less to go wrong. The output was raised by installing a nitrous oxide injection system that boosted power to 1,700hp.

The internal combustion engine works by burning oxygen and fuel. Air has an oxygen content of about 20 per cent, which governs the amount of fuel consumed and the power produced. Supercharging increases power by cramming in more usable air. An alternative to this is nitrous oxide (N_2O), which is made up of nitrogen (64 per cent) and oxygen (36

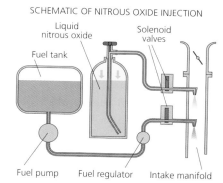

SCHEMATIC OF NITROUS OXIDE INJECTION

Liquid nitrous oxide

Solenoid valves

Fuel tank

Fuel pump   Fuel regulator   Intake manifold

per cent). When stored under pressure it remains in liquid form but when injected into the intake system of an engine it immediately vaporises at −88.48°C. This increases the oxygen content, which allows proportionately more fuel to be burned, resulting in large increases in power.

When finished, *Spirit of Rett* began its record-breaking campaign by taking the prize in three classes with speeds of up to 392.503mph. Charlie Nearburg had achieved his aim but the story did not end there. With engine displacement increased to 8.7 litres, he drove it to an average of 414.316mph on 21 September 2010. This was ratified by the FIA in the same class (AI-II-11) as the Summers brothers' *Goldenrod* and so the 45-year-old record was finally officially broken. Al Teague's car had run a single supercharged engine on fuel in A/BFS while the Burkland Streamliner ran two blown engines on fuel in AA/BFS, both in different classes.

Even someone with the determined

work ethic of Charlie Nearburg could never have imagined that his very personal odyssey on the salt flats would achieve so spectacularly: *Spirit of Rett* had become the fastest normally aspirated single-engine car ever, owning the four fastest SCTA unblown records at the same time and conquering the most sought-after record in land speed history. Rett's memory had been well and truly honoured.

SPECIFICATIONS

Vehicle	Spirit of Rett
Origin	America
Weight	4,017lb (1,822kg)
Length	401in (10.19m)
Width	31.0in (0.79m)
Height	33.2in (0.84m)
Transmission	Five-speed
Powerplant	Chevrolet V8
Engine capacity	8.7 litres
Horsepower	1,700hp
BHP per litre	195/1
Power/weight ratio	1/2.4
Venue	Bonneville
Speed	414.316mph

spirit of rett

arlie

weight or an increase in power output   power output will theoretically get the car   practice is to make only small changes at

VENTURI BUCKEYE BULLET 3 • ROGER SCHROER

The idea of automobiles competing for a land speed record was instigated by the rivalry generated between Count Gaston de Chasseloup-Laubat and Camille Jenatzy in 1898. Their battery-powered machines amazed the world but commercial success for electric vehicles was short-lived as they soon lost out to the internal combustion engine in the popularity stakes for personal transport. The inherent problem of heavy, short-range batteries saw electric cars fade from the market.

SPECIFICATIONS

Vehicle	Buckeye Bullet 3
Origin	America
Weight	7,480lb (3,393kg)
Length	444in (11.28m)
Width	41in (1.04m)
Height	62in (1.57m)
Transmission	Two-speed gearboxes
Powerplant	Electric motors x2
Horsepower	3,000hp
Power/weight ratio	1/2.5
Venue	Bonneville
Speed	341.4mph

In the latter part of the twentieth century there was a resurgence of interest in electric vehicles that offered a zero-pollution solution to public transport and

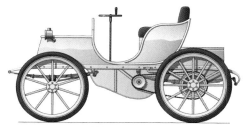

1898 JEANTAUD

great strides have been made. As a result it is not surprising that this power source has made itself felt in the quest for speed. Technology has come a long way since the Count's horseless carriage.

The first electric car to exceed 200mph,

Ed Rannberg's beautifully designed *Lightning Rod*, which set a record of 213.084mph in 1997, provides a contrast between the Jeantaud and the longer, lower, narrower paradigm created by the Summers brothers. Including 26 sealed lead-acid batteries that weighed 800lb, *Lightning Rod* tipped the scales at 2,310lb, had a frontal area of just 5sq ft and a single motor powering the rear wheels.

The challenge was taken up by the Ohio State University Center for Automotive Research (CAR) under the direction of Giorgio Rizzoni, who took up his position in 1999, and in partnership with Venturi Automobiles, a Monaco-based specialist car manufacturer. Engineering students have run the ongoing electric

vehicle project, gaining valuable practical experience and setting numerous records in the process.

The project entered the new millennium with the *Venturi Buckeye Bullet 1* (*VBB1*). The name derived from the state of Ohio's nickname, the 'Buckeye State', from the prevalence of buckeye trees in the area. The original concept was developed through *Buckeye Bullets 2* and *2.5* with speeds reaching 307mph. The

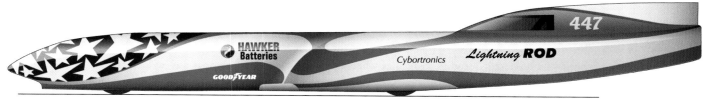

1997 LIGHTNING ROD

next in the series, *Venturi Buckeye Bullet 3*, had four-wheel drive with two motors at the front and two at the rear. Powered by 2,000 lithium-iron-phosphate pouch cells, it delivered 3,000hp. The running weight of the car, including 3,584lb of batteries, was 7,480lb.

This made *VBB3* heavier than all streamliners since *Goldenrod* (with its four engines) and highlights the different parameters that relate to electric cars. Rocket cars could expend a ton of fuel in 20 seconds, thus drastically reducing weight on a run. Piston-engine cars did not carry a large weight of fuel in the first place. Electric cars, however, had to deal with the penalty of having to haul heavy batteries even when their power was almost expended. In other words, the car weighed the same at the end of a run as at the start. Although cutting-edge batteries and motors were used, *VBB3*'s carbon-fibre bodywork was similar to the shape of *Dieselmax* and not much removed from Mickey Thompson's *Autolite Special* from decades before.

After two years of disappointment on shortened tracks with poor surface conditions and in unsuitable weather, the 25-strong team returned to Bonneville in 2016. They were gunning for their own, FIA-sanctioned record of 307.666mph that Roger Schroer, test driver at the Ohio Transportation Research Center, set in *VBB2.5* seven years earlier. The available course was 11 miles long and the car was fully prepared. Schroer was strapped into the cockpit and arrowed down the track and back within the specified hour to set a record of 341.4mph. The young engineering students, using this rejuvenated technology, had made their own significant contribution to the rich history of land speed record breaking.

True to the spirit of *La Jamais Contente*, those who commune with Munro's God of Speed find that they are often inexorably drawn to the next elusive milestone. With four times the power of previous cars, the *Buckeye Bullet*'s power-to-weight ratio compared favourably with cars such as *Goldenrod*, *Spirit of '76* and *Spirit of Rett*. Having already exceeded 350mph as a peak speed, the team nowadays feels that there is enough potential in the car to give the old timers a run for their money in a race to 400mph. Given a suitable track that is long enough, who is to say they cannot do it?

Should an electric vehicle make it into the select 400mph club, which has only 10 wheel-driven members, it might tilt the axis of perception in the world of speed. And in today's world, as the use of fossil fuels diminishes, the story of record breaking with electric vehicles looks set to have a long way to run.

CHALLENGER 2 • DANNY THOMPSON

Mickey Thompson's attempt with the *Autolite Special* was rained out at Bonneville back in 1968. Suffering further disappointment when his main sponsors — Ford, Gulf Oil and Reynolds Aluminum — withdrew their support, Thompson put the car in storage while he developed his many demanding business ventures.

When remotivated in 1988, Thompson laid plans to resume the challenge with

his son Danny as driver. However, this came to a sudden halt with his untimely death and Danny put the car back in storage, where it became a case of 'out of sight, out of mind'.

Danny Thompson concentrated on his father's business interests and also made a name for himself as a competitor in motocross, off-road racing, sprint cars and circuit racing before

Mickey Thompson's endurance records that still stand.

Captivated by the spirit on the salt, he returned each year. In 2010, the 50th anniversary of his father's first attempt with *Challenger 1*, Danny resolved to resurrect the *Autolite Special* and fulfil his father's ambition to break the piston-powered, wheel-driven record. Renamed *Challenger 2*, the car that was built in just six

months had remained inanimate for decades. It took a 25-strong team of volunteers several years to rebuild. With sponsorship and his own savings, Thompson replaced the two original Ford engines with normally aspirated, fuel-injected 500 cu in aluminium Hemi V8s, each engine driving one set of wheels. Updating the internals included three-speed gearboxes and upgraded driveshafts together with modern safety equipment.

SPECIFICATIONS

Vehicle	Challenger 2
Origin	America
Weight	5,700lb (2,585kg)
Length	384in (9.75m)
Width	34in (0.86m)
Height	58in (1.47m)
Transmission	Three-speed
Powerplant	Chrysler Hemi V8 x2
Engine capacity	16.4 litres
Horsepower	5,000hp
BHP per litre	305/1
Power/weight ratio	1/1.4
Venue	Bonneville
Speed	448.757mph

MICKEY THOMPSON'S ORIGINAL AUTOLITE SPECIAL IN 1968

retiring from motorsport in 1995. It was not until 2003 that he became interested in Bonneville when he was invited to drive the Bill Burke *Pumpkin Seed*, a streamliner that had once belonged to his father, and became a member of the 200mph club. More records followed as Danny added his name to record books peppered with

Having decided against the use of superchargers, the necessary gains in power output were achieved by the use of nitromethane. An 80/20 per cent mix of nitro and alcohol produced 2,500hp per engine at a moderate 7,200rpm — more than twice the output of *Speed Demon*. To make this kind of power requires huge quantities of fuel. To put this into perspective, a contemporary hatchback will burn one gallon of petrol in one hour at about 50mph whereas with a wide-open throttle *Challenger 2* burns a bewildering one gallon of fuel every second. Its two 30-gallon fuel tanks hold just enough to

| Goldenrod | Burkland | Ack Attack | Speed Demon | Challenger 2 | Turbinator II |

make one pass taking about 68 seconds. Without a radiator or ice tank system, the massive fuel flow is itself responsible for engine cooling.

Apart from alterations to the stabilising tail fin and other smaller modifications, the chassis and bodywork are original. The twin-engine set-up with four-wheel drive, and with the front engine mounted backward to drive the front wheels, is still Mickey Thompson's basic configuration. As the diagram above shows, there have

been various designs of nose cones with debates ranging from technical discussions on von Karmann/Ogive curves to the hot rodder's mantra of punching a hole in the air and driving through it. Mickey Thompson's way of doing things was about to prove as good as any.

In 2016 *Challenger 2* turned the clock back and returned to Bonneville. Danny Thompson began his campaign in poor weather running the almost

inevitable gauntlet of setbacks: problems with a snapped con rod, failed valve springs and a broken driveshaft, which caused a near disaster by destroying a rear tyre. Out of these misfortunes, however, came a record of 448.757mph set on 12 August 2018. Danny Thompson's motivation to vindicate his father's design was fulfilled as he made the 50-year-old car the fastest piston-powered vehicle on earth. And then walked away.

TURBINATOR II • DAVE SPANGLER

The Vesco family's odyssey into the realms of speed began in 1933 with John Vesco racing his jalopy across the dry lakes of Southern California. By 1949 he had graduated to racing a belly tank that reached 170mph within a few years but was destroyed in a crash.

In designing a new car, Vesco made a conceptual leap by giving it an extended wheelbase and a narrow track of only 24in, with the wheels enclosed within the streamlined bodywork. At Bonneville in

1957 it pre-dated the Summers brothers and their *Goldenrod* by several years and was so unusual it ran in the experimental class. With homespun aerodynamics and powered by a Model B four-cylinder engine equipped with a Riley overhead valve conversion, *Little Giant* became the pattern for all future streamliners and began its

impressive record-breaking career.

Vesco's two sons, Don and Rick, grew up to the background noise of open-exhaust headers and both raced in their teens with motorbikes and later cars. Rick set his first record of 131mph aged 16 and older brother Don went on to dominate the fastest two-wheel records before turning

to the absolute wheel-driven record.

Over the decades *Little Giant* underwent many engine changes and constant bodywork development while setting dozens of records with different drivers, including Dave Spangler. The Vesco family steadily amassed a fund of knowledge and hard-won experience that has few

JOHN VESCO'S LITTLE GIANT

SPECIFICATIONS

Vehicle	Turbinator II
Country	America
Weight	4,950lb (2,245kg)
Length	432in (10.97m)
Width	36in (0.91m)
Height	46in (1.17m)
Transmission	Clutch
Powerplant	Gas turbine
Horsepower	5,000hp
Power/weight ratio	1/1
Venue	Bonneville
Speed	482.646mph

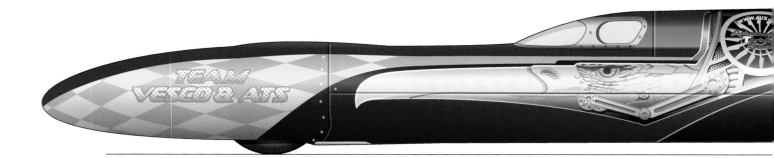

imitators. By 2011 *Little Giant* had propelled both Rick and his daughter Rhonnie into the select 300mph club and put three generations of Vescos into the record books.

Rick's challenge for the outright wheel-driven record began when he designed a streamliner with twin V8 engines in 1988. Don joined forces with his brother to speed things up and take care of the driving duties. The expense of maintaining the piston engines led to their opting for a change of power source and they bought a gas-turbine engine from Art Arfons. They

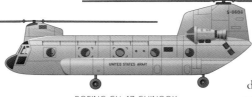

BOEING CH-47 CHINOOK

renamed the car *Turbinator*. After Don took the four-wheel-drive car to a world speed record in 2001, he succumbed to illness and died, believing that 500mph was possible in *Turbinator*.

Rick Vesco continued the quest in memory of his brother. In addition to modifications already started, the car was extended

Rick Vesco

by another 3ft with new carbon-fibre bodywork, engine, gearbox and driveline. The new engine was a modified T55-L-712 Shaft Gas Turbine normally used in the Chinook military helicopter. It produced 5,000hp.

Long-time friend Dave Spangler, who was part owner of Hooker Headers, provided funding and took the driver's seat. The finished vehicle, *Turbinator II*, clearly showed its *Little Giant* heritage. The 40 years of development on a careful budget,

which did not allow wind-tunnel testing or traction control, paid off in September 2018 when Spangler piloted the turbine missile to an average of 482.646mph. The following October it clocked a peak recorded speed of 503.332mph.

At the age of 76, Dave Spangler became the oldest man ever to set the wheel-driven record and the only one to exceed 500mph in such a car. Team Vesco intends to continue its quest for an official 500mph record. The Vesco story has been running for over 60 years and is an epic saga in itself.

DANGER! SALT ADDICTION

The Bonneville Salt Flats in Utah are part of the remains of a prehistoric lake that has been reduced to a bed of pure salt through an endless cycle of flooding and evaporation. In summertime the harsh sunshine dries it out into a smooth, hard surface. Standing in this vast area it is possible to see the curvature of the earth. In this perfectly silent and desolate place there is no sign of life — in any direction.

Motorists first came here in the early part of the twentieth century. In 1914 Teddy Tetzlaff propelled his thunderous *Blitzen Benz* to a speed of 142.8mph. By 1935 it had become the mecca for Malcolm Campbell, George Eyston and John Cobb in their pursuit of the absolute record. Cobb set his last record in 1947 with one run clipping the 400mph mark.

Back in California there was plenty of activity on the dry lakes of Muroc, El Mirage and a few others. These areas, only a couple of hours' drive from civilisation, were ideal places for pushing modified cars to their limit. The Southern California Timing Association (SCTA) had been set up in 1937 to organise such gatherings and create safety guidelines. In 1949 the SCTA extended its activity to Bonneville to accommodate the post-war boom of the hot rod culture. Bonneville had the advantage of a longer track and better traction than the dry lakes. The introduction of Speed Week, each August, ensured Bonneville's reputation as the open-air cathedral of speed.

An increase in activity of all kinds of vehicles followed through the 1950s: roadsters, coupes, belly tanks, lakesters and streamliners, each searching for that elusive record in their class. Many found that after just one visit they caught the bug and were unable to resist the quest.

It gained a name — 'salt addiction' or 'salt fever' — and in some cases has been passed from generation to generation to the present day. The addiction is often a devotion to a particular kind of engine, model of car or class designation, which is subjected to home-brewed technology and ingenuity. Many of the chosen vehicles are chopped, channelled, sectioned, lowered and lengthened, fitted with highly modified engines of various displacements, equipped with different types of superchargers and powered with alternative fuels. The result is a multitude of unique vehicles that look like no other but all conform to the rules of their individual classes.

Since the last thrust-powered record set by *Blue Flame* in 1970, Bonneville has been entirely the domain of wheel-driven cars. The participants regard themselves as the true believers in the quest and regard jets and rockets as a different contest.

In this activity, if the question 'Why?' is posed, then one could ask that about any sport. But in other professional sports the

SOUTHERN CALIFORNIA TIMING ASSOCIATION

rewards can amount to millions without actually winning anything. In land speed competition there is little or no financial return — quite the opposite in most cases.

The possibility of serious injury or death is factored into the decision to take part in the first place and, furthermore, to set an official record a driver must run not once but twice — a tall order given the risks.

What motivates those who become intoxicated by the quest for speed? The answer is a variation on George Mallory's famous response to why he climbed Everest: 'Because it's there.' And as with climbing, part of the thrill is the inherent danger and adrenalin rush. Many consider it gives a true purpose to their lives. Those men and women behind the tiny *Buddfab* or *The Flying Pickle* wanted to take something ordinary and do something extraordinary with it, regardless of whether the world at large was watching. Besides the lack of financial reward, the cost to the contestant can be high in terms of time, money and social life, not to mention pressures on relationships.

At Bonneville success is simply registered on a timing slip. There are no grandstands full of cheering crowds waiting for a trophy to be lifted at the moment of glory. There are some peripheral benefits such as displaying the car at exhibitions and getting your name on *Hot Rod* magazine's trophy for fastest time of the week. But nothing is guaranteed. These gladiators of speed devote decades of their lives using their own funds and scraping up a little sponsorship for the privilege of risking all. Living legend Al Teague, known as 'Mr Bonneville' to his peers, was a working man who devoted all his spare time and money to developing his car over a period of 17 years. Yet his total investment was less than some of today's professional footballers earn in a week.

Hot rod heritage has left us today with stunning cars that sometimes test our comprehension. If Henry Ford had been told that one day his Model T engine would power a car to over 200mph, he would have given the look normally reserved for the fools that he never suffered gladly. As it happened the Model T was the personal obsession of Joel Young, who acquired the old *Thermo King* diesel streamliner and planned to use a Model T engine of circa 1927 vintage to set records in the V4F/BFS class. The streamliner was rebuilt and the ancient four-cylinder engine block was highly modified and turbocharged. In 2012 Young took his car, now named *Matrix Machine*, into the record

DAVE DAVIDSON'S '34 BLOWN FUEL ROADSTER

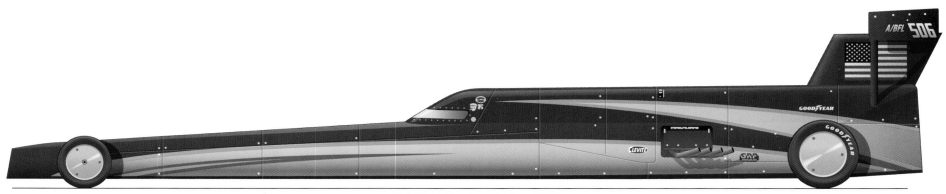

WOLFE-STRASBURG BLOWN FUEL LAKESTER

books with a speed of 214.749mph.

Edsel Ford would have been no less bewildered if someone had suggested that in the future one of his '34 Ford Roadsters would exceed 300mph with a Chrysler engine pumping out in excess of 4,000hp.

CLASS	ENGINE DESCRIPTION
XF	Flathead Fords
XXF	Flathead Fords with overhead-valve conversions
XO	'59-older overhead-valve in-line engines and non-Ford/Mercury flatheads
XXO	XO class with specialty heads
V4F	'34-older flathead in-line four-cyl
V4	V4F class with specialty heads
Omega	Engines that run on anything other than the Otto cycle

Dave Davidson is the present-day owner and driver of such a car. The roadster-class regulations stipulate a stock body and allow fender removal but little in the way of streamlining. To move this blunt object quickly through the air requires an engine of fearsome output. Davidson employed an ex-drag racing Keith Black Chrysler Hemi with a GMC blower, running it on a 60-per-cent-plus load of nitro. Although the engine is detuned from its drag-racing specification, the team has worked a miracle in making it survive for 45 seconds without exploding while consuming 30 gallons of fuel on each pass. In 2010 Davidson set an A/BFR record of 301.150mph, making it the world's fastest

roadster and the only one to top 300mph.

Fame itself is not a prime motive for those involved. Outside the community of the Bonneville faithful they are little known. Even when Don Vesco, whose family's exceptional exploits have been covered in these pages, put the wheel-driven record almost out of sight, it passed without much comment. Which prompted Don to produce T-shirts with the legend 'Who the #$!% is Don Vesco?'

Fame certainly was not the object for Allen Strasburg, who built a Ford with nephew Bryant and raced it at Bonneville in 1962. Having caught salt fever, he passed it on to his sons Lindsay, Mike, Jeff and Tim. The Strasburg boys currently own and

run the Strasburg Automotive Machine shop, building engines and transmissions. All four have made it into the Bonneville 200mph club, which is no easy task. To

CLASS	CUBIC INCHES	LITRES
AA	501.00 and over	8.21 and over
A	440.00–500.99	7.21–8.19
B	373.00–439.99	6.11–7.19
C	306.00–372.99	5.01–6.10
D	261.00–305.99	4.27–5.00
E	184.00–260.99	3.01–4.26
F	123.00–183.99	2.01–3.00
G	93.00–122.99	1.51–2.00
H	62.00–92.99	1.01–1.50
I	46.00–61.99	0.76–1.00
J	31.00–45.99	0.51–0.75
K	30.99 or less	0.50 or less

CLASS	VEHICLE DESCRIPTION
BFS	Blown Fuel Streamliner
BFR	Blown Fuel Roadster
BFL	Blown Fuel Lakester
FS	Fuel Streamliner
FL	Fuel Lakester
GL	Gas Lakester
BGL	Blown Gas Lakester
BFMS	Blown Fuel Modified Sports

ORIGINAL HAMMOND LAKESTER 77

gain entry requires a two-way run over the measured mile and the setting of a class record in the process.

For the Strasburg brothers, this was no cure for their affliction. At present with Monty Wolfe, who supplied the car, they campaign in the lakester class. Currently they are inked into the three top records for AA, A & B in the BFL class with a top speed of 373.582mph. The Strasburgs' annual excursion to Bonneville involves the whole family, sometimes including four generations, to what they regard as a home from home.

Seth Hammond is the patriarch of another family that succumbed to the siren call of the salt. It all started in 1965 when Seth was invited to Speed Week, where he met people such as Burt Munro and became captivated by the whole idea. He set his first record in 1976 and in 1981 bought an old lakester built by Tim Rochlitzer that dated back to the early 1960s. The car was numbered 77 and its meticulous development over the next 30 years put more people in the 200mph club than any other. It also propelled his wife, Tanis, to 304.516mph in 2002. A year later Hammond survived a 300mph crash that destroyed the 77 lakester when it pencil-rolled half a dozen times. A lot of bruises and a vertebra fracture simply gave Hammond time during his recovery to conceptualise a better machine.

A modified roadster that used parts salvaged from the lakester set more records in the next few years. In the meantime, Hammond's son Channing taught himself to use 3D computer technology and designed the new car. Starting with a clean sheet, the chassis was made from chrome-moly tubing with a glass-fibre and carbon-fibre body, with thought given to making engine swaps easier. First appearing in 2007, the new 77 lakester ran V8 engines

NEW HAMMOND LAKESTER 77

in different classes and now holds the top three records in both FL and GL classes. It has powered Seth, wife Tanis, son Channing and daughter Tegan to records of over 300mph. With four family members in the 300mph club, another son, Colin, is awaiting his chance to make it a straight family flush.

Colin may have to bide his time because of his father's concerns over the condition of the salt. The problem is that the salt layer is often too thin and tyres that break through this layer to the dirt underneath can lose traction. At speeds of 300mph and above the tyres are spinning at four or five times the speed of those on a normal

5050 NEBULOUS THEOREM IV

car cruising along a highway. Thick layers of rubber cannot withstand the centrifugal forces inflicted at these speeds so the tyres used have just a few millimetres of rubber. Wheelspin will strip off this thin layer and eat through the corded skin underneath in seconds, creating a life-threatening situation. Waiting for suitable conditions is a big part of land speed racing and consequently efforts are being made to counteract the problem.

Jack Costella's bout of salt addiction, predicated on his mechanical creativity,

eventually became incurable. He contracted the condition in 1969 when he took three mini bikes to Bonneville and returned with two records. After lying dormant for many years, the affliction broke out again in 1989, by which time he had built the first of a series of innovative vehicles, *Nebulous Theorem I*. 'Nebulous theorem' translates as 'a vague hypothesis', which fits Costella's motto: 'Don't do what everyone else is doing'.

His experience with research and development in the glass-fibre industry helped to produce two-, three- and four-wheel vehicles that defied convention. The result was needle-shaped projectiles

that were long, low and light, with small-diameter solid front wheels to keep the nose off the ground. The engines used ranged from 50cc through to 1,000cc for motorcycle classes and anything from half a litre to seven litres for the four-wheel classes — more than 20 different displacements in all. Over the next 30 years Costella machines set over 100 records at Bonneville and the dry lakes in dozens of different classes. No one has achieved as many in the history of land speed racing.

The 5050 *Nebulous Theorem VI* is one example of a Costella creation. Its flat underbody is just half an inch off the ground and anyone who has nearly tripped over the knee-high machine must have

788 NEBULOUS THEOREM III

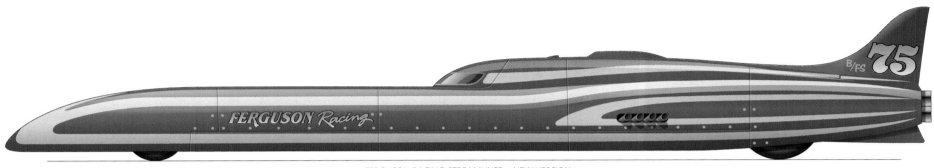

FERGUSON RACING STREAMLINER – NEW VERSION

wondered what it was. With just enough room for the driver to lie prone inside, it has set 13 records, including a top speed of 198.904mph with a 250cc engine.

At the other end of the scale is the very compact 788 *Nebulous Theorem III*, which has set 33 records in a career of more than 20 years. The most recent and fastest was 384.657mph in E/BGS running just a 4-litre engine, set in 2018.

In the modern digital world some view the activities of Costella and his peers as the hobby of yesterday's men clinging to outdated, fossil-fuel technology. The view of participants is quite different. They see land speed racing as pushing the boundaries of ingenuity and innovation by making ancient engines go faster than

modern supercars, often using alcohol, which is a cleaner fuel than petrol. There is no reason why Costella's vehicles cannot be regarded as artistic creations with three-dimensional moving parts working in time and space and closely aligned with human endeavour. Beauty, in any case, does not have to be visual. We can appreciate the

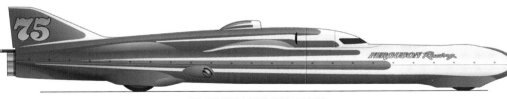

FERGUSON RACING STREAMLINER

beauty of maths, physics and chemistry combining to do something special just as we can a baseball pitcher or bowler in

cricket delivering a beautiful ball.

For some perspective, compare Jeff Koons's 3ft tall, inanimate stainless steel sculpture, based on an inflatable balloon rabbit, which sold at auction for $91.1 million in 2019, to a record car whose cost to build in human and financial resources brought no guarantee of any return. The vast sum of money paid for Koons's creation is enough to stock a whole museum with historic land speed cars.

Yet this could only happen in a country embracing freedom of opinion and activity.

Another family to embrace that freedom are the Fergusons and what better way to keep the name in the record books than having a son and grandson called Don and a second grandson named Randy Ferguson to keep the pressure on. Don Ferguson Senior grew up and set records in the hot rod era. His salt fever and mechanical ability flowed down the family tree. The 'family' streamliner, similar in design to the Vesco *Little Giant* and specialising in vintage flatheads and six-cylinder engines, put Don Ferguson Junior, Don Ferguson III and Randy Ferguson into the record books and the 200mph club. Forever aiming at higher speeds, a new streamliner was built. Going up the scale in engine size to a 7-litre V8, Don Junior's B/FS ran 349.939mph in 2016. The name Ferguson currently appears 13 times in the Bonneville records.

The racing continuum of families such as the Vescos, Strasburgs, Hammonds and Fergusons has helped to inject younger blood into an activity that at present has an average age of 55. Dave Spangler drove *Turbinator II* to a record at the age of 76; Jack Costella gave up driving at 75 but continues to build cars into his 80s;

George Poteet, Danny Thompson and Charlie Nearburg, the fastest men in the world in wheel-driven cars, are all senior citizens. As concerns also grow about the condition of the salt at Bonneville, there is the possibility that the era of land speed racing will slowly disappear.

Robert Dalton's decades-long passion eventually led to gunning his engine in pursuit of Poteet's *Speed Demon* record in A/BFS. A glance at *Flashpoint* shows that Dalton's approach to the problem is very different and, again, that technology does not follow a predetermined course. Apart from a few exceptions, such as the Strasburg lakester, aerofoils were

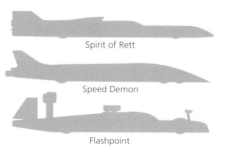

Spirit of Rett

Speed Demon

Flashpoint

largely avoided in the past because of the considerable obstruction they cause to the airflow at high speed. Dalton's approach was to forego the finer points of streamlining and opt for brute force in the style of the Davidson Roadster. He added aerofoils to prevent the nose from lifting and to exert massive downforce on the rear

wheels to prevent destructive wheelspin. His brute force came from a detuned drag-racing supercharged Hemi running on nitro. The visual result was very different from the sleek profiles of single-engine cars such as *Spirit of Rett* and *Speed Demon*.

Using this combination in 2018, Dalton laid down a pass of 436mph with an exit speed of 451mph, which put him in serious contention for a record. However, on the second run his luck ran out. A rear tyre exploded, sending the machine spinning and then into a series of pencil rolls, spreading debris over a mile of track. Miraculously, Dalton emerged from the wreckage completely unhurt and the

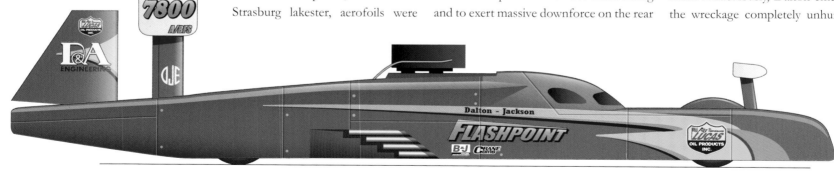

7800 FLASHPOINT STREAMLINER

consensus is that rather than be deterred he will regard the integrity of the roll cage and safety equipment as an inducement to keep going.

This next example is enough to stretch the bounds of credibility even for Bonneville aficionados. Keith Copeland's first visit to the salt was in 2006 with a modified Bocar, a small glass-fibre sports car dating from around 1960. In 2008 he flipped the car at high speed and suffered eye damage that required surgery and an 18-month convalescence. Like so many, the shadow of injury or death did not cool his ambitions. Learning from the experience, he resolved to continue running

in the Blown Fuel Modified Sports class and began construction of a new car. The rules for BFMS require that the vehicle is

1971 TRIUMPH GT6

based on a production two-seater sports car. Regulations also allow a roof chop, bodywork modifications from the firewall forward, an extended wheelbase and either front- or rear-wheel drive, but no wings. Supercharged engines can be anything from AA through to H in size. Copeland's

choice of car was the British-made 1971 Triumph GT6, an affordable poor cousin to Jaguar's E-type. Its 0–60mph time of 12 seconds is unimpressive compared with the E-type and even the Jaguar could not live with muscle cars of the period such as the Dodge Charger. Copeland gave his GT6 a 5in roof chop, extended the wheelbase to 130in, fitted a 6-litre Chevy small-block and installed front-wheel drive, which was almost unheard of at Bonneville.

Under the Black Salt Racing banner, the car made an immediate impact in 2011 and by 2012 Copeland had set a record of 364.051mph

with an exit speed of 380mph. Although it did not conform to what cars are supposed to look like, it represented a classic case of form following function. The little swan turned into an ugly duckling and did go to the ball. The stock rear bodywork is 57in wide, more than double most streamliners, and with front-wheel drive it may create a new avenue for land speed cars.

When Teddy Tetzlaff thundered across Bonneville in his *Blitzen Benz* over a century ago he was probably unaware that the salt was three or four feet thick. Today it is measured in inches. The racing community has raised concerns for over 30 years that nearby potash mining and climate conditions have been eroding the salt. So far action to have the situation remedied has had little effect. But now the State of Utah has agreed $5 million in funds with a further $45 million contribution from the government. At last serious efforts are under way to save this historic site of human endeavour.

BLACK SALT RACING GT6

THE LAST FRONTIER

Andy Green's immense achievement in 1997 of breaking the sound barrier and exceeding the land speed record by such a large margin might have persuaded all-comers that the quest had run its course. Yet in the years since three more cars have been under construction. The epoch-making speed of sound is now transcended by the ambition to travel at 1,000mph, over 200mph faster.

Ed Shadle's initiation at Bonneville in 1991 led to a record in a lakester and entry to the 200mph club. In 1998 he became fixated with the absolute record. With Keith Zanghi the idea was born to adapt a jet fighter, rather than start from scratch. A search unearthed an F-104A Starfighter in a sorry state at a scrap yard. It was rescued

and work commenced on giving it a second life. In its first incarnation it turned out that it had had a rich history as a chase plane flown by a number of notable test pilots at Edwards Air Base. On the premise that the supersonic plane had undergone extensive testing and had proved itself in flight, the wings were removed, panels repaired, wheels engineered and a J79 turbojet fitted. The aim was to go supersonic and beyond even though by the time the project neared completion the airframe and engine technology were almost 60 years old. This was a very different proposition from *Thrust SSC*, which had been designed and engineered from a clean sheet.

In running condition the car weighed 6.5 tons with 19,000lbf of thrust. This

was more weight and less power than Breedlove's *Sonic Arrow*, which had run at 676mph by the time he terminated the project, and *Thrust SSC*, although heavier and wider, had a better power-to-weight ratio with its twin engines. Common sense dictated that the original estimates should be revised down to 800mph and the initial aim should be the women's outright record of 512.710mph held by Kitty O'Neil.

Shadle had already made a single run at 515mph and Jessi Combs was recruited to take the controls. In 2013 Combs reached 398mph to break Lee Breedlove's long-standing record, making her the fastest woman on four wheels. Three years later she hit 479mph on a one-way pass.

The project had been going for 17

years when Shadle died in 2018. The under-funded, 50-strong team of part-timers resolved to continue but with their ambitions trimmed back from shooting for the absolute record. Over the years dozens of engine tests and test runs had been

SPECIFICATIONS

Vehicle	North American Eagle
Origin	America
Weight	14,500lb (6,577kg)
Length	672in (17.07m)
Powerplant	General Electric J79
Thrust	19,000lbf
Thrust/weight ratio	1.3/1

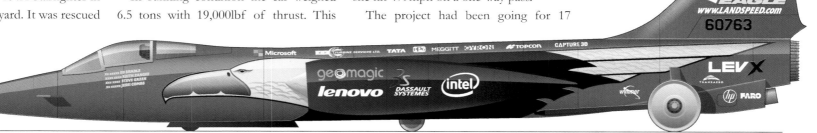

NORTH AMERICAN EAGLE

carried out with no dramatic increase in speed. So, for the moment, a further tilt at the women's record would be their aim. It ended in tragedy. On 27 August 2019, Combs powered the North American Eagle across the Alvord Desert in Oregon at over 500mph. On another run, as Combs was approaching 550mph, her vehicle's front-wheel assembly collapsed, causing a violent crash. Combs died in the impact and the wreckage was engulfed in flames. The Eagle's decades-long quest was over.

A six-year-old Richard Noble caught the bug when he saw John Cobb testing his jet-powered boat *Crusader* at Loch Ness. Noble, who was born in Edinburgh and went to Winchester College, grew up to steer *Thrust 2* to success and then mastermind breaking the sound barrier with *Thrust SSC*. The British had owned the record since 1983 and Noble was unlikely to settle for a life more ordinary. Andy Green had driven *Thrust SSC* to the ragged edge and had since taken the diesel record. Both men

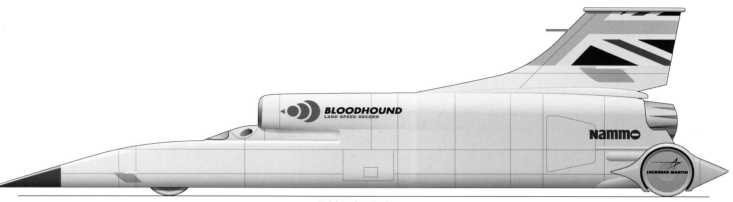

BLOODHOUND LSR

were still entranced by the spell of speed, so it was hardly surprising that they seized the chance when in 2008 the team behind a new project, *Bloodhound SSC*, came calling. The team, which included Ben Evans, Mark Chapman and Ron Ayers, stated their objective: a speed of 1,000mph, a magical figure that helped attract sponsorship.

To achieve their ambition, the four-wheel car was designed with a narrower profile than *Thrust SSC* and equipped with a single EJ200 jet engine, as used in the Eurofighter. It delivered 20,232lbf of thrust. Ayers knew that this alone would not be enough, which is why he integrated a Nammo hybrid rocket motor into the specification. The rocket, using hydrogen peroxide with polybutadiene as

a secondary fuel, would generate a further 27,820lbf. The intention was that this would boost the car to the projected speed after the jet engine had got it up to 500mph or more. The team scrapped plans to run at Black Rock Desert in Nevada because the site was no longer viable and decided on Hakskeenpan in the Kalahari Desert in South Africa, even though that track, at 12 miles, is shorter.

After ten years of development with an investment running into tens of millions *Bloodhound SSC* ran out of money and went into administration. Needing another £25 million to complete the task, it seemed at a dead end. Which it was until Ian Warhurst, a businessman from Barnsley in Yorkshire, stepped forward. Noble

was initially retained as a director and the project, renamed *Bloodhound LSR*, was now back on track with a planned first test run at Hakskeenpan.

Testing would show whether the car would behave as predicted by CFD and accelerate quickly enough on the shorter track. The budget for reaching 1,000mph, compared with a relatively modest

SPECIFICATIONS

Vehicle	Bloodhound LSR
Origin	Britain
Weight	14,158lb (6,422kg)
Length	504in (12.80m)
Powerplant	Eurojet EJ200
Auxiliary power	Rocket motors
Thrust	48,000lbf in total
Thrust/weight ratio	3.4/1

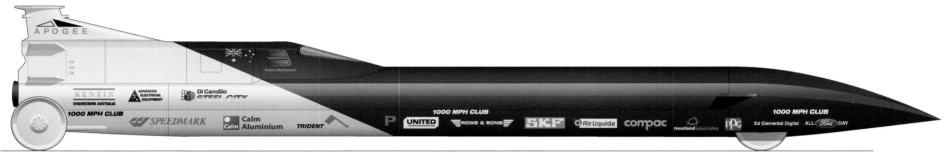

£2.8 million for *Thrust SSC*, had risen exponentially. Problems, too, had grown. Things that are less troublesome at lower speeds — such as small debris on the track, aerodynamic inconsistencies and gusts of wind — become dramatically pronounced in the supersonic zone.

In October 2019 the whole operation moved to the Hakskeenpan for testing. Over a period of four weeks the car made several runs using only the jet engine,

SPECIFICATIONS

Vehicle	Aussie Invader III
Origin	Australia
Weight	20,600lb (9,344kg) loaded
Fuel load	6,272lb (2,845kg)
Length	624in (15.85m)
Powerplant	Rocket motor
Thrust	62,000lbf
Thrust/weight ratio	3/1

increasing the speed each time. The last run reached a maximum of 638mph. The team then returned to the UK to develop the additional rocket engine and raise the necessary funding to make a serious attempt on the record a year later.

The challenge from Australia is the brainchild of Rosco McGlashan. His CV includes drag-racing bikes and jet cars plus two previous attempts at the land speed record. His inspiration came at the age of 12 from watching Donald Campbell set his hard-won record on Lake Eyre in South Australia in 1964.

McGlashan's first attempt in 1995 with *Aussie Invader II*, built on the *Thrust 2* model, ended with the car going off course and being damaged beyond repair. Rosco returned with an improved version in 1997 to make a run of 638mph but was unable

to back it up due to poor conditions. Shortly after that Andy Green put the record out of reach — immediate reach, anyway — with *Thrust SSC*. With the bar raised yet again, McGlashan spent ten years considering designs with much more power. By 2009 his ideas had crystallised and construction work began on *Aussie Invader 5R*. The planned propulsion system is simplicity itself. It consists of a large rocket motor fuelled by white-fuming

nitric acid and turpentine, delivered by pressurised nitrogen, all of which instantly ignites when mixed to create 62,000lbf of thrust. Apart from valves, there are no moving parts. The car's innovative structure features a chassis on the outside like an exoskeleton, comprising a steel tube of 36in diameter and 10mm thickness. This was given a V-shaped underbody to deflect shock waves. The finished look resembles an enlarged version of the 50-year-old *Blue*

AUSSIE INVADER III

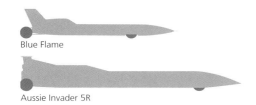

Blue Flame

Aussie Invader 5R

Flame but the new machine produces three times as much power. Significantly, though, it is three times the weight, has a bigger frontal area, more skin friction and a lot

the *Budweiser Rocket* has also obscured the creative engineering skills of Bill Fredrick. Both *Bloodhound* and *Aussie Invader* use the solid alloy wheels pioneered by Fredrick. Other concepts include the use of polybutadiene rings as a secondary fuel, an auxiliary rocket motor to provide boost, and a V-shaped underbody. Fredrick also understood only too well the need to

obvious in the comparison between *Turbinator II*, which produces 5,000hp to reach 500mph, and *Thrust SSC*, which had the equivalent of 100,000hp. So to go 50 per cent faster requires 20 times more power. This explains why streamliners at Bonneville, which have minimal frontal area, have made only small increases in speed over long periods and other factors

this page may provide an interesting study in power-to-weight ratios and frontal areas from a theoretical point of view. Bigger is not always better. Leaving abstract calculations aside, the two current teams also face daunting practical problems. The *Bloodhound LSR* team needs huge sums of money to continue and is handicapped by the shorter track at Hakskeenpan, which leaves less room to accelerate and, just as important, to slow down. *Aussie Invader 5R* has less of a problem as its power comes on instantly but is sustained for a shorter period. In both cases the teams need perfect conditions.

THRUST/WEIGHT RATIO AND FRONTAL AREA COMPARISON

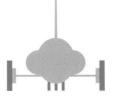

Blue Flame 2.5/1   Budweiser 4/1   Thrust SSC 2.1/1   North American Eagle 1.3/1   Bloodhound 3.4/1   Aussie Invader 3/1

more rolling resistance. Serious testing has yet to take place. Whether *Bloodhound* or *Aussie Invader* can reach their goals remains to be seen.

These cars may seem to be at the cutting edge of 21st-century technology but the cloud of controversy surrounding

reduce frontal area to a minimum and the dramatic escalation of power required to increase speed.

When entering the transonic zone, with all other things equal, a ten per cent increase in speed requires as much as a 100 per cent increase in power. This becomes

such as traction and track condition have become critical. When talk turns to 1,000mph the mind boggles at the amount of power necessary. Even McGlashan's optimistic estimate of 200,000hp is not as much as it might seem.

A look at the comparison diagram on

Now and for the future the odds are stacked ever higher against the protagonists. Sheer cost is an obstacle that *Bloodhound* found almost insurmountable. The participants are above the average age for this activity. At the time of writing Andy Green is 58 and Rosco McGlashan is 70. As for finding a suitable place to fulfil their ambitions, perhaps the Earth is no longer big enough.

THE SOURCE OF POWER

The path from Count Gaston de Chasseloup-Laubat to the sound barrier did not, from the very beginning, follow a predictable course.

Even at the early stage the approach varied as the emerging internal combustion engine overtook electric motors and Léon Serpollet's flash-tube boiler system. Walter C. Baker's advanced streamlining ideas withered as automobile companies took up the challenge with production engines that were modified for the popular vogue of road racing. The era of the piston engine established itself. The power units of that period were low revving and their poor volumetric efficiency produced only about 10hp per litre, so they had to be of a large displacement by today's standards in order to produce any significant power. Anything from 10 to more than 20 litres was not unusual.

Because the cost of designing and developing an engine was so high, it was rare for automobile companies to produce a one-off specifically for record breaking. The exceptions were the purpose-built 25.4-litre Darracq V8 and the 28.35-litre Fiat S76, the largest automobile engine ever made. Yet, with output per litre stalling at about 10hp, even this was not enough and the search for more powerful engines began. Anomalies in this period were the complex opposing-piston design of the Gobron-Brillié and the dramatic return of steam power with the streamlined *Stanley Steamer*. Neither, though, changed the adopted paradigm.

Looking for ever more output, the participants turned to aero engines. The advent of flight gave manufacturers the incentive to invest in such engines. Ralph DePalma was the first to set a record with a V12 Packard. There followed a whole series of aero-engine cars, not always affiliated to motor companies, using whatever was available. Sunbeam, Delage, Fiat, Liberty, Napier and Rolls-Royce all found their aviation engines mounted in land speed cars. These engines were improved over the years to provide up to 60hp per litre or more (see Fig. 1). The well-designed Napier Lion proved to be the most successful

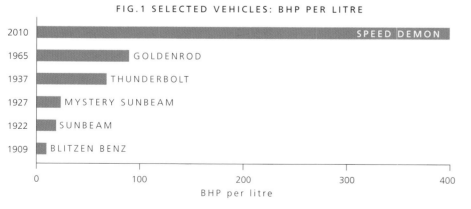

FIG.1 SELECTED VEHICLES: BHP PER LITRE

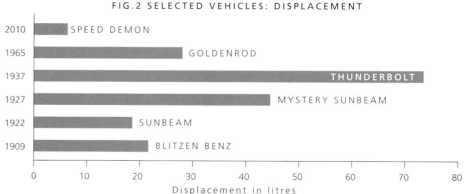

FIG.2 SELECTED VEHICLES: DISPLACEMENT

with its cylinders arranged in three banks of four and this engine powered five different cars to success. By the time John Cobb drove it to its last record, the original design was 30 years old. To do this, Reid Railton had mounted two Lions displacing a total of 47.8 litres and producing 3,000hp to drive all four wheels. George Eyston's *Thunderbolt*, using Rolls-Royce engines, was even bigger at 73.4 litres and a total of 5,000hp (see Fig. 2).

There were more anomalies during the age of these leviathans, demonstrated first by Tommy Milton's *Double Duesy*. This used two eight-cylinder engines of only 4.86 litres each that reached 3,800rpm, which was higher than bigger opponents. Then came Sunbeam's *Ladybird*, which was propelled by the smallest-displacement engine to set the land speed record. Its 12-cylinder, 3,976cc supercharged engine spun even higher to 5,300rpm. Last came the ill-fated Frank Lockhart. He engineered two supercharged straight-eight engines side by side for a total of only 3 litres and these could be pushed to 8,000rpm and a stunning 128hp per litre. These examples were the forerunners of post-war thinking: smaller, supercharged, high-revving power units combined with smaller, more efficient body shapes.

The Napier Lion ruled the piston-engine record for 19 years until the Summers brothers appeared with *Goldenrod* and a different way of doing it. By placing their four engines in line, the brothers created a much more efficient shape that needed less brute force (see Fig. 3). As with most protagonists, the choice of powerplant had to come from what was available. In their case it was the Chrysler Hemi, which was introduced in 1951. With four of these on loan from Chrysler, the British stranglehold on the wheel-driven record was broken and when Danny Thompson pushed the record to 448.757mph in 2018 using only two Hemis the engine design was 67 years old.

Master craftsmen such as Keith Black undertook the development of this engine. He started with drag boats and understood the need to prevent potentially disastrous

FIG.3 SELECTED VEHICLES: POWER OUTPUT

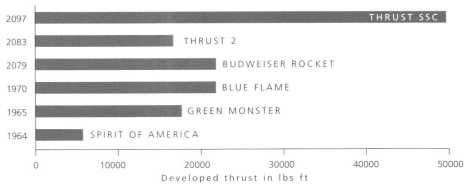

engine seizures. To do this he blueprinted the engines. This meant taking the engine apart, checking that all the machined tolerances were exactly the same, making all the matched components — such as connecting rods and pistons — the same weight and balancing rotating parts. The result was a much more reliable engine and the release of 20 or so hidden horsepower. Drag racers soon became aware of this and Black found himself much in demand.

Over the years everything was improved and replaced to include purpose-built engine blocks so that today a Hemi can be built without using any original parts. According to the 'Ship of Theseus' principle, this posed the question: is it still a Hemi? Ultimately it is not what it is made of that defines the Hemi but a series of measurements. The Chevy small-block, introduced in 1955, has been subjected to the same process and still powers the turbocharged *Speed Demon*, among many other cars.

Blueprinting had improved mechanical efficiency. And supercharging, high-lift cams and larger valves had increased volumetric efficiency. Next in the search for ever more power, the hot rodders turned to chemistry.

Alcohol was well known as a fuel but then they discovered nitromethane, which had been used experimentally in aircraft. They learned the right way to use it the hard way, routinely exploding engines, sometimes with dire consequences. It proved to be safer to use super-rich mixtures of nitro rather than too little of it and run dangerously lean. Eventually figures of 1,000hp per litre were attained as compared to the *Blitzen Benz* output of around 10hp per litre. The price for this is a phenomenal rate of fuel consumption in terms of gallons per second. Nitrous oxide was also used in the Second World War in aircraft experiments. Hot rodders rediscovered it in the late 1950s and Charlie Nearburg successfully adopted

Keith Black

it for his non-supercharged *Spirit of Rett* record breaker. It is clear that the current record holders are all using old technology and this is particularly the case in the lower classes, where 90-year-old engines are still achieving astonishing speeds. Modern multi-cylinder, double-overhead-camshaft, multi-valve engines do not have much of a presence.

While Mickey Thompson's *Challenger 2* put 5,000hp through four wheels, *Speed Demon* has gone as fast as that with one engine and just rear-wheel drive. This and the fact that the record has increased by only 50mph in 70 years shows that other things besides sheer power have become the limiting factors.

Although it is possible to mount four blown, nitro Hemis on a chassis to create a 16,000hp car, the problems of tyres, traction, weight, size, time and expense virtually rule out the notion.

Don Vesco's choice of gas-turbine engine, the Avco Lycoming T55, was designed in the 1950s. It was an upgraded version of this unit that powered Dave Spangler past 500mph in 2018. The turbine was by then more than 60 years from the drawing board.

When jets appeared on the salt in the 1960s, Breedlove used a General Electric J47 turbojet that was 15 years old in design terms. The J79 used by Breedlove and Arfons was over a decade old and in 1983 Richard Noble's Avon 302 was a 37-year-old concept. Andy Green's Rolls-Royce Spey engines had been around for over 30 years and *Bloodhound*'s Eurojet EJ200 was also designed a generation previously.

When *Thrust SSC* improved on *Blue Flame*'s record by 20 per cent, it took more than double the power to do it (see Fig. 4). The exponential power increase needed to go ever faster (see Figs. 5 & 6) suggests that to reach speeds approaching 1,000mph would need more than double the power of *Thrust SSC*. The only jets capable of 100,000lbf or more are the

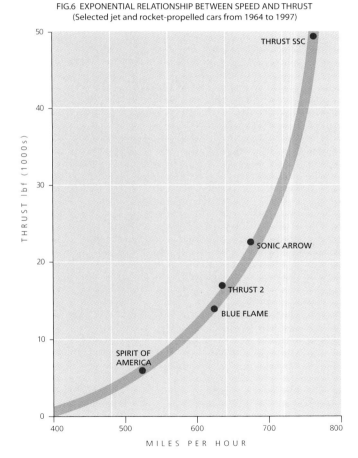

FIG.5 EXPONENTIAL RELATIONSHIP BETWEEN SPEED AND HORSEPOWER
(Selected open-wheel cars with rear-wheel drive from 1902 to 1935)

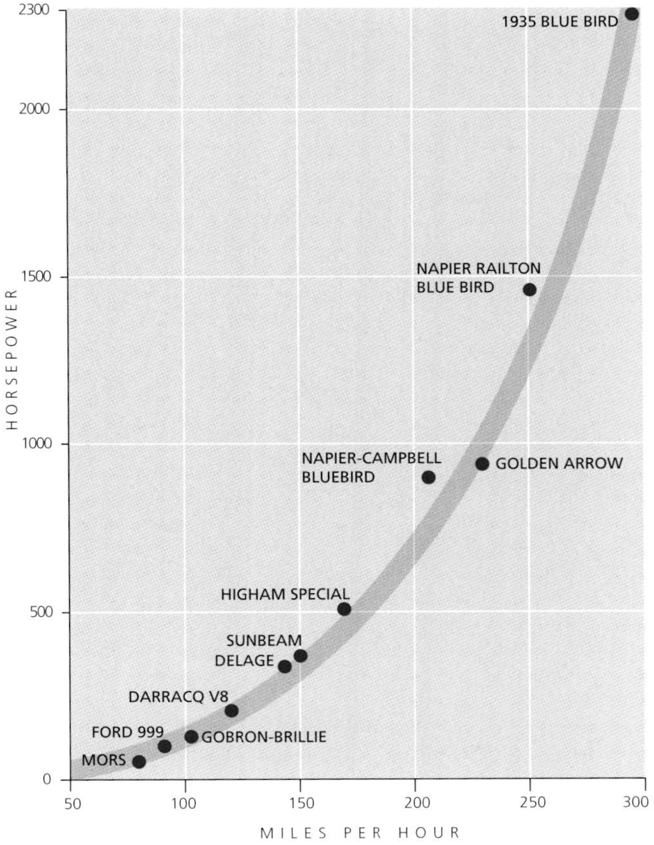

HORSEPOWER

2300
2000
1500
1000
500
0

1935 BLUE BIRD

NAPIER RAILTON
BLUE BIRD

NAPIER-CAMPBELL
BLUEBIRD   GOLDEN ARROW

HIGHAM SPECIAL

SUNBEAM
DELAGE

DARRACQ V8

FORD 999   GOBRON-BRILLIE
MORS

50   300
MILES PER HOUR

FIG.6 EXPONENTIAL RELATIONSHIP BETWEEN SPEED AND THRUST
(Selected jet and rocket-propelled cars from 1964 to 1997)

THRUST lbf (1000s)

50
40
30
20
10
0

THRUST SSC

SONIC ARROW

THRUST 2

BLUE FLAME

SPIRIT OF
AMERICA

400   500   600   700   800
MILES PER HOUR

turbofan engines found on modern long-haul aircraft with a typical diameter of 10ft and weight of eight tons — a seemingly self-defeating proposition.

Rockets introduced new chemistry to conjure with in the form of high-test hydrogen peroxide (up to 98 per cent pure) and using liquid gas or polybutadiene as secondary fuels. Their dramatic performance was short-lived, partly because high-test hydrogen peroxide became hard to source. However, the same power principles apply to rockets. With all things being equal, it would appear that *Aussie Invader* will need at least 82,000lbf of thrust to reach 1,000mph.

Yet, time and again, inventive minds have overcome things that were thought to be impossible. But all things come to pass. Supersonic passenger planes and moon landings have come and gone.

As current contenders look to the far horizon, there is a feeling that we may be witnessing the last frontier in the epic quest for speed.

175

ALL APPLICANTS WELCOME

This particular club has no imposing building, no impressive entrance where a plaque could be affixed. It does not discriminate against age, gender, class or ethnicity. Of the seven and a half billion people on earth, anyone can take part providing they show a proficiency to drive. And of the two billion or so motor vehicles ever built, any one of them could take part in speed trials as long as it meets safety regulations. The objective is simple: to drive a specific class of vehicle faster than anyone has done before. Membership is the possession of a slip of paper that looks like a grocery receipt but is inscribed with a verified record time.

In the field of human endeavour there have been many historic milestones. Since the first men reached the North and South Poles, thousands have made these trips. Five thousand people, most with the benefit of guides, have climbed Mount Everest. The International Space Station has welcomed over 239 visitors and there have been 12 astronauts to have walked on the surface of the moon, all thanks to the efforts of tens of thousands of people and billions in government funding. In this history of the quest for speed only 16 people have made it into the Bonneville 400mph chapter and only eight are known to have exceeded 600mph driving a wheeled vehicle on the Earth's surface.

If land speed racing is regarded as a form of sport, it is different from most others in that there is an ever-present risk of serious injury or death. Over the past 100 years some 'greats' have survived, such as Malcolm Campbell, Art Arfons and Craig Breedlove. Others such as Frank Lockhart, Lee Bible and Athol Graham did not. Even comparatively moderate speeds of 200mph at Bonneville are over double what any normal person would ever experience in a car and mechanical or tyre failure at this level is life-threatening.

The participants have come from all walks of life: moneyed counts and barons, barnstormers, multi-millionaires, novices with no previous experience, entrepreneurs, racing drivers, stunt people, jet pilots, regular working men, college students and hot rodders. The common denominator has been an obsession with speed. Some involved visionaries, brilliant designers and qualified engineers; others were backyard virtuosos. Craig Breedlove built *Spirit of America* in a garage. Some had vast budgets; others ran shoestring operations with secondhand tyres, scrapyard parts and borrowed engines. But all wrote their names and the names of the cars they drove into the record books to become members of this conceptual club. Motivation varied a great deal. Ray Keech did it for the money; Craig Breedlove gambled everything.

Within the saga there are unique achievements that are hard to match. Aviation pioneer Glenn Curtiss is the only man to have held the absolute record with a motorcycle. Malcolm Campbell broke the record nine times. And when his son, Donald Campbell, persevered his way to success in Australia the Campbells became the only father and son to hold the absolute wheel-driven record. Taking perseverance to extreme lengths, Burt Munro spent over 30 years, and took to working on his motorcycle full-time, before reaching his promised land — a record at Bonneville. Half brothers Art and Walt Arfons competed with each other and both held the absolute record with jet-propelled vehicles. Craig and Lee Breedlove are the only husband and wife to have held the absolute record for men and women.

Danny Thompson fulfilled his father's ambition in 2018 with the same car that Mickey Thompson had built 50 years previously. In other classes there are families such as the Vescos, Strasburgs, Hammonds and Fergusons who can boast wives, sons, daughters and even grandchildren in the record books.

The age span starts with Karlee Cobb who, at the age of 14, qualified for a South Dakota driving licence and promptly set a motorcycle record of 110mph in 2008, adding to the records her mother and sister had already set. At the upper end of the scale 76-year-old Dave Spangler drove *Turbinator 2* to a spectacular result in 2018.

In this rarefied atmosphere there are even more exclusive members. Don Vesco is the only person to have held both the

```
   BONNEVILLE NATIONALS INC.
        2108 SpeedWeek
  LONG COURSE 1 *RECORD* RU
  Vehicle #        Class
        492         AA/FS
  Date-12-18       Time
  08-12-18         07:49
  Location         Speed
  Mile 2           326.062mph
  2-1/4            372.675mph
  Mile 3           391.174mph
  Mile 4           428.592mph
  Exit Speed       459.588mph
  Mile 5           450.909mph

  Wind:7mph from the N
  TEMP: 75.2F    HUMID: 24%
  SP:25.74in     DA: 6382ft
```

Facsimile of the Danny Thompson 'grocery' receipt that backed up a previous run to validate an average speed of 448.757mph for *Challenger 2*, making it the fastest piston-powered car on the planet.

motorcycle and wheel-driven car records. Gary Gabelich is the only person to have broken the absolute record with a rocket-powered vehicle. Kitty O'Neil is the only woman to have exceeded 600mph. Dave Spangler is the only person to have travelled at 500mph in a wheel-driven car. And at the top of the pyramid is Andy Green, the only person to have officially broken the sound barrier.

Many of these achievements are not likely to be equalled in a pursuit whose costs, dangers and complexities are unique. The average age for those actively involved is over 50. Significantly the drivers who hold some of the highest records, such as Dave Spangler, Danny Thompson, George Poteet and Charlie Nearburg, are all senior citizens. Of the 16 members in the 400mph chapter, all but three are either no longer with us or retired from the sport. Most of them had their origins in the hot rod era, which is now part of automotive history. Today few people fix or modify their own cars. There are too many other

distractions for younger people and the likelihood of enough of them spending decades building up experience with nitro-burning monster V8 engines seems slim.

Those racers still active will continue to face the difficulties of adverse track surfaces and climate conditions. If the salt flats in Utah are not suitably reclaimed, the only recourse is places like the salt pan at Salar de Uyuni in Bolivia. And the expense of transport and accommodation would rule out most of the Bonneville faithful.

When the current generation passes, it will take with it a vast amount of accumulated knowledge and experience. It will leave some protégés and competition in the smaller classes will continue. But as far as the big stage is concerned, the feeling is that limits are close to being reached and the number of new members of the club will diminish.

The absolute title is at present British property and has been for 37 years. First reclaimed by Richard Noble and consolidated by Andy Green, it has not

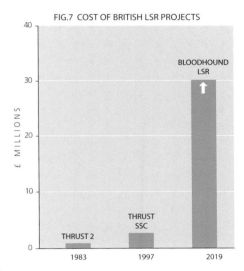

been cheap. The *Thrust 2* budget was £1 million, *Thrust SSC* cost £2.8 million and *Bloodhound LSR* is running at about £30 million so far — and remains some way from making a serious run (see Fig. 7). It is clear that costs have become exponential, even taking inflation into account. This is a high price to pay for a slip of paper. Perhaps the reason for doing it is gradually fading away.

ACCREDITED SPEED RECORDS

From the electric Jeantaud horseless carriage and hand-held stopwatches to the massive twin-jet engines of *Thrust SSC*, electronic timing systems, accurate to a thousandth of a second, and the sound barrier, this graphic encapsulates 120 years of the epic saga of the quest for speed.

It illustrates the close contest of the earlier years followed by the age of the aero-engine leviathans and continues to the quantum leaps of the fire-breathing jets and rockets.

Camille Jenatzy's phrase 'The never satisfied' encapsulates the constant progress over these 120 years, from Walter C. Baker's perilous *Electric Torpedo* to the present day, always fraught with danger.

The introduction of gas turbines and diesel-powered cars is depicted along with the return of modern electric and steam power.

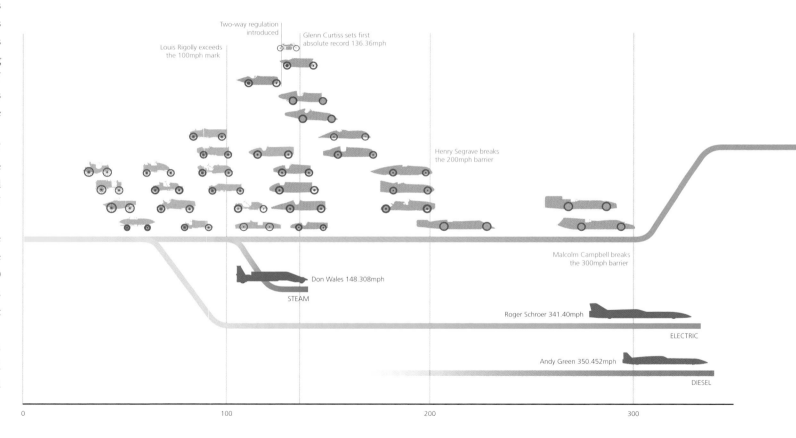

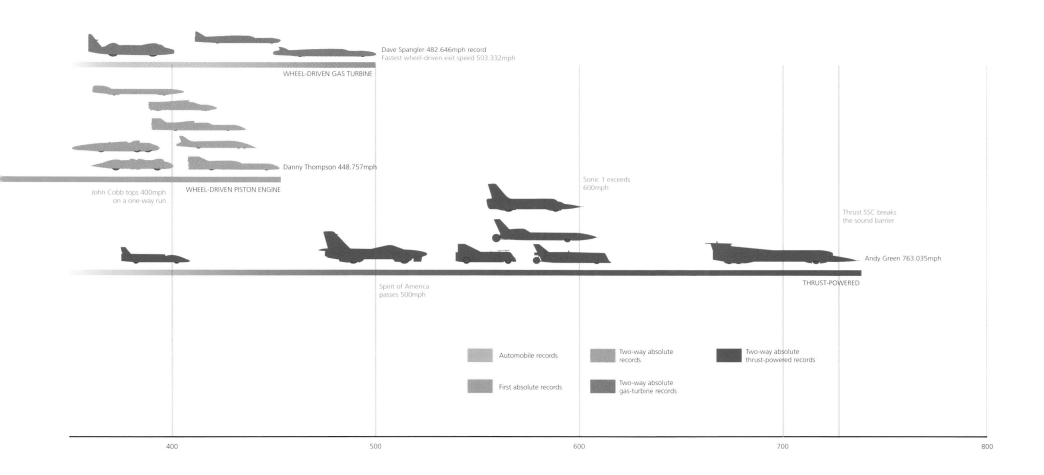

Dave Spangler 482.646mph record
Fastest wheel-driven exit speed 503.332mph

WHEEL-DRIVEN GAS TURBINE

Danny Thompson 448.757mph

John Cobb tops 400mph
on a one-way run

WHEEL-DRIVEN PISTON ENGINE

Sonic 1 exceeds
600mph

Thrust SSC breaks
the sound barrier

Andy Green 763.035mph

Spirit of America
passes 500mph

THRUST-POWERED

Automobile records

First absolute records

Two-way absolute
records

Two-way absolute
gas-turbine records

Two-way absolute
thrust-powered records

400   500   600   700   800

GLOSSARY–ABBREVIATIONS

DC	Direct current	OBE	Order of the British Empire	LNG	Liquefied natural gas
AAA	American Automobile Association	SCTA	Southern California Timing Association	CV	Curriculum Vitae
ACF	Automobile Club de France	GMC	General Motors Company	SSC	Supersonic car
AEG	Allgemeine Elektricitäts-Gesellschaft	MG	Morris Garages	AMC	American Motors Corporation
RPM	Revolutions per minute	SCORE	Southern California Off Road Enthusiasts	CFD	Computational fluid dynamics
BTU	British thermal unit	MT	Mickey Thompson	LSRV	Land speed record vehicle
BHP	Brake horsepower	NHRA	National Hot Rod Association	JCB	Joseph Cyril Bamford
HP	Horsepower	AMA	American Motorcyclist Association	RAF	Royal Air Force
MPH	Miles per hour	BP	British Petroleum	NASA	National Aeronautics and Space Administration
AIACR	Association Internationale des Automobile Clubs Reconnus	FIA	Fédération Internationale de l'Automobile	NACA	National Advisory Committee for Aeronautics
TDC	Top dead centre	FIM	Fédération Internationale de Motocyclisme	LPG	Liquid petroleum gas
RAC	Royal Automobile Club				
IMCA	International Motor Contest Association	JATO	Jet assisted take-off	DRCE	Drag race competition engine
KLG	Kenelm Lee Guinness (spark plugs)	AGA	American Gas Association	CAR	Ohio State University Center for Automotive Research
MC	Military Cross	IGT	Institute of Gas Technology		

SCTA CLASS DESIGNATIONS

E	Electric vehicle	GR	Gas roadster	BMMP	Blown modified mid-mini pick-up
T	Turbine vehicle	BSTR	Blown street roadster	MMP	Unblown modified mid-mini pick-up
BFS	Blown fuel streamliner	AIR	American iron roadster	CBFALT	Classic blown fuel altered coupe
FS	Fuel streamliner	STR	Street roadster	CFALT	Classic fuel altered coupe
BGS	Blown fuel streamliner	BVFCC	Blown vintage fuel competition coupe	CBGALT	Classic blown gas altered coupe
GS	Unblown gas streamliner	BVFALT	Blown vintage fuel altered coupe	CGALT	Classic gas altered coupe
DS	Diesel streamliner	BFCC	Blown fuel competition coupe & sedan	CBGC	Classic blown gas coupe
BFL	Blown fuel lakester	FCC	Fuel competition coupe & sedan	CGC	Classic unblown gas coupe
FL	Fuel lakester	BGCC	Blown gas competition coupe & sedan	CPRO	Classic production coupe & sedan
BGL	Blown gas lakester	GCC	Gas competition coupe & sedan	CPS	Classic production supercharged
GL	Gas lakester	BFALT	Blown fuel altered coupe		coupe & sedan
BFMR	Blown fuel modified roadster	FALT	Fuel altered coupe	PRO	Production coupe & sedan
FMR	Fuel modified roadster	BGALT	Blown gas altered coupe	PS	Production supercharged
BGMR	Blown gas modified roadster	GALT	Gas altered coupe	BGT	Blown grand touring sports
GMR	Gas modified roadster	BGC	Blown gas coupe	GT	Unblown grand touring sports
BFRMR	Blown fuel rear-engine modified roadster	GC	Unblown gas coupe	PP	Production pick-up
FRMR	Fuel rear-engine modified roadster	BFMS	Blown fuel modified sports	PMP	Production mid-mini pick-up
BGRMR	Blown gas rear-engine modified roadster	FMS	Fuel modified sports	DT	Diesel truck
GRMR	Gas rear-engine modified roadster	BGMS	Blown gas modified sports	MDT	Diesel truck
BFR	Blown fuel roadster	GMS	Gas modified sports	UDT	Diesel truck
FR	Fuel roadster	BMP	Blown modified pick-up		
BGR	Blown gas roadster	MP	Modified pick-up		

INDEX